ODDBALL FLORIDA

ODDBALL FLORIDA

A Guide to Some Really
STRANGE PLACES

JEROME POHLEN

CHICAGO
REVIEW
PRESS

Library of Congress Cataloging-in-Publication Data

Pohlen, Jerome.
   Oddball Florida : a guide to some really strange places /
   Jerome Pohlen.—1st ed.
     p. cm.
   Includes bibliographical references and indexes.
   ISBN 1-55652-503-6
    1. Florida—Guidebooks. 2. Curiosities and wonders—Florida—Guidebooks.
    3. Florida—History, Local—Miscellanea. I. Title.
F309.3.P636 2004
917.5904'64—dc21

2003010819

The author has made every effort to secure permissions for all the material in this book.
If any acknowledgment has inadvertently been omitted, please contact the author in care
of the publisher.

All photographs courtesy of Jerome Pohlen unless otherwise noted.
Cover and interior design: Mel Kupfer
Cover photo: Courtesy Jungle Adventures (see page 160)

© 2004 by Jerome Pohlen
All rights reserved
First Edition
Published by Chicago Review Press, Incorporated
814 North Franklin Street
Chicago, Illinois 60610
ISBN 978-1-55652-503-2
Printed in the United States of America

FOR JIM
AND TERESA

CONTENTS

INTRODUCTION

Contrary to what you may have been led to believe by the best marketing minds in the world, the state of Florida is not a wholly owned subsidiary of the Walt Disney Company ... at least not yet. If you ignore everything in the state emblazoned with big, round ears, you'll still find gator wrestlers, school bus demolition derbies, wax presidents, fan boats, and Hemingway wannabes. But that's not all. Florida's also where you'll find such one-of-a-kind attractions as the Fountain of Youth, the Nudist Hall of Fame, Humphrey Bogart's *African Queen*, a drive-in church, and a utopian community based on the premise that the earth is a sphere, but that we live on the *inside*.

The Magic Kingdom suddenly sounds a little less magical, doesn't it?

Oddball Florida leaves Disney veneration to the other travel guides, and focuses instead on the stuff you *really* want to see: a rooster graveyard; the original Batmobile; the World's Smallest Police Station; the World's Largest Alligator Statue; the three-wheeled Hamburger-Harley; an island overrun with Playboy bunnies; and museums dedicated to seashells, oranges, teddy bears, sponges, bowling ball art, air conditioning, hamburgers, and one very old petrified cat. Who needs Space Mountain when, for a fraction of the price, you can explore Dante's Inferno at the Miracle Strip Amusement Park? Why stand in line for hours to ride Dumbo (in circles!) when you can cruise the Atlantic in the NautiLimo, the world's only seaworthy stretch limo? And who in their right mind would claim that Cinderella's Castle is more interesting than Solomon's Castle, a recycled Camelot sided with aluminum printing plates that shimmers like a soda can in a swamp near Ona?

But wait—there's more! For those of you looking for the gritty underbelly of this not entirely sunshiny state, *Oddball Florida* answers the twisted travel questions that local civic boosters would just as soon leave unanswered. Where did Jim Bakker first meet Jessica Hahn (in the Biblical sense)? Why did St. Pete retiree Mary Reeser spontaneously combust? What does a female urinal look like, and how does it work? Who shot Old Joe, and why did his friends stuff his carcass and put it on public display? What ever happened to Katherine "The King Maker" Harris? And will Florida's refurbished, more comfortable electric chair ever be used?

You're about to find the answers to these questions and more, but not if you're distracted by you-know-what. Resist the mighty Mickey! Trust me on this one: Tinkerbell is a fictitious marketing tool, but the mermaids at Weeki Wachee Springs are 100 percent real!

While I've tried to give clear directions from major streets and landmarks, you could still make a wrong turn. If you want to avoid being sucked into a swamp, like the tourist vortex of Orlando's theme parks, here are a few Oddball travel tips:

- **Stop and ask!** For a lot of communities, their Oddball attraction might be their only claim to fame. Locals are often thrilled that you'd drive to their little town in the middle of the swamp to marvel at their underappreciated shrine. And remember, old cranks at the town cafe are good for reliable information; teenage clerks at the 7-Eleven are not.

- **Call ahead.** Few Oddball sites keep truly regular hours. Many Florida sites are seasonal, and can sometimes close up at a moment's notice, particularly if there's an approaching hurricane. Always call. And if there's a hurricane, bring a surfboard.

- **Don't give up.** Think of the woman whose small museum is slowly being throttled by an enormous entertainment megapark just down the road. She could have sold out or, failing that, have thrown herself in front of a tour bus, but she didn't. Neither should you.

- **Don't trespass!** Don't become a Terrible Tourist. Just because a guy turned his front yard into a year-round Christmas display, that doesn't mean he wants you knocking on his door. If it's not open to the public, stay on the road. Besides, have you forgotten about all the free-roaming gators?

• **Coupons, coupons, coupons.** If you plan to visit Florida and return with your kids' college funds still untapped, you've got to clip a few coupons. Don't worry, there's no shame in it. Quite the contrary— ticket-cashiers often look at you funny if you *don't* present them with a coupon. Any attraction that costs more than $5 will likely issue discount coupons. A five-minute stop at a tourist information center or the flyer rack in a motel lobby could easily save you $100 over the course of a week—not a bad hourly wage.

Do you have an Oddball site of your own? Have I missed anything? Do you know of a location that should be included in a later edition? Please write and let me know: c/o Chicago Review Press, 814 N. Franklin Street, Chicago, IL 60610.

ODDBALL FLORIDA

Eglin Air Force Base
Air Force Armament Museum
So many air force museums focus on the *air* portion of the military branch; here's one that demonstrates the *force*. Guns, bombs, missiles, more bombs, this place is armed to the hilt. Need a Gatling gun that fires 4,200 rounds per minute? They've got it. A cruise missile to launch at Osama bin Laden? They've got a few left over from Desert Storm. A pistol to hide in your boot, just in case you get shot down behind enemy lines? Check out the Sikes Pistol Collection—it's bound to have a gun that's just right for you.

Oh, they've got their fair share of planes at this museum, too. An SR-71 Blackbird spy plane is parked out front. Inside you'll find a B-17 Flying Fortress, an F-105 Thunderchief, and a P-51 Mustang, among others. But the emphasis is always on stuff that shoots or blows up. They even explain how World War I biplanes fired machine guns through their turning propellers without hitting the blades. Now that's timing!

100 Museum Dr., Eglin Air Force Base, FL 32542

(850) 882-4062 or (850) 651-1808

Hours: Daily 9:30 A.M.–4:30 P.M.

Cost: Free

Directions: Between the airport and Ft. Walton Beach on Rte. 85, just outside the base's West Gate.

Gulf Breeze
The Gulf Breeze UFO Flap
To ufologists, the eerie sightings at Gulf Breeze in the late 1980s rank up there with the Roswell crash as the best evidence yet that we are not alone in this universe. And let me tell you, if the scores of reports are true, our neighbors are running down the property values.

The story begins in November 1987 when Ed and Frances Walters spotted a mysterious craft hovering outside their Gulf Breeze home. Ed grabbed a camera and snapped five Polaroids before being paralyzed by a beam of blue light. Two of the shots were anonymously published in the *Gulf Breeze Sentinel* a week later, and the Martian toothpaste was out of the tube. Reports of mysterious lights flooded into the paper and local police departments—some of them made by state troopers. A craft was spotted over the Pensacola Bay bridge, and across the border in Alabama. A crop circle appeared in the grass at Shoreline Park. The *Sentinel* did its part by reporting them all, with photos, which only encouraged additional "witnesses" to come forward. One resident said he'd gotten a message that the town would be vaporized by the intruders if his story wasn't published. The newspaper printed the story—better safe than sorry.

Still, the Walters family seemed to bear the brunt of the aliens' attention. A big-eyed, silver creature stared through their windows. A UFO shot a blue beam of light at Frances, just missing her (which Ed captured on film). Sometimes, when the UFO appeared, Ed unexpectedly began dreaming of dogs who were speaking Spanish! And the aliens even followed Ed to work, causing his pickup to break down. Scariest of all, Ed had several episodes when he could not account for his whereabouts, yet he had marks on his body suggesting he had been abducted and examined—mostly bruises, not the classic anal probes. Eventually, the Walterses left town.

Great story, right? Too bad it now appears to have been an elaborate hoax. Ed managed to wrangle a six-figure advance from a publisher wanting to tell his story. The new owners of the Walters' home found a UFO model stashed in the attic that bore a striking resemblance to the craft seen in Ed's photographs. Soon, a local kid, Tommy Smith, fessed up that he had helped Walters fake the photos. And then neighbors revealed that during the entire flap they had been trying to get anyone to listen to *their* story: before this all started, Ed Walters was famed in the community for making double-exposure photos of ghosts. Ooops! (Later, photographic experts pointed out that in several of Ed's daytime photos you can see reflections of everything *except* the UFO in nearby car windows and fenders—either the flying saucers were imposed on the film earlier, or they were vampires.)

But how does that explain all the others who saw lights in the skies over Gulf Breeze? Take a quick look at a map of the area around Gulf Breeze and you'll see no fewer than 21 air fields, civilian and military, from Fort Walton Beach to Mobile, Alabama—it would be odd if folks *didn't* see lights in the night sky.

Still, the believers are convinced they haven't been duped. You can still find groups after dark in Shoreline Park with binoculars, looking skyward, cameras at the ready. Most are looking for "Bubba," a large red orb they claim hovers over the waters, and a faceless man who sometimes parks his black sedan in the adjoining lot. The crowds are smaller than they used to be—sometimes nobody shows up—leaving the cosmic door wide open for a Martian invasion.

Shoreline Park, Shorline Dr., Gulf Breeze, FL 32561

No phone

Hours: After dark

Cost: Free

www.skiesare.demon.co.uk/gbdocs.htm

Directions: Turn south on Shoreline Dr. from Rte. 98/30, two lights south of the Pensacola Bay Bridge, and follow it to the access road leading left, just past the South Santa Rosa County Recreation Center.

JESUS IS COMING . . . IN A UFO!!

When a Ouija board spirit named Safire talked to Vance Davis, telling him that The End was near, Davis knew just what to do: head for Gulf Breeze! He'd heard about the UFO sightings, and so too had the disembodied spirit. At the time, Davis was an army intelligence officer with the 701st Military Intelligence Brigade based in West Germany. Somehow he was able to convince five other military personnel to go AWOL, and they all hopped aboard a U.S.–bound flight on July 9, 1990.

The army was understandably nervous that six of its most intelligent had disappeared. They were eventually apprehended in a van at a Gulf Breeze campground. First investigated for espionage, they were demoted and honorably discharged as loonies. Why did the army make such a harsh assessment? According to the runaways, the Ouija board had told them that a Middle East war was about to break out (when *isn't* it?), New York would soon be leveled by a gas explosion, Jesus would soon return to Earth (at Gulf Breeze) on a UFO, and that they had been chosen to fight the Antichrist. Who was the Antichrist? None other than Ed Walters!

Lakewood
As High as You Can Get in Florida

As states go, Florida is about as low as you can get. If any place should be concerned about the Greenhouse Effect, it's the Sunshine State, as no part of it is more than 345 feet above sea level. And where is it highest? Britton Hill, just outside of Lakewood on the Florida–Alabama border. Britton Hill is not too impressive—after all, there are apartment complexes in Miami Beach that are higher—but this bump offers you a low-impact option to brag to your friends about climbing a state's highest mountain. Don't mention that it wasn't in Colorado.

What does the future hold for this geographic region? Perhaps a land boom. If the ice caps start melting in a big way, and Florida residents want to remain in their income tax–free state, they should probably look into real estate near this Panhandle peak.

Britton Hill, Lakewood, FL 32538

No phone

Hours: Always visible

Cost: Free

americasroof.com/fl.html

Directions: Along Rte. 285, watch for the sign.

IT WASN'T IN LAKEWOOD

The official Florida state seal, adopted in 1868, showed a sun setting between two mountain peaks. It wasn't until 1985 that the imaginary topography was corrected.

CHUMUCKLA

The village of Chumuckla hosts a Redneck Parade each December, when a King and Queen Redneck are crowned.

DEFUNIAK SPRINGS

Lake DeFuniak in DeFuniak Springs is one of only two perfectly round natural lakes in the world. It is exactly one mile in circumference.

Marianna
Florida Caverns

With as many rivers, springs, and sinkholes as there are in Florida, you might expect to find more cavern systems here. Unfortunately, the state's topography never rises more than 300 or so feet above sea level, so any cave that does get started is very near the surface and usually collapses into a sinkhole.

The Florida Caverns are an exception. They were "discovered" in March 1937 by Oliver Chalifoux, who happened to look through a hole he found under a fallen tree. Chalifoux had refound a cave system that had been used by Native Americans for centuries; evidence of early human activity has been discovered deep inside the cave. Also, during the Civil War Battle of Marianna, residents from the town sought shelter here.

Today this hole carved by the Chipola River is open to visitors and the bats who perch here during daylight hours. You can see typical stalactites and stalagmites, as well as flowstone, soda straws, and columns. It's no Mammoth Cave, but it's the best you'll find in these parts.

3345 Caverns Rd., Marianna, FL 32446

(850) 482-9598

Hours: March–September, daily 9 A.M.–4:30 P.M., October–February, daily 9 A.M.–4 P.M.

Cost: $3.25/vehicle, Adults $5, Kids (3–12) $2.50

www.dep.state.fl.us/parks/district1/floridacaverns/index.asp

Directions: Three miles north of town on Rte. 166, turn left on Caverns Rd.

Panama City
Gideon's Trumpet

One of the fundamental rights afforded you under America's modern judicial system is the right to be represented by a lawyer in a court of law. Were it not for a 51-year-old drifter who got railroaded four decades ago in Panama City, you might not have that.

Clarence Earl Gideon was accused of burglarizing the Bay Harbor Poolroom on June 3, 1961, stealing money from the cigarette machine and jukebox. Because Gideon was not charged in a capital case, and because he was *poor*, he was forced to defend himself in court. The state's case hinged on the eyewitness testimony of Henry Cook. Gideon did not explore contradictory statements made by his accuser on the stand, and failed to uncover evidence pointing to Cook's potentially questionable motives. As a result, Gideon was found guilty and sentenced to five years in prison.

But Gideon didn't accept his verdict as the final word. He applied for a writ of *habeas corpus* to the Florida Supreme Court, saying he had been illegally imprisoned. The court rejected it. He went over the court's head and filed a writ of *certiorari* with the U.S. Supreme Court. Amazingly, the justices decided to hear his case. This time it was argued by Abe Fortas (who would later be named to the highest court). On March 18, 1963, the court ruled in *Gideon v. Wainwright* that Gideon was entitled to a new trial, but this time with a lawyer.

The second time Gideon was tried in the Panama City Courthouse, Cook's original testimony fell apart under cross-examination. Gideon wasn't the only victor at the end of the trial on August 5, 1963; the judicial system was a winner as well.

109 N. Everitt Ave., Panama City, FL 32401
No phone
Hours: Never visible; torn down
Cost: Free
Directions: Five blocks west of Rte. 98/30, at Cherry Ave.

MARIANNA
Florida governor John Milton committed suicide at his Marianna plantation, Sylvania (Rte. 164, 4.2 miles east of town), on April Fools' Day, 1865, as Union troops raised the American flag over the capitol building in Tallahassee. His last message to the Florida legislature was "Death would be preferable to reunion." Milton was buried at the St. Luke's Episcopal Church Cemetery (4362 Lafayette Street) in Marianna.

MUNSON
An 11-foot alligator was captured along Coldwater Creek in the Blackwater River State Forest near Munson on August 15, 1995. It had been tracked using the electronic dog collar worn by its final victim, Flojo. Five other collars were in its stomach, but estimates put the number of its hunting dog victims at 25.

Come to Hell!
Courtesy Miracle Strip Amusement Park

Panama City Beach
Dante's Inferno and the Abominable Snowman
You've gotta hand it to the folks at the Miracle Strip Park. While everyone else in Florida seems to be rushing to Disney-fy their operations, they have

the courage to stand by their classic amusement park. And what a park it is! In 1963, Miracle Strip started with the Starliner, a classic wooden roller coaster. It expanded to include dozens of other rides you might find in a traveling carnival, but they dressed them up with funky exteriors. Step through the open mouth of a gigantic devil's head and into Dante's Inferno, the best of the bunch. It's a covered Trabant ride (sometimes called a Mexican Hat), with a light show set to rock 'n' roll music, and each time your seat rises you swear you're going to hit the ceiling. You'll be minding your p's and q's after that one!

Need to cool off from the fiery pits of hell? Take a walk over to the Abominable Snowman, where you enter the ride between the legs of a 20-foot yeti. This Scrambler is located inside a deep freeze, and you almost forget about the nasty bumble over the door.

And there's more—the Haunted Castle, the Dungeon, Hilda's Hotel of Horrors—not to mention its original wooden roller coaster, the Starliner, a log flume, and several dozen other classic carnival rides without the scary traveling carnival operators. Who needs Disney World? Mickey Mouse can go to Dante's Inferno!

Miracle Strip Amusement Park, 12000 Front Beach Rd., Panama City, FL 32407

(850) 234-5810

E-mail: info@miraclestrippark.com

Hours: March–August, Sunday–Friday 6 A.M.–11 P.M., Saturday 1–11:30 P.M.

Cost: Gate Fee $5.50, All-Day Pass $18 (includes Gate Fee)

www.miraclestrippark.com

Directions: On Rte. 98A (Front Beach Rd.), at Miracle Strip Rd.

NICEVILLE
The town of Niceville hosts a Boggy Bayou Mullet Festival each October when a Queen of the Mullet is crowned. The mullet they celebrate is the fish, not the haircut.

PANAMA CITY
Panama City received its name because it is located on a direct line connecting Chicago and the Panama Canal.

Hole-y ground

Miniature Golf Mecca

Lee Koplin was a genius. Back in 1958, this visionary single-handedly shifted the prevailing miniature golf paradigm from one of minimized putting greens to a maximized golfing pleasure. Though the silly sport had been around since the 1920s, mostly known as Tom Thumb Golf, nobody had the vision to dress up the tiny fairways.

But then came Lee Koplin. In 1958 he built a course in Panama Beach and added a replica of the Great Sphinx. And a giant monkey. And an Easter Island head, and a few dinosaurs, and a beached fish, and a stucco spider web, and so on, and so on. . . . He called this miraculous complex Goofy Golf.

Leonardo da Vinci. Albert Einstein. Lee Koplin.

Soon, goofy courses were popping up everywhere, their names only slightly altered to avoid legal complications: Goony Golf, Wacky Golf, Spooky Golf, Magic Carpet Golf. But none did it as well as the one who did it first. The best part of the story is that Koplin's course *is still around*! Koplin passed away in 1988, but Goofy Golf is still run by his son. The statues get a fresh coat of paint each spring, as well they should. This isn't just a bunch of kitschy crap, it's roadside hole-y ground.

Goofy Golf, 12206 Front Beach Rd., Panama City Beach, FL 32407

(850) 234-6403

Hours: March–August, Monday–Friday 9 A.M.–10 P.M., Saturday–Sunday 8 A.M.–10 P.M.

Cost: $5/round

Directions: On Rte. 98A (Front Beach Rd.), at Miracle Strip Rd.

Just around the corner from Goofy Golf is another old-style course, not as magnificent . . . but darn close. Location is everything—it's sandwiched between Goofy Golf and the Miracle Strip Amusement Park—and it's worth stopping by for nine holes.

The greens at Shipwreck Golf wrap around a central mountain topped by an enormous orange octopus, its tentacles snaking through the bushes and around the greens. You'll also find enormous skulls, tiki heads, and a full-size Loch Ness Monster scattered around the park.

Shipwreck Golf, 12000 Front Beach Rd., Panama City Beach, FL 32407

(850) 234-3912

Hours: March–August, daily 10 A.M.–10 P.M.

Cost: $5/round

Directions: On Rte. 98A (Front Beach Rd.), at Miracle Strip Rd.

Scuba Doobie Do

The Museum of Man-in-the-Sea should rightly be called the Museum of Man-*Under*-the-Sea, for this unique museum focuses on humankind's exploration beneath the oceans' waves. Owned by the Institute for Diving, the large collection contains artifacts from as far back as the 1500s.

The museum has diving bells, deep-sea capsules, hand-cranked air pumps, and scuba gear. Parked outside are several submarines.

And if you wonder why humans have been so interested in diving, you need look no further than the booty these folks have pulled up from the deep: Spanish doubloons, gold ingots, and other valuable artifacts. If you catch the diving bug, the Institute of Diving will be glad to set you up in a training class.

Museum of Man-in-the-Sea, 17314 Panama Beach Pkwy., Panama City Beach, FL 32413
(850) 235-4101
Hours: Daily 9 A.M.–5 P.M.
Cost: Adults $5, Kids (6–16) $2.50
www.diveweb.com/iod/mmits.html
Directions: A quarter mile west of Rte. 79 on Back Beach Rd.

All tourists on deck!
Photo by author, courtesy National Museum of Naval Aviation

Pensacola
National Museum of Naval Aviation

You've no doubt had a chance to see the Blue Angels sometime in your life, but probably not as close as you can in the atrium at the National

Museum of Naval Aviation. That's right, *naval* aviation. Contrary to what you might expect, the world's second-largest air force (after the U.S. Air Force) belongs to the U.S. Navy. Those aren't air force flyboys landing on the decks of aircraft carriers—they're navy pilots.

Dozens of vintage and modern aircraft are crammed onto the two wings of this enormous museum, as well as outside. One wing is dedicated to both early and modern aircraft, while the other features planes from World War II and the Korean Conflict, all of which appear to be sitting on the flight deck of the USS *Cabot*. On the second floor, on the balconies surrounding the airplanes, are exhibits on dirigibles and blimps, cockpit trainers (which you can try your hand flying!), and spacecraft, including the command module from the *Skylab II* mission.

Scattered everywhere are hundreds of smaller artifacts from U.S. Navy history; for example, the helmet the future Senator John McCain was wearing when he was shot down over Vietnam on October 26, 1967, as well as the peasant clothing he and his fellow POWs wore at Hoa Lo Prison, better known as the Hanoi Hilton. They've also got the seal fur coat and mukluks worn by a pilot on a 1926 flight across the North Pole, and a rubber raft in which several gobs bobbed around in the south Pacific for 34 days in 1942. And because so many early astronauts were navy veterans, the museum also has displays tracing the evolution of space suits and the men and women who wore them.

1750 Radford Blvd., NAS Pensacola, Pensacola, FL 32508

(850) 452-3604

Hours: Daily 9 A.M.–5 P.M.

Cost: Free

www.naval-air.org

Directions: Enter the base via Rte. 295 (Navy Blvd.), follow the signs on the base.

PENSACOLA

The city of Pensacola changed national hands so many times the British House of Lords referred to it as a "lady of impure fashion."

It is against the law to roll barrels along the streets of Pensacola.

Krusty kitty.
Photo by author, courtesy T. T. Wentworth, Jr., Florida State Museum

Petrified Cat

T. T. Wentworth, Jr., was a poor-man's Robert Ripley, but nevertheless he amassed an impressive collection of weird artifacts and delightful doodads, many of which are on display in the Pensacola museum that now bears his name. The most popular item is the well-preserved carcass of a cat accidentally sealed into the walls of a home built in 1850 but not discovered until 1946. This Morris-shaped mummy, the "Petrified Cat," rests in a case with Robert Wadlow's left shoe (Wadlow was the world's tallest man at 8'11", and wore a size 37 shoe), a helpful gas mask instruction booklet, commemorative coins and plates, and lots of World War II booty. Sadly, Wentworth's most prized possession, a shrunken head from South America, is not on display. Bad taste, you know . . .

The T. T. Wentworth, Jr., Florida State Museum, located in the old 1907 City Hall, is just part of the larger Historic Pensacola Village. Your ticket also gains you entry to 10 other historic sites in the immediate downtown area, including the Museum of Commerce (print shop, toys, buggies, hardware), the Museum of Industry (trains, lumber, fishing), and the homes of several Pensacola founders.

T. T. Wentworth, Jr., Florida State Museum, 330 S. Jefferson St., Pensacola, FL 32501
(850) 595-5985
Hours: September–May, Monday–Friday 10 A.M.–4 P.M.; June–August,
  Monday–Saturday 10 A.M.–4 P.M.
Cost: Adults $6, Seniors (65+) $5, Kids (4–16) $2.50
www.historicpensacola.org
Directions: Three blocks south of Garden St. (Rte. 98 Business), three blocks east of
  Spring St., on the east side of the Plaza Ferdinand.

World's Longest Fishing Pier

Rather than tear down the old Pensacola Bay Bridge when the new causeway was built, city planners came up with a better idea: turn it into the World's Longest Fishing Pier. To avoid parking congestion at either end, they decided to allow folks to drive onto the old road and park wherever they like.

The fishing pier is two miles long and runs parallel to the new bridge connecting Gulf Breeze and Pensacola. It can be entered from either end; just pay your fee at either toll booth. There are bathrooms along the pier, so you don't have to worry about having to hang over the railing when nature calls.

Pensacola Bay Fishing Pier, 1750 Bayfront Pkwy., Pensacola, FL 32501
(850) 444-9811
Hours: Sunday–Thursday 5 A.M.–Midnight, Friday–Saturday open 24 hours
Cost: $2.50/person + $1.50/car
www.fishthebridge.com
Directions: Along Rte. 98/30, on the east side of the bridge.

PENSACOLA BEACH

Apache warrior **Geronimo** was imprisoned in Old Fort Pickens (1400 Fort Pickens Road) from 1886 to 1888 on Pensacola Beach's Gulf Islands National Seashore, at the eastern end of Santa Rosa Island.

Seaside
The Truman Show Town

Even if you never saw *The Truman Show*, Seaside would look kind of creepy. Developer Robert Davis wanted a new kind of town for the 1990s, where folks got to know one another, where you could walk to the market or the school, where white picket fences surround energy-efficient homes on brick-paved streets. So he hired architects Andres Duany and Elizabeth Plater-Zyberk, champions of New Urbanism, and Seaside was born.

The result is . . . well . . . disturbing. Sure, most people want a clean, comfortable, and energy-efficient America, but not if it looks like *this*. Where is the greasy diner? Where is the cranky old geezer who won't mow his lawn or paint his garage door? Where is the teen hangout, and the trashy No Tell Motel? In short, where is Seaside's *personality*? After seeing it, if some newspaper ran a hoax saying Seaside residents were robots, you'd probably do a double-take.

Seriously.

Is it any wonder that a movie about a contained, idyllic, TV-set town was filmed right here, and that set designers barely had to change a thing? You can still see the Truman house (31–39 Natchez Street, the last lane at the west end of town), pretty much the same way it looked when the Peter Weir film was released in 1998. Just watch out for falling studio lights.

County Road 30A, PO Box 4730, Seaside, FL 32459

(888) SEA-SIDE

Hours: Always visible

Cost: Free

www.seasidefl.com

Directions: At the intersection of Rtes. 395 and 30A.

PENSACOLA BEACH

Surgeons successfully reattached the arm of an eight-year-old boy who was attacked by a bull shark at the Gulf Islands National Seashore in Pensacola Beach in the summer of 2001.

Tallahassee
Helping Out the Undertaker

Calvin C. Phillips liked to plan ahead. During his twilight years he had a mausoleum constructed in Oakland Cemetery, complete with a minaret atop a 20-foot sepulcher. When the tomb was finished, Phillips had a cherrywood coffin placed inside. When the time seemed right, he handed a friend a key to the crypt, crawled into the coffin, and died.

Today the site is haunted, supposedly giving people and animals an uneasy feeling when they are near the Phillips Mausoleum. Is it any wonder?

Oakland Cemetery, 4th & Bronough Sts., Tallahassee, FL 32303

No phone

Hours: Daily 8 A.M.–5 P.M.

Cost: Free

Directions: West of Bronough between Brevard and 4th Sts.

Missionary Artist Mary L. Proctor

Mary L. Proctor's life and work are a testament that beauty can grow out of tragedy. Back in the early 1990s her aunt, uncle, and grandmother perished in a trailer fire. Proctor was having a difficult time making sense of the deaths. While she was praying under an oak tree in her front yard in February 1995, a bright light appeared to her and spoke. The message was simple: Paint doors. Lots of doors.

So Proctor bought herself some paint, and she hasn't stopped painting since. Doors, she's figured out, are "escape hatches from suffering and into peace." Her creations are large and elaborate and usually have a personal thought about life or love or salvation from the artist. Proctor uses tubes of caulking compound to affix discarded objects—canceled stamps, beads, scraps of cloth, trimmed soda cans, you name it—to her works. As soon as she's finished, she stacks the piece in her work area and starts on a new one.

Her largest work to date is called the *Hall of Presidents.* Each chief executive, dressed in a suit of old Coke cans, is given his own red, white, and powder blue door. Proctor researched their lives in order to write and illustrate a thick book on each of her subjects. The books are thick because the pages are made out of cardboard covered in aluminum sheeting.

Proctor is around her museum/gallery most days—her work never stops—but it's a good idea to call ahead if you're interested in looking at her work. Even if she's there, she's oftentimes too wrapped up in her painting or praying to hear the bell at the front gate.

American Folk Art Museum and Gallery, 3919 Woodville Hwy., Tallahassee, FL 32311

Mailing Address: PO Box 7597, Tallahassee, FL 32314

(850) 656-2879

Hours: Always visible; call ahead for a tour

Cost: Free

www.marysart.com

Directions: North of Rte. 263 (Capitol Circle Dr.) on Rte. 363 (Woodville Hwy.).

Tallahassee Antique Car Museum

The Tallahassee Antique Car Museum would be an otherwise common auto attraction were it not for three pieces in its collection, only one of which is an actual car off an assembly line. That's the 1948 Tucker Torpedo, a relic of the short-lived Tucker Auto Company, which was used in the filming of the movie *Tucker*. The museum also has the space-age Batmobile from *Batman Returns*, so overcustomized as to hardly be a car at all, and an 1860 hearse, which was used to transport the body of President Abraham Lincoln after his assassination.

The rest of the museum is filled with beautiful classic vehicles from the early 1900s on, but they're the kind of cars you'll see at most auto museums. Owner Devoe Moore sees these cars as the embodiment of the free enterprise system, something he thinks is sorely lacking in the 21st century. Why else would he ask you (as he does on his Web site) to contemplate the question: "Under the oppressive constraints, rules, and regulations forced on us by the 1990s political bureaucrats, can 'we the people' achieve the goals and regain the freedom outlined in the Constitution of the United States of America that is so vital to our existence in a healthy free enterprise system?" Sounds like somebody got a doozy of a property tax bill!

3550A Mahan Dr., Tallahassee, FL 32308

(850) 942-0137

Hours: Monday–Saturday 10 A.M.–5 P.M., Sunday Noon–5 P.M.

Cost: Adults $7.50, Teens (11–15) $5, Kids (10 and under) $4

www.tacm.com

Directions: Northeast of downtown on Rte. 90 (Mahan Dr.), just past Phillips Rd.

Weirdness ahead.

Vernon

Vernon, Florida

Back in 1980, filmmaker Errol Morris tried to make a documentary about a group of Florida scam artists who cut off portions of their own limbs to collect insurance settlements. *Nub City* was almost finished when these not-too-bright stumpy folk wised up just enough to realize a movie about their tactics might get them in hot water. When they threatened to kill Morris, he decided to take his camera elsewhere. Quick.

He landed in nearby Vernon, Florida, and the result was a movie that bears its name. The residents of Vernon didn't possess the same can-do, entrepreneurial attitude as the folks in *Nub City*, but at least they still had their fingers and toes. Morris turned on the camera and let the town tell its own story. One resident went on at length about the gobbling habits of the wild turkeys, day after day after day after day. Vernon's only cop proudly showed off his new two-way radio, though he admitted it would be more useful if a second cop were at the other end. A couple showed their photos of a trip to White Sands National Monument and a souvenir jar of sand they *swore* had been expanding since they brought it home. And a local preacher gave a full-length sermon on the significance of the word *therefore*.

Morris's 1981 film is a hard-to-find cult classic. It's almost easier to stop by Vernon, plop down on a bench outside the store, and ask a local about any topic under the sun. You won't be disappointed, although you might be confused.

Rte. 79, Vernon, FL 32462
No phone
Hours: Always visible
Cost: Free
Directions: All over town.

SUMATRA
A single burning cannonball destroyed Fort Gadsen near Sumatra on July 27, 1816, when it landed in the fort's ammo dump. Fired by troops under the command of American Colonel Duncan Clinch, it ended up killing 270 of the 300 people inside the British-controlled fort.

TALLAHASSEE
Tallahassee was the only Confederate capital not captured by the North during the Civil War.

Tallahassee recorded a temperature of −2°F on February 13, 1899, the lowest ever recorded in the state.

Wakulla Springs
Old Joe

It's a mystery that has hung over this quaint country lodge for more than a quarter century: who murdered Old Joe? On August 1, 1966, his body was found lying at the bottom of Wakulla Springs, a single .22-caliber bullet between his eyes. A $5,000 reward for information pointing to his killer was offered, but police uncovered nothing. The folks at the Wakulla Springs Lodge decided to honor Old Joe in the best way they knew how: they stuffed him and put him in a Plexiglas case in the lobby.

Did I forget to mention that Old Joe was an alligator? Not just any alligator, but 650 pounds and 11 feet, 2 inches of rompin' stompin' reptile. (Some estimates say he was 300 years old.) Actually, he didn't really romp or stomp. As large as he was, he couldn't move much more when he was alive than he does now. These days he sometimes wears a Santa hat during the holidays.

A local sheriff claimed he got a confession from a local ne'er-do-well, "Skebo" Ross, in 1982; Ross claimed he'd shot Old Joe by accident while hunting for smaller gators. The sheriff didn't pursue the case, as Ross was also accused of killing his wife with a hammer.

Wakulla Springs isn't just known for reptilicide. It is also one of the world's largest and deepest (185 feet) freshwater springs, gushing 400,000 gallons of clean, clear water every minute. It is also home to Henry, a trained fish who pole-vaults on command. To see Henry's trick you have to take the glass-bottom boat tour. Movie buffs will be interested to learn that some of the early *Tarzan* films starring Johnny Weissmuller were shot at the springs, as were some scenes from *The Creature From the Black Lagoon* and *Airport '77*.

Wakulla Springs Lodge, 1 Spring Dr., Wakulla Springs, FL 32305

(850) 224-5950

Hours: Always open

Cost: Free; Rooms $79–$99

www.dep.state.fl.us/parks/district1/wakullasprings/index.asp or
  www.wakullacounty.com/wakulla-5.htm

Directions: Just southeast of the intersection of Rtes. 61 and 267.

TALLAHASSEE
It's illegal to drive a train through Tallahassee faster than a person can walk.

ERECTED IN GRATEFUL RECOGNITION OF THE ROLE THE
NORTH AMERICAN POSSUM, A MAGNIFICIENT SURVIVOR OF
THE MARSUPIAL FAMILY PRE-DATING THE AGES OF THE
MASTADON AND THE DINOSAUR, HAS PLAYED IN FURNISHING
BOTH FOOD AND FUR FOR THE EARLY SETTLERS AND THEIR
SUCCESSORS. THEIR PRESENCE HERE HAS PROVIDED A SOURCE
OF NUTRITIOUS AND FLAVORFUL FOOD IN NORMAL TIMES AND
HAS BEEN IMPORTANT AID TO HUMAN SURVIVAL IN TIMES OF
DISTRESS AND CRITICAL NEED.

THE 1982 SESSION OF THE FLORIDA LEGISLATURE
FURTHER RECOGNIZED THE POSSUM BY PASSING A JOINT
RESOLUTION PROCLAIMING THE FIRST SATURDAY IN AUGUST
AS POSSUM DAY IN THE GREAT STATE OF FLORIDA.

ERECTED
BY
WAUSAU COMMUNITY DEVELOPMENT CLUB
AUG. 7, 1982

DESIGNED AND ERECTED BY:
SAPP MEMORIAL, INC.
COTTONDALE FLA.

Them's good eatin'.

Wasau
Possum Monument

To many, possums seem like oversized rats, but without any of the rats'
good looks. To others, like the good folk of Wasau, possums represent
something else: vittles. Not everyday eats, but more for special occasions

such as, say, the Great Depression. The town has erected a granite monument to this North American marsupial that reads, in part, "Their presence has provided a source of nutritious and flavorful food in normal times and has been an important aid to human survival in times of distress and critical needs."

Each year, on the first Saturday in August, the town throws a Possum Festival. Locals compete for the title of Possum King and Possum Queen, the tackier the outfit, the better. (Contestants are also required to submit a possum recipe to the judges.) Other Possum Day events include a hog-calling contest, a cornpone bake-off, and 5K-meter race, called the Possum Trot.

200 Washington St., Wasau, FL 32463

No phone

Hours: Always visible

Cost: Free

Directions: On Rte. 77 (Washington St.) at 2nd Ave., across from the gas station.

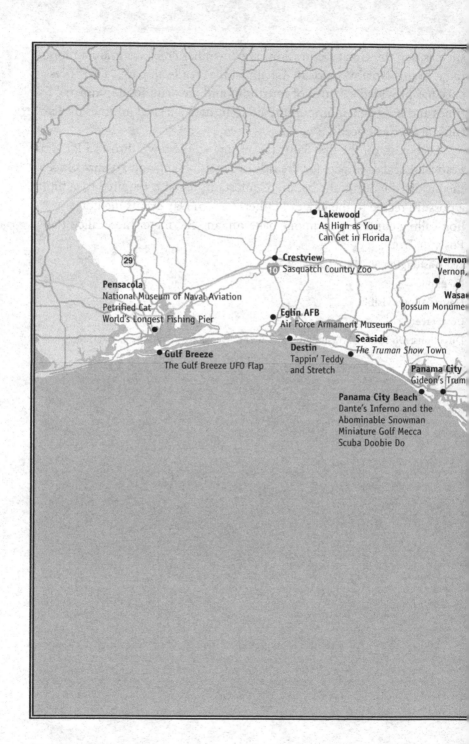

Lakewood
As High as You
Can Get in Florida

Crestview
Sasquatch Country Zoo

Vernon
Vernon,

Pensacola
National Museum of Naval Aviation
Petrified Cat
World's Longest Fishing Pier

Wasa
Possum Monume

Eglin AFB
Air Force Armament Museum

Seaside
The Truman Show Town

Gulf Breeze
The Gulf Breeze UFO Flap

Destin
Tappin' Teddy
and Stretch

Panama City
Gideon's Trum

Panama City Beach
Dante's Inferno and the
Abominable Snowman
Miniature Golf Mecca
Scuba Doobie Do

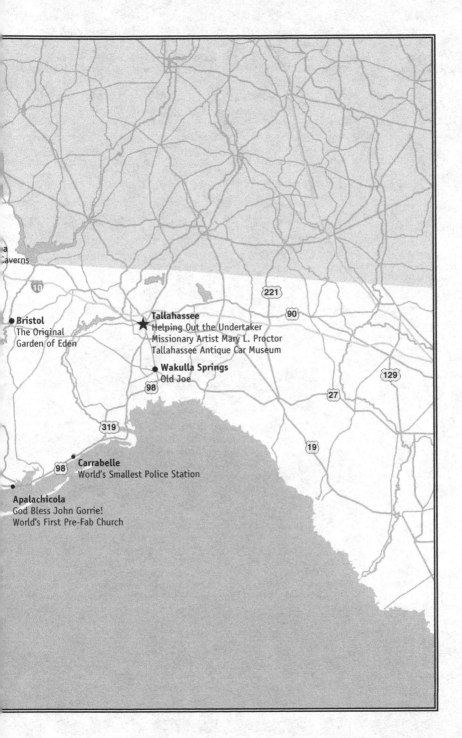

2

THE NORTH

There's a saying around Florida that the farther north you go, the farther South you go. The attitude, the culture, the *speed*. Northern Florida is a lot like Georgia, which can be both a good and a bad thing.

First the good news. Folks in the Southern north have much better manners than those in the Northern south—good luck trying to find somebody, *anybody*, in Miami to hold a door for you. But in Jacksonville? No problem.

On the other hand, the region is quite a bit more "country" than the rest of the state, even in the big cities. A few years ago, a $16 million F-18 at the Jacksonville International Airport struck, at 160 MPH, two wild pigs that were mating on the runway. The plane veered out of control and crashed—a total loss. Think that would happen at New York's LaGuardia? Nope. Welcome to Jacksonville and the great Southern north!

Bardin
Bardin Booger

It's hard to say which is a worse name for Florida's Bigfoot: Skunk Ape or Bardin Booger. To the folks of Bardin, there's no debate. They love their Booger and have turned it into a local celebrity, selling T-shirts, stuffed animals, and Booger Burgers to anyone willing to buy them.

The first Bardin Booger sighting came during the 1970s. The man who spotted it, Randy Medlock, delayed filing a report, and by the time a search got underway the trail had grown too cold to follow. A posse searched a local swamp and found nothing, and the story still made it to Walter Cronkite. All the attention must have frightened it away, because it wasn't until 1980 that a motorist spotted it again, this time farther east, along I-95.

Realizing that most folks won't be lucky enough to see a Booger, a few local folks have taken to dressing up like the mysterious creature for Wal-Mart openings and the like. Ask around for the next appearance—nobody will think you're nuts, at least not in Bardin.

All Over Town, Bardin, FL 32177
No phone
Hours: Nobody knows
Cost: Free
Directions: Look around.

AMELIA ISLAND
Amelia Island is called the Isle of Eight Flags because over the years it has been under the control of France (1562–1565), Spain (1513–1562, 1565–1763, 1783–1812, 1812–1817, and 1819–1821), England (1763–1783), the East Florida Patriots (1812), the Green Cross of Florida (1817), Mexico (1817–1819), the Confederacy (1861–1862), and the United States (1821–1861, 1862–Present).

DOCTORS INLET
Pumsy, a dragon puppet, has been banned from the Doctors Inlet elementary schools. Parents are worried that Pumsy had New Age undertones and might put children in a trance.

BOOGERS, BOOGERS EVERYWHERE

Bardin isn't the only community besieged by the mysterious Skunk Ape; reports have been filed since the 1920s. Most are harmless encounters. But in 1973 a man claimed he'd struck a Skunk Ape with his car. This report prompted the Florida Legislature into action, passing a law making it illegal to harass or molest a Skunk Ape. It is clearly endangered and needs to be protected. Here are a few reports (many more at www.floridaskunkape.com) from the lucky few who have come across the creature:

★ A woman changing a tire near **Brooksville** in November 1966 was watched, at a distance, by a Skunk Ape. It made no effort to assist.

★ In July 1967, a trucker was dragged half out of his cab by a Skunk Ape after stopping to snooze along I-75. The creature was scared away when the trucker blew the rig's air horn.

★ In the fall of 2001, a woman near Myakka River State Park east of **Sarasota** noticed that apples were being stolen from her porch, and a few nights later took two photographs of the culprit: a seven-foot-tall Skunk Ape! She sent the pictures with an anonymous note to local authorities who have yet to identify her or the creature lurking behind a stand of chest-high palmettos.

GAINESVILLE

Gainesville was once known as Hogtown.

Rocker **Tom Petty** was born in Gainesville on October 20, 1953. His first band was called Mudcrutch.

HASTINGS

Hastings is "The Potato Capital of Florida."

Electrisaurus rex

Jacksonville
Dinosaur Electric

Who knew dinosaurs even needed electricity? Perhaps that's why they became extinct . . .

Well, that's a question for paleontologists to figure out. This much is sure: one extremely large green dinosaur *does* have electricity because it's the mascot for Jacksonville's Dinosaur Electric. The concrete creature stands in a small lot next to the company offices. With its out-of-proportion head it looks less like something you'd see in *Jurassic Park* and more like something you'd see on *The Flintstones*.

1931 Blanding Ave., Jacksonville, FL 32210

(904) 630-4356

Hours: Always visible

Cost: Free

Directions: At the intersection of Lexington Ave. and Rte. 21 (Blanding Blvd.), one block north of San Juan Ave.

Karpeles Library

Surprisingly, not all of this nation's important documents are held by the National Archives or the Library of Congress. Many are in the hands of private collectors, such as David Karpeles, who has a strong sense of historic and civic responsibility. Not only are the items in his collection available for viewing by the public free of charge, but the foundation ships replicas of the originals to schools everywhere as part of its Mini-Museums program. Karpeles's goal is to put history into the hands of America's students, and he does.

The Karpeles foundation constantly rotates its artifacts among its seven museum/libraries nationwide, so each time you visit you're likely to see something new (which is really old). A recent exhibit at the Jacksonville Library focused on the official papers and personal letters of Juan and Eva Peron. In one document, Juan asks the minister of war for permission to marry Eva Duarte. In another, Eva asks the head of the Buenos Aires Zoo for a job for her brother-in-law. And for those wondering about Eva's winning smile, the Karpeles Library also has Eva's dental records: six cavities and a missing molar (#7).

Compared to other items in the museum's holdings, the Peron papers seem almost inconsequential. The Karpeles collection includes a draft of the Bill of Rights, a page from Noah Webster's original dictionary, George Washington's declaration making Thanksgiving a holiday, the original draft of Lincoln's Emancipation Proclamation, Roget's *Thesaurus*, Beethoven's *Emperor Concerto*, the first draft of the Constitution of the Confederate States of America, and Einstein's description of the Theory of Relativity.

101 W. First St., Jacksonville, FL 32206

(904) 356-2992

Hours: Tuesday–Saturday 10 A.M.–3 P.M.

Cost: Free

www.rain.org/~karpeles/jax.html

Directions: One block west of Rte. 1 (Main St.), three blocks north of State St.

The King Had No Clothes

. . . but he didn't start out that way.

Elvis Presley made the mistake of saying, "Girls, I'll see you all back-stage," at the end of his May 13, 1955, concert at the Gator Bowl, and a bunch of fans decided to take him up on it. The King had been escorted to the dugout locker room to change, but before he could relax, fans broke through a window and started to tear at his clothes. Elvis retreated to a high wall in the showers, but not before losing his jacket, his shirt, his belt, his boots, and his socks. The women were clawing at his pants when the police broke up the melee.

Gator Bowl, 1 Gator Blvd., Jacksonville, FL 32202
(904) 798-1700
Hours: Always visible
Cost: Free
www.gatorbowl.com
Directions: Off Rte. 1, just north of the St. John's River.

"Lift Every Voice and Sing"

As far back as the Civil War, the Johnson family of Jacksonville played an integral part in this community, and eventually in American history. Helen Louise Johnson was Florida's first African American teacher, and began teaching at Stanton School shortly after it was founded in 1868. It was the first Jacksonville school for African American students, and one of her prize pupils was her son, James Weldon Johnson.

James went on to graduate from Atlanta University in 1894, then returned to Stanton to become its principal, serving until 1902. While working here, Johnson studied law and passed the Florida Bar in 1897, the first African American to do so in Florida. Somehow he found time to write the poem "Lift Every Voice and Sing." His brother Rosamond later set it to music and it was adopted by the NAACP as its official song.

After leaving Stanton, Johnson wrote more songs, including *Under the Bamboo Tree*, and several books, including *Autobiography of an Ex-Colored Man*. He also served in the U.S. foreign service in Venezuela, Haiti, and Nicaragua.

Edwin M. Stanton School, 521 W. Ashley St., Jacksonville, FL 32202
Private phone
Hours: Always visible; view from street
Cost: Free
Directions: Five blocks west of Rte. 17 (Main St.), two blocks south of Rte. 23 (Union St.).

Redneck Mecca

Lynyrd Skynyrd Town

Like most gym teachers of the 1960s, Leonard Skinner had little patience for kids with long hair. One particular group he singled out for abuse was a bunch of hippie kids that had formed a band called My Backyard. They later changed the name to The Noble Five: Ronnie Van Sandt, Larry Steele, Allen Collins, Gary Rossington, and Bob Burns. But that name didn't sound quite right either. Though they couldn't agree on a name, they did agree on how much they despised their gym teacher. Somebody got the idea to twist Skinner's name around, and the band's new name was born: Lynyrd Skynyrd.

Skinner didn't stay with teaching forever; he went on to sell real estate. A photo of his office at 1702 Osceola Avenue was used for the album *Nuthin' Fancy*. But his high school terror campaign against long-hairs is what he will be best remembered for.

Robert E. Lee High School, 1200 S. McDuff Ave., Jacksonville, FL 32205

(904) 381-3930

Hours: Always visible

Cost: Free

Directions: Seven blocks northwest of St. Johns Ave. (Rte. 211), approximately five blocks northeast of Edgewood Ave.

Under the direction of Ronnie Van Sant, Lynyrd Skynyrd grew to become what some called "America's Rolling Stones." Band members came and went. The ones that went turned out to be the lucky ones. On October 20, 1977, the band's plane crashed in a Mississippi swamp, killing Ronnie Van Sant, Steve Gaines, and Cassie Gaines (Steve's sister, and one of the band's "Honkette" backup singers), as well as the band's personal assistant, Dean Kilpatrick.

Van Sant and the Gaineses were buried just south of Jacksonville in Orange Park. Their mausoleum is easily identified by the "Freebird" logo, and is located just north of the cemetery offices. On June 29, 2000, the graves were vandalized; Ronnie's casket was pulled out of the mausoleum and Steve's ashes were spilled. That was enough for their families—the Freebirds were moved to an undisclosed location and reburied, though the old markers remain. Leave all the flowers you want, but just know that the plots are empty.

Jacksonville Memory Gardens, 111 Blanding Blvd., Orange Park, FL 32073

(904) 272-2435

Hours: Daily 9 A.M.–5 P.M.

Cost: Free

Directions: Just south of the Orange Park Mall at I-295 on Rte. 21 (Blanding Blvd.).

Fans of the band (www.lynyrdskynyrd.com) can find plenty of merchandise at the Freebird Cafe in nearby Jacksonville Beach. The Cafe is the town's main performance venue, so call ahead for a schedule of upcoming acts.

Freebird Cafe, 200 N. 1st St., Jacksonville Beach, FL 32250

(904) 246-BIRD

Hours: Performances vary; check the Web site

Cost: Prices vary

www.freebirdcafe.com

Directions: At the corner of 1st St. and 1st Ave. N, near the beach.

Mandarin
Aunt Harriet's Cabin

Harriet Beecher Stowe, author of *Uncle Tom's Cabin*, was once identified by Abraham Lincoln as "the little woman who started the Civil War." Others thought so, too, so it seems all the more remarkable that just after the war she decided to spend her winters in a small cottage near Mandarin, starting in 1867. Her son had previously moved south to the Sunshine State to recover from his war wounds and planted an orange grove along the St. John's River.

Rather than lead a life in hiding, as Elvis does today, she charged tourists 75¢ to visit with her. Some of her guests included Mark Twain and William Cullen Bryant. Stowe eventually wrote a book about Florida called *Palmetto Leaves*, which attracted even more tourists to the state.

Stowe never returned to Florida after her husband died in 1886. Her home was eventually torn down, though one of the original property's outbuildings remains as part of a community club on the site today, at the northwest of the parking lot.

12247 Mandarin Rd., Mandarin, FL 32223

No phone

Hours: Torn down; only one outbuilding remains

Cost: Free

Directions: Turn south on Rte. 13 from I-295, turn right (east) on Mandarin Rd.

Marineland
Marineland of Florida

Marineland ain't what it used to be. Depending on your point of view, that could be a good thing or a bad thing. The facility was originally built by descendants of Cornelius Vanderbilt and Leo Tolstoy to shoot underwater films—it was called Marine Studios—but movies weren't covering all the bills. To bring in additional income, it began opening its doors to tourists in May 1938, making it the World's First Oceanarium. The studio's first shows featured a dolphin named Flippy—that was original—and later an albino named Snowball. But one of the park's most popular residents was Static, an electric eel. A handler would prod him with a pole, and Static would fight back with 600 volts of zapping eel fury, all clearly registered on a voltmeter inserted into the tank.

Marineland went bankrupt in 1998, and it looked as if this out-of-date park would be one for the history books. But it was retooled to be more educational and interactive. Marineland reopened a year later, and is still wowing audiences today. Now, with reservations (and a hefty fee), you can swim with the dolphins as part of the new Dolphin Encounter exhibit.

9600 Oceanshore Blvd., Marineland, FL 32080

(888) 279-9194 or (904) 460-1275

Hours: Wednesday–Monday 9:30 A.M.–5 P.M.

Cost: Adults $14, Kids $9; Dolphin Encounter $120

marineland.net

Directions: South of St. Augustine Beach on Rte. A1A, just past the Matanzas Inlet.

Ponte Vedra Beach
The Germans Have Landed

Four German tourists tossing around a beach ball on a Florida beach wouldn't normally be cause for alarm, but the four men frolicking at Ponte Vedra Beach on June 17, 1942, were an exception. These cleverly disguised men—each was in swimwear—had arrived at the beach early that morning on a German U-boat. Looking for all the world like beach bums (but carrying $174,000 in cash), the foursome boarded a bus for Jacksonville and points beyond.

Meanwhile, on New York's Long Island, four more men landed and were headed for the Big Apple. The plan was for the eight men to rendezvous in Cincinnati, then break off in pairs to sabotage America from the inside out: blow up a hydroelectric dam in Muscle Shoals, Alabama; destroy railroad lines in the Midwest; burn down aluminum plants from Illinois to Tennessee; foment unrest among German Americans; and poison New York City's water supply with hydrogen cyanide . . . nasty stuff.

Luckily, there was a snitch among the Long Island crew, George Dasch, who called the FBI as soon as he reached New York. The FBI thought he was a crank, so he went to the bureau's Washington headquarters. Within days, the FBI had apprehended all the invaders. A secret military court found them guilty and ordered their execution. Before the sentence was carried out, FDR commuted the sentence of Dasch and one other, Ernst Burger, both of whom had helped in the investigation. The FBI objected, claiming all credit for their capture, not acknowledging that the case had been handed to them on a silver platter . . . twice. The other six Germans got the electric chair on August 8. The story never made it to the American public until after the war was over.

Modern saboteurs would have a difficult time coming ashore at Ponte Vedra Beach today. Most of the shoreline is blocked by multimillion-dollar homes with gated security systems. Of course, those high fences aren't designed to keep the foreign riffraff out, but the American riffraff—folks like you—off "their" beaches.

Ponte Vedra Blvd., Ponte Vedra Beach, FL 32004

No phone

Hours: Always visible

Cost: Free

Directions: Along Rte. 203 (Ponte Vedra Blvd.) between Jacksonville Beach and Mickler Landing.

St. Augustine
Caddyshack

Back in 1979, the movie *Caddyshack* achieved the impossible: it made golf look exciting. It did it with a dancing gopher and a lot of explosions, neither of which you're likely to see watching the Masters. The movie was filmed at the Rolling Hills Golf and Country Club (3501 W. Rolling Hills Circle) in Davie, near Fort Lauderdale. Unfortunately, that place is off-limits to bounders like you, so you're going to have to settle for the two next best things, both in St. Augustine.

First, Bill Murray and his brothers have opened a movie-themed restaurant called Murray Bros. Caddyshack. (If you're one of those people who think Bill's brothers are tagalongs, you should know that brother Brian Doyle Murray helped write the screenplay.) Murray Bros. Caddyshack offers the traditional 19th green fare: sandwiches, which they call sand-wedges; salads, known as The Greens; and pizza, The Slices.

Murray Bros. Caddyshack, 455 S. Legacy Tr., St. Augustine, FL 32092

(904) 940-FORE

Hours: Sunday–Thursday 11:30 A.M.–10 P.M., Friday–Saturday 11:30 A.M.–11 P.M.

Cost: $6–$15

www.wgv.com/shopdine/d_murray.html

Directions: Take the International Golf Pkwy. west from I-95, then right on World Golf Village Way and follow it around to the right.

Murray Bros. Caddyshack is by far the favorite restaurant at the World Golf Village (the second stop), home of the World Golf Hall of Fame and IMAX Theater. That's right, if you think watching golf on television is exciting, wait until you see it on a six-story screen! The adjacent World Golf Hall of Fame is located between the resort's front and back nines, giving you time to browse around while waiting for your tee time. Inductees are honored in the awesome Tower Shrine.

World Golf Village, 500 S. Legacy Trail, St. Augustine, FL 32092

(888) 446-5301 or (904) 940-8000

Hours: Monday–Saturday 10 A.M.–6 P.M., Sunday Noon–6 P.M.

Cost: Adults $12, Seniors (55+) $11, Kids (5–12) $7

www.wgv.com

Directions: Exit 95A (International Golf Pkwy.) from I-95, follow the signs.

Castle Otttis—the extra *t* is for . . . for . . . *what*'s it for?

Castle Otttis

Rusty Ickes is a dreamer, and what's more, he's done something about it. Some time ago he started having elaborate visions when he slept; the plots varied, but they all took place in and around a medieval castle.

Ickes, who is half Lakota Sioux, had been taught to trust his visions, so he and his friend Ottis Sadler (who also plays together with Ickes in a reggae band) set out to build the castle he'd imagined. Without formal plans or permits, Ickes and Sadler started constructing the structure out of recycled stonework in Ickes's backyard.

The dreamer named the castle after his reggae bud, with one slight modification: he added a *t*. Why three *t*'s? Many reasons, mostly having to do with Christian symbolism—three crosses (that look like *t*'s) on Calvary, three members of the Trinity, and so on. The structure also contains another significant number, 88: the number of keys on a piano, the number of windows in the walls, and the year in which the castle was finished, the same year as the nearly forgotten Harmonic Convergence.

Castle Otttis (pronounced AH-tis) eventually caught the attention of a city building inspector who was kind enough to classify it as some type of garage or sculpture because the interior was never entirely finished. Lee Carpenter, himself a carpenter, was hired to finish the interior chapel with an altar and pews, but no electricity or running water was ever installed. Today this "garage" remains unfinished, but it is clean enough to host weddings, which it does several times a year. It is also open one Sunday every month.

103 Third St., PO Box 1754, St. Augustine, FL 32085

Private phone

Hours: Exterior always visible; interior the third Sunday of each month

Cost: Free

Directions: Just west of Rte. A1A, at the north end of town, opposite Villano Beach.

JACKSONVILLE
Singer **Pat Boone** was born Charles Eugene Boone in Jacksonville on June 1, 1934.

ST. AUGUSTINE
Ray Charles attended the Florida School for the Deaf and Blind (207 N. San Marco Avenue) from age 7 to 15. Here he learned to play the piano and read Braille, and he once tried to drive a maintenance truck across campus.

Fountain of Youth

Historians rarely argue about where Ponce de León's fabled Fountain of Youth is really located—Wakulla Springs, Silver Springs, Green Cove Springs—because most are convinced it isn't *anywhere*; it's a myth.

Louella MacConnell would have called that poppycock. She knew where it was: smack in the middle of her St. Augustine beachfront property, that's where! There was a small spring on the lot, a spring the former owner had dubbed Ponce de León Spring. MacConnell knew in her gut it was the *true* Fountain of Youth, and she planned to turn it into a tourist attraction.

Now MacConnell understood the value of a novelty—she had a diamond set in her front tooth—and she had the brains to exploit it. She was one of America's first female doctors. She set out to prove her fountain was *the* fountain. According to her retelling of events, while she was off in Spain in 1904, researching her bold theory, a tree next to the spring on her property toppled over, exposing a cross made of coquina stones embedded in the ground. The longer piece was laid out east–west, with 15 stones, while the north–south piece had 13 stones: 15 . . . 13 . . . 1513, the year Ponce de León set foot on the Florida shore! Excavators also found a silver salt chamber with a piece of parchment, supposedly written by a crew member, authenticating Ponce de León's landing on the spot. Wasn't that convenient?

You can still see the stone cross and the salt chamber at the Fountain of Youth today. Even if you don't believe the dubious claims made by MacConnell, the attraction is well worth a visit. The spring continues to ooze water from the Anastasia Aquifer, the same aquifer used by St. Augustine, though the city extracts the sulfur odor. Visitors are offered a paper cup and told, with a wink, the story of the spring's youthful properties. Inside the Spring Building is a mechanized diorama showing Ponce de León's first meeting with a very tall Timacuan Indian on April 2, 1513, while his ship bobs in the waves offshore. Your guide tells you this native tribe practiced a custom of having the two tallest men mate with the two tallest women each year, thus breeding an uncharacteristically tall population. Could this be why the runty Spanish explorer felt he'd discovered the fountain he sought?

You're left wondering as you move along to the next stop on the tour: the Explorer's Discovery Globe. Housed in its own structure, this bright blue sphere, 56 feet in circumference and illuminated from within, rotates on its axis while a disembodied Godlike voice tells you of the first 100 years of European exploration of the New World. Ships sail along lighted courses across the Atlantic, and Spanish missions appear—the effect is truly stunning.

Less impressive is the Navigator's Celestial Planetarium, the next stop on the tour. It's a smaller version of most planetariums, but it does contain a ship's mast to give you the sensation of sailing the seas at night, guided by your trusty astrolabe. You almost forget that the crew has scurvy.

11 Magnolia Ave., St. Augustine, FL 32084

(800) 356-8222 or (904) 829-3168

Hours: Daily 9 A.M.–5 P.M.

Cost: Adults $6, Seniors $5, Kids (6–12) $3

www.fountainofyouthflorida.com

Directions: East of Rte. A1A, east of the Old Jail, at the intersection of Williams and Magnolia Sts.

The Glob!

What was it? On the night of November 30–December 1, 1896, the decomposing remains of a seven-ton sea creature washed up on St. Augustine Beach. Those who saw it estimated its "tentacles" to have been 200 feet long. Nobody did much but stare and poke at the glob, and during the next high tide, it floated away. But then it washed up again, a day later, this time without its tentacles. Under the direction of Dr. DeWitt Webb, a physician and founder of the city's scientific society, locals tried to lash it down to prevent it from disappearing yet again. Tissue samples and photos were taken. Eventually, as it rotted and grew stinkier, they untied it and let it return to its watery grave.

Dr. A. E. Verrill of Yale studied the samples and publicly announced they came from a giant octopus, *Octopus giganteus verrill*, named after himself. Because no such mega-octopus was (or is) known to exist, his superiors suggested that he recant his findings, and he did. Other scientists, from the Smithsonian, came forward to dismiss the glob as nothing more than the gooey, shredded remains of a half-decomposed sperm whale.

End of story . . . or cover-up? The photographs taken of the carcass later disappeared under mysterious circumstances. The tissue samples also vanished. Sounds fishy . . . or octopussy.

So even though nobody is willing to come out and claim a colony of gigantic octopi are living just off St. Augustine Beach, if you feel something slithering around your legs while taking a dip here, you might want to get out of the water.

St. Augustine Beach, Rte. A1A, St. Augustine, FL 32084

No phone

Hours: No longer visible . . . but it could return

Cost: Free

Directions: Four miles south of town along A1A.

Gomek!

What do you do if your star performer up and dies on you? Do what the St. Augustine Alligator Farm did when Gomek, its 17-foot 9-inch Indo-Pacific saltwater crocodile, died in 1997: they stuffed him and put him back on display! Gomek had been captured in New Guinea in 1968, where he was known to locals as Louma Whalla Coremana Dikana, meaning "Fierce Giant with an Evil Nature." It was a cool name, but it was too long and too difficult to pronounce. His captors changed it to match an Australian cartoon character: Gomek.

For years he wowed the Aussies—the World's Largest Crocodile in Captivity! In 1989 he retired to the St. Augustine Alligator Farm, which has its own record to boast: Florida's Oldest Continuously Operating Tourist Attraction. It first opened in 1893 when two trolley-line employees looking for fun, gathered unsuspecting gators along their route and penned them inside an abandoned beach house. They soon noticed that tourists loved being able to look at these enormous reptiles up close . . . as long as they were protected from attack by chicken wire.

The farm moved to its present location a few years later, and in the 1920s bought out the stock of the nearby Ostrich Farm. The farm's animal menagerie continued to grow, including at least one specimen of all 23 species of crocodilian.

From the day he arrived, Gomek was the park's big draw even though he did little more than recline on the sand of his pen and wait for his next feeding. He weighed 1,900 pounds and handlers estimated his age at between 60 and 80 years. No wonder he died of a heart attack. Taxidermists mounted Gomek in a more active pose than most people ever saw him while alive: he's raised on his front legs with his mouth wide open, forever waiting to chomp on an unfortunate New Guinean villager.

St. Augustine Alligator Farm, 999 Anastasia Blvd., St. Augustine, FL 32084

(904) 824-3337

Hours: June–August 9 A.M.–6 P.M., May–September 9 A.M.–5 P.M.

Cost: Adults $14.95, Kids (5–11) $8.95

www.alligatorfarm.com

Directions: On Rte. A1A (Anastasia Blvd.) at Old Quarry Rd.

Johnny, you're a dummy. No, *really*.
Photo by author, courtesy Oldest Wooden School House

Oldest Wooden School House Robots

It might seem like a strange idea to fill the nation's oldest wooden schoolhouse with robots but ... but ... but ... OK, it *is* strange, but isn't that why you bought this book in the first place?

Clang, clang, clang! A female android, bell in hand, appears in an upper window along St. George Street in the old Spanish Quarter. Line up and pay your entry fee—it's time for school to start! And don't think you're going to be coddled like today's youth; this is public education circa 1763.

The first indication of how times have changed sits in a makeshift prison cell beneath the schoolhouse stairs. It appears that one young pupil has been very, very naughty and has been thrown into the "dungeon" by the headmaster robot. A sign around the child's neck professes his innocence, but since he's a mannequin instead of a talking robot, nobody pays him much mind. In the front of the class, a boy named Johnny wears a dunce cap, the standard head decoration for scatterbrained youth of yore. Be sure to laugh and point at Johnny; it'll make him try harder the next time. But don't worry that this Colonial-era role-playing will have any lasting effect on Johnny. Remember, he's just a robot, he has no feelings . . . yet.

14 St. George St., St. Augustine, FL 32084

(888) OLD-SCHL

Hours: Daily 9 A.M.–5 P.M.

Cost: Adults $2.75, Seniors (55+) $2.25, Kids (6–12) $1.75

Directions: One block south of the City Gates, off Castillo Dr. (Rte. A1A), at Tolomato Lane.

Potter's Wax Museum

Wax museums were once as common in tourist-trap towns as temporary tattoo parlors are today, but most have long since melted away. One of the few that remains just happens to be the first ever built in the United States: Potter's Wax Museum. George L. Potter opened the doors to his St. Augustine attraction in 1949. Many of his early wax sculptures had been made in England and flown stateside on commercial flights, each figure with its own seat. The original George L. Potter World of Wax was a much larger operation, with more figures. It was housed just up the street from its present location. Potter died in the 1980s, and the operation was eventually sold to its current owner, Gary White.

About 160 figures are in the collection today, shoehorned into various small galleries. In Arts & Sciences, Walt Disney, Leonardo da Vinci, Michelangelo, and Rembrandt share a cozy room. In Royalty & Empire, dozens of European monarchs flaunt their crown jewels and lavish clothing, barely aware that many will soon lose their heads involuntarily. Poor Princess Di might have requested that—her noggin appears to have been recycled from an old Barbra Streisand model! Around the corner, an optional gallery awaits those who are not faint at heart: the Chamber of Horrors. Nothing too ghastly, but there is plenty of fake blood oozing from the victims. In the American Century gallery, Al Capone looks left and right, providing the only animation in this museum, while Machine Gun Jack McGurn stands ready to shoot. And finally, in the Today's Stars gallery, the cast of *Seinfeld* upstages an old Sly Stalone dummy. Hey—that's waxy show biz.

17 King St., St. Augustine, FL 32084

(800) 584-4781 or (904) 829-9056

Hours: September–May, Sunday–Thursday 9 A.M.–5 P.M., Friday–Saturday 9 A.M.– 9 P.M.; June–August, daily 9 A.M.–9 P.M.

Cost: Adults $7.95, Seniors (55+) $6.95, Kids (6–12) $4.75

www.potterswax.com

Directions: Two blocks west of the Bridge of Lions on King St.

Ripley's Believe It or Not! Museum

St. Augustine's Ripley's Believe It or Not! Museum, the company's flagship attraction, is housed in the city's historic Castle Warden, constructed in 1887 by William Warden, a Standard Oil business partner of John D. Rockefeller. For some time the castle was also home to Florida's best-known writer, Marjorie Kinnan Rawlings—quite a step up from her cracker cabin at Cross Creek.

Pfffffftttt!! History, shmistory—nobody comes to Ripley's for an edumacation. Where's that 10.6-ounce feline hairball? A 13-pound local cat named Sashay coughed up this 8-by-4-by-4-inch hairball some years back and set a new world's record! But that's not all you'll see. Look, there's a sculpture of the *Last Supper* by B. W. Crawford of Denton, Texas, and it's made entirely out of pecans. And a bottle of fetal field mice wine from China. And the World's Largest Erector Set Ferris Wheel. And a cannibal's fork from Fiji. And Willie Wonka's hat and walking cane from the movie. And the intricate paintings of Linda Lee Curtiss . . . done entirely on potato chips!

Ghouls will appreciate the gallery on medical accidents—photos and X-rays of some very lucky survivors of some very unlucky accidents. See the Thai boy with a sword stuck in his forehead, or the Nevada man with a ½-inch auger drilled through his back. Just around the corner are strange animals to make your stomach go flip-flop, a two-faced kitten, a six-legged cow named Beauregard, and a chicken from Neenah, Wisconsin, that smoked cigarettes. (It probably started as a youth, trying to impress the chicks.)

Finally, just before you head out the door and into the gift shop, you'll come across a nude female mannequin stepping out of a bathtub. A sign tells you of a ghost that haunts Castle Warden, that of a female boarder who died in a fire here in April 1944. The mannequin's back is turned, and when you scurry to get a full-frontal view from the next alcove, she disappears!

19 San Marco Ave., St. Augustine, FL 32084

(904) 824-1606

E-mail: ripleys@aug.com

Hours: June–August, daily 9 A.M.–9 P.M.; September–August, daily 9 A.M.–7 P.M.

Cost: Adults $9.95, Seniors (55+) $7.95, Kids (5–12) $5.95

www.ripleys.com/bion/staug.html

Directions: At the intersection of Rte. A1A (San Marco Ave.) and Castillo Dr.

Starke
Old Sparky

Old Sparky is as faithful an employee as the Florida Department has ever known, and though he's pushing 75, he still gets the job done. No, he's not a septuagenarian sentinel; Old Sparky is the state's electric chair, based right here in Starke. In the last three-quarters of a century the three-legged device has been used to execute 240 prisoners, including Ted Bundy. On three different occasions—October 19, 1936; October 6, 1941; and March 23, 1942—four prisoners were executed in a single day.

Old Sparky's recent performance has given Florida legislators pause—even those who are strong proponents of capital punishment. On May 4, 1990, double murderer Jesse Joseph Tafero's head burst into flames. Each time it did, the executioner turned off the juice. Tafero wasn't declared dead until the third jolt four long minutes later. Some said it was the wet sponge on his head that caught fire, not his noggin. Prison officials promised it would never, ever, ever happen again.

Then, on March 25, 1997, flames leapt from the skull of Pedro Medina, igniting his death mask. The blue and orange fire burned for 10 seconds and smoke filled the death chamber. The repeat performance encouraged Florida to pass legislation offering lethal injection to death row inmates, though the state rejected one congressman's proposal to offer the guillotine as well.

However, Old Sparky is still an option for criminals with a sense of the dramatic. In 1999, the state was preparing to put prisoner Allen Davis to death and was worried the 350-pound triple-murderer might break the weathered old chair. So they had a new chair built and put the old electrodes on it. The new Old Sparky has an adjustable headrest and a wider, more comfortable seat. One death row inmate commented, "I can hardly wait to sit in Old Sparky. I'm curious about it. I think it's spiffy."

Florida State Prison, Starke, FL 32091

Contact: 7819 NW 228th St., Raiford, FL 32026

(904) 368-2500

Hours: Prison visible at all times

Cost: Free

www.dc.state.fl.us/facilities/region2/205.html

Directions: Eleven miles west of town on Rte. 16.

IT COULD BE WORSE

Sure, having your skull ignited by 2,200 volts of electricity can ruin your day, but at least the suffering is over in relatively short order. Not so with other punishments in several Florida prisons:

★ Unruly prisoners at two prisons are fed "confinement loaf," a mixture of carrots, dehydrated potato flakes, navy beans, tomato paste, spinach, whole-wheat toast, vegetable oil, and nonfat dry milk.

★ Florida prisoner Douglas Jackson sued the state in the 1990s because he didn't have access to public television but was forced to watch "junk TV."

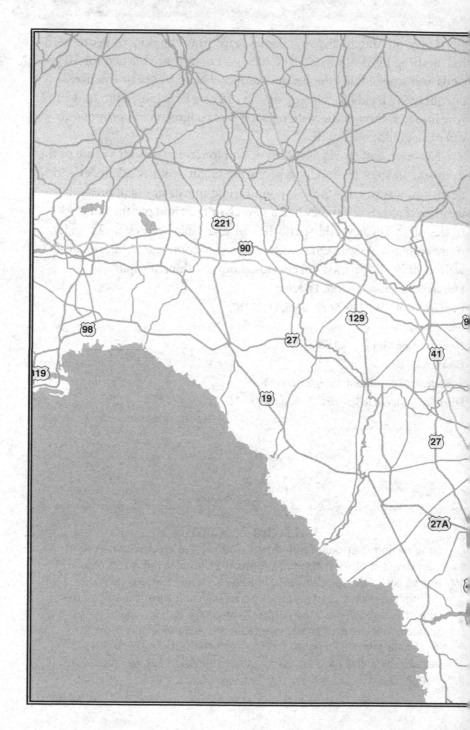

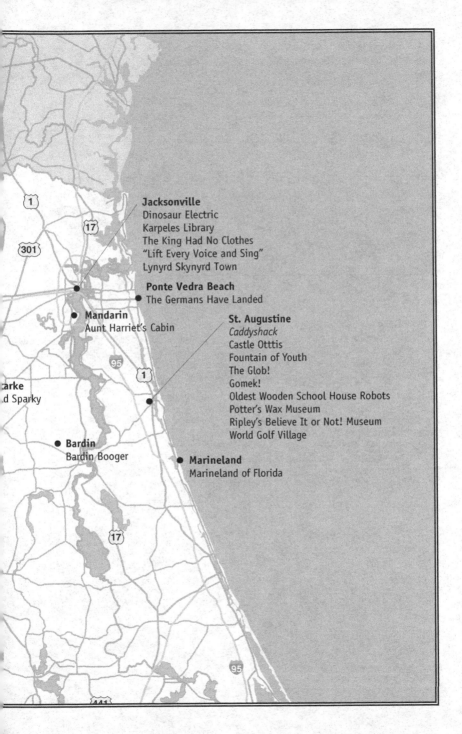

Jacksonville
Dinosaur Electric
Karpeles Library
The King Had No Clothes
"Lift Every Voice and Sing"
Lynyrd Skynyrd Town

Ponte Vedra Beach
The Germans Have Landed

Mandarin
Aunt Harriet's Cabin

St. Augustine
Caddyshack
Castle Otttis
Fountain of Youth
The Glob!
Gomek!
Oldest Wooden School House Robots
Potter's Wax Museum
Ripley's Believe It or Not! Museum
World Golf Village

Bardin
Bardin Booger

Marineland
Marineland of Florida

arke
.d Sparky

3

THE GULF COAST

Life on Florida's western coast is a lot like the water just off shore: placid. Still, there are oases of excitement to be found. Have you ever met a mermaid? Do you want to see how a female urinal works? Would you believe me if I told you the earth was spherical, like a ball, but that we live on the *inside* of that sphere? How would you like to visit the site where Ozzy Osborne was nearly killed in a kamikaze attack? Are you suddenly and unexplainably intrigued? Then read on . . .

Bartow
Wonder House

Conrad Schuck was given a death sentence by his Pittsburgh doctor in the early 1920s, so he moved to a warmer climate to live out his final days. But when he began feeling better, he started to build a home. Using materials he found on his land, he constructed what would later be named the Wonder House. He finished the building in 1925.

What was so wondrous about it? In a state where summers are unbearably hot, it had a unique air-conditioning system that used a central fireplace to create a draft through the rooms, a draft cooled by rainwater captured from the roof. The Wonder House also had several bathtubs on its secluded porches, and a system of mirrors that allowed those inside to see who was at the front door from any room in the house.

Those mirrors got Schuck in trouble during the early days of World War II. Rumors circulated that he was using the fireplace and mirrors to signal German planes. To quell the rumors, he bricked up the fireplace.

You're not going to be able to see the fireplace, bricked over or not, because the private home is not open to the public. But you can see the impressive exterior of the house, and when you do, you'll know that somewhere inside the building is its current owner, watching your every move in a mirror.

1075 Mann Rd., Bartow, FL 33830
Private phone
Hours: Always visible; view from street
Cost: Free
Directions: One-half mile south of Georgia St. on Rte. 17, turn west on Mann Rd.

BROOKSVILLE
Hernando was renamed Brooksville in 1859 for Congressman Preston Brooks of South Carolina who, on May 20, 1856, beat Yankee Senator Charles Sumner of Massachusetts nearly to death with his walking cane on the Senate floor.

Arrrrrrrgh!

Bonita Springs
Ship Building

Ahoy, mateys! An Italian galleon named the *Tony Franco* seems to have washed ashore in Bonita Springs and drifted a considerable distance inland. On closer inspection, it turns out not to be a ship at all, but a concrete building made to look like one, complete with masts, rigging, sails, and cannons.

The Bonita Rib Room & Club Royale was built using the plans from a similar ship-shaped structure in Saugus, Massachusetts. In its early days it was a pirate-themed restaurant, but its swashbuckling servers were made to walk the plank to make way for this semiprivate dinner club. Visitors are welcome, but there's a cover charge for nonmembers and a strict dress code—jackets are required.

Wait a second—what kind of pirate wears a dinner jacket? They should require patrons to wear eye patches, stuffed parrots, or peg legs instead. Now *that* would be a royale experience!

The Bonita Rib Room & Club Royale, 24080 S. Tamiami Trail, Bonita Springs, FL 34134

(239) 947-3333

Hours: Always visible; Meals, daily 5–10 P.M..; Music, daily 9 P.M..–1 A.M.

Cost: Free; Meals $18–$30

Directions: On Rte. 41 (Tamiami Tr.) north of Rte. 865 (Beach Rd.).

Captiva Island
Bubble Room

If you're the kind of person who feels uncomfortable with forced jocularity, the Bubble Room might not be right for you. But if you don't mind ordering food from an adult wearing rainbow suspenders and a jester's hat with jingle bells, then come on by. Your server is called a Bubble Scout because beneath all those goofy buttons, he or she is wearing a scouting uniform. Your Bubble Scout will explain the menu because the dish names only hint at the ingredients: Porky Pig à la Bobby Philips, the Judy Garden, Artie "Choke" Shaw and His Bubble Band, the Maltese Falcon, the Little Rascals, and Guava Gabor. (Despite the nonserious names, the food is seriously fantastic.)

Every square inch of the restaurant's three floors is covered in kitschy movie memorabilia, antique toys, and Floridiania. Model trains run on tracks around the ceiling. The rotating chandeliers have Christmas bubble bulbs in their sockets. Even the tables are filled with tchochkes; each glass top reveals hundreds of items in a shadow box below. After your meal, you're encouraged to walk around the place, check out the balcony overlooking Santa's Workshop, and pose for a photo in the boat emerging from the Tunnel of Love.

15001 Captiva Dr., Captiva Island, FL 33924

(239) 472-5558

Hours: Lunch, daily 11:30 A.M.–2:30 P.M.; Dinner, Monday–Saturday 4:30–10 P.M.,
  Sunday 4:30–9:30 P.M.

Cost: Meals $10–$27

www.bubbleroomrestaurant.com

Directions: At the far northern end of Captiva Island, at Wrightman Lane.

Clermont
Citrus Tower

When the Citrus Tower first opened in 1956, there were a lot more orange groves in central Florida. But killing frosts and far more destructive housing developments have wiped out most of the fruit trees. Today, when you take the elevator to the top of this 226-foot tower, all there is to see are the roofs of recently built homes and highways radiating out from Orlando.

Not that it isn't worth the trip to the top, but just understand that if you're only looking for citrus it's in the ground-level gift shop. The glass-enclosed observation deck is rather spartan, having little more than wall-to-wall carpet and a hole labeled "Wishing Well." Drop a penny in the slot and listen at the tube as the coin clinks down a series of slides to the bottom.

The Citrus Tower will likely be here for many years to come. The architects used five million pounds of concrete and 149,000 pounds of reinforced steel to build a structure that can withstand 190-MPH winds. If only orange trees were that strong.

Citrus Tower, Inc., 141 N. Highway 27, Clermont, FL 34711

(352) 394-4061

Hours: Monday–Saturday 9 A.M.–6 P.M., Sunday 11 A.M.–5 P.M.

Cost: Adults $3.50, Kids (3–15) $1

www.citrustwer.com

Directions: Just northeast of town along Rte. 27.

BROOKSVILLE
Brooksville claims to be the Home of the Tangerine.

CHARLOTTE HARBOR
A boomerang found in Little Salt Spring near Charlotte Harbor is the oldest boomerang found anywhere in the world, and the only one of its kind found in North America.

ELOISE
Singer **Jim Stafford** was born in Eloise on January 16, 1944.

GEORGE H.W. BUS
1989–199

A bunch of troublemakers
Photo by author, courtesy of Presidents' Hall of Fame

Presidents' Hall of Fame

You know you're in for something special when you pull into the parking
lot at the Presidents' Hall of Fame. The building looks like Mt. Vernon,
but a seated replica of Abe from the Lincoln Memorial has been placed
between the front columns. Inside, this attraction looks like a wax museum
crossed with a jumbo-size dollhouse crossed with a presidential garage sale.

Anything and everything having to do with the nation's chief executives is on display. Look, there's a model of the White House while it was being built. And there's Ron and Nancy's sofa pillows from the family quarters, cross-stitched with their Secret Service code names, "Rawhide" and "Rainbow." (You're left to assume that Ronnie was "Rawhide," but you never know.) Check out the champagne glasses used to toast Soviet leader Gorbachev when he traveled to Washington. The display points out that the glasses still have the leaders' original "residue and lip prints," which could come in handy if anyone ever wants to clone either of them (see page 187). Less impressive is Bill Clinton's blue leather travel bag; it looks like something you might win on *The Price Is Right*.

The Presidents' Hall of Fame includes dollhouse models of the Oval Offices of our most recent commanders-in-chief, and full-sized wax figures of all 43 men who have held the position. The museum is also the home base of the 60-foot scale replica of the White House (the World's Largest Doll House!), though it is rarely on display here; it's usually out touring the nation's malls, airports, and convention centers.

123 N. Highway 27, Clermont, FL 34711

(352) 394-2836

Hours: Daily 9 A.M.–6 P.M.

Cost: Adults $9.95, Kids (5–11) $4.95

Directions: Northeast of town along Rte. 27, just south of the Citrus Tower.

FROSTPROOF
The town of Frostproof was bombed by American pilots several times during World War II. Trainees mistook the town's one-light main intersection for an *X* at the nearby Avon Park Bombing Range.

HAINES CITY
A glowing green UFO landed near a police cruiser in Haines City on March 19, 1992. Patrolman Luis Delgado said the disk-shaped craft landed between Robinson Drive and Roe Road along 30th Street.

It all seems so clear.
Photo by author, courtesy Koreshan State Park

Estero
Koreshan State Park

Don't try to say Cyrus Teed was no brain surgeon, because he *was*. Born and raised in upstate New York, he pursued a career as a noggin doctor until an angel, dressed in purple and gold, appeared to him in 1870. "The earth is concave," the Mother of the Universe revealed. "You live on the inside of a 'macroscopic egg,' and the stars, the sun, and the heavens are floating around inside the void." (Those were not her exact words, but they're close enough.)

With a little mathematical checking, Teed was convinced. Off he went to Chicago to recruit followers to his new religion: Koreshanity. (*Koresh* is Hebrew for "Cyrus," a shepherd.) Over the years he converted 4,000 into believers, but he pissed off a whole lot of nonbelievers, not so much with his hollow egg talk, but because of the group's more progressive stances on equality of the sexes, racial tolerance, ecological conservation, and communal property.

Teed decided the best strategy to advance his church was to found a utopian community, and in 1894 he found a plot of ground near Fort Myers that he said had special magnetic qualities. He convinced the owner, Gustave Damkohler, to donate the land and join the church. Teed dubbed the colony New Jerusalem. There was to be no drinking, no smoking, no gambling, no swearing, and no sex on its grounds. He only persuaded 200 to join him.

The prophet tried to prove his concave earth theory in 1897 using a device called a Rectilineator, a straight-line beam running along the earth's surface. He claimed that if it hit the ground in two points, his theory was confirmed. Sure enough, when it hit the sand twice on Naples Beach, Teed announced that the Mother of the Universe had been vindicated. He offered $10,000 to anyone who could disprove his data, but nobody ever tried, much less collected.

The locals were not amused by their new neighbor, nor were they happy to have a significant voting block controlled by a person they felt was a raving lunatic. So it was not surprising that the sheriff's son and several others roughed Teed up at the Fort Myers train station in 1906. Teed would die two years later, some say from the injuries received in the beating. But before he died, Teed claimed he would rise again. His flock put Teed's coffin on the stage of the community's Art Hall. Nothing happened. The county coroner demanded that Teed be removed and buried for health reasons. He was placed in a tomb on nearby Estero Island where followers maintained a 24-hour vigil.

Still nothing.

Thirteen long years and many, many, many prayers later, a 1921 hurricane washed away Teed's coffin, which was never to be found again. His followers rejoiced, "See? He rose from his tomb!" Everyone else said, "Whaaaaa???"

The dwindling Koreshan community got an unexpected influx in the 1930s when Hedwig Michel, a Jewish woman run out of Hitler's Germany, came to Florida and fixed up the place. Oddly enough, Hitler also believed, at least in part, in Teed's theories. He even sent a team to the Baltic Sea in early 1945 to point its telescopes skyward in a last, desperate attempt to spy on the British Navy. (Is it any wonder they lost the war?)

A state park was built around the sect's eight remaining commune buildings. Inside the old Art Hall, where Teed was put on deathly display, is a working model of the macroscopic egg. See if you can figure it out. If you're still confused, there are still a few followers of Koreshanity in an office across the highway from the park.

Koreshan State Historic Site, PO Box 7, Estero, FL 33928

(941) 992-0311

Hours: Daily 8 A.M.–5 P.M.

Cost: $3.25/car; $1/pedestrian or bicycler

www.dep.state.fl.us/parks/district4/koreshan/index.asp

Directions: Just south of Estero on Rte. 41, turn west on Corkscrew Rd.

Fort Myers
Tom and Hank

Fort Myers was a sleepy little village of 350 back when inventor Thomas Alva Edison showed up in 1885. Though he was only in his late 30s at the time, his doctor had warned him to stop burning his filament at both ends and to get some rest, and suggested the inventor take a vacation in a climate warmer than Menlo Park, New Jersey. Edison picked Fort Myers because he thought it a good place to find the bamboo he needed for his lightbulb filaments. So much for doctor's orders.

Warmed and rejuvenated by the Florida climate, Edison decided to set up a new laboratory on the Gulf Coast, and arranged for a home to be built . . . in Fairfield, Maine. The building was shipped to Fort Myers in pieces and reassembled in 1886, making it the town's first trailer park, sort of. He dubbed the home Seminole Lodge and illuminated it with electric chandeliers that you can still see today, with their still-working original bulbs! Edison offered to illuminate Fort Myers with streetlights, but the town turned him down for fear the lights would keep the free-roaming cows awake at night. In 1900, Edison had hundreds of royal palms imported from Cuba and gave them to Fort Myers. Many still line the city's boulevards.

In 1900, Edison built what is believed to be America's first modern swimming pool, fed by an artesian spring, using Edison Portland Cement. Henry Ford, Edison's biggest fan, bought a relatively modest two-story home next door in 1916 so that he could hang out with the great inventor. Ford named his home Mangoes.

Fort Myers has long since gotten over its distrust of street lights and, on the weekend closest to Edison's birthday each February, the town hosts a Festival of Lights. Both the Edison and Ford homes are open to the public today, still connected by their Friendship Gate. The laboratory at the Edison estate is only a replica; Ford moved the original lab to his Greenfield Village museum in Dearborn, Michigan, in 1929.

Edison-Ford Winter Estates, 2350 McGregor Blvd., Fort Myers, FL 33901

(941) 334-3614

Hours: Monday–Saturday 9 A.M.–4 P.M., Sunday Noon–4 P.M.

Cost: Adults $14, Kids (6–12) $7.50

www.edison-ford-estate.com

Directions: Seven blocks southwest of Rte. 41 (Cleveland Ave.) on Rte. 867 (McGregor Blvd.).

Inglis
Local Government at Work

With all the issues that elected officials have to keep them busy, you'd think that fighting the devil would be the least of their worries. But you're looking at it the wrong way, according to Inglis mayor Carolyn Risher. Think BIG: if you banish Satan, all your town's troubles will be solved!

And that's just what Mayor Risher did. In late 2001 she signed a proclamation that the Prince of Darkness, Mephistopheles, Beelzebub, the guy on the canned ham label, was banned from the city. The proclamation was duplicated and sealed inside four monuments placed along the four roads that connect the town to the outside world.

One of those roads, Route 40 heading toward Yankeetown, would have been an unlikely entry point for Lucifer, even without the mayor's handiwork; in 1996 the local government renamed the road Follow That Dream Parkway to honor Elvis's long ago visit to the area to film *Follow That Dream*. During shooting, the King stayed at the Port Paradise Resort (1610 S.E. Paradise Circle, (904) 795-3111) in Crystal River. Were the devil to try to approach Inglis on this rock 'n' holy road, he would no doubt burst into flames!

Inglis Town Hall, 135 Highway 40W, Inglis, FL 34449

(352) 447-2203

Hours: Always visible

Cost: Free

Directions: Four blocks west of Rte. 19.

One way to save gas.

Lake Wales
Spook Hill

If only scientists could harness the mysterious force on a street in this sleepy Florida burg, all the world's energy problems might be solved. Believe it or not, cars actually roll *uphill* on Fifth Street, better known as Spook Hill.

A local legend says that an alligator's ghost is to blame. The reptile was killed by a Seminole warrior years ago, and has never stopped trying to drag humans away, uphill, to eat them. If you are interested in being among its potential victims, park your car in front of the Spook Hill sign, read the legend, then slowly drive forward to the line on the pavement. Stop, put on your parking brake, then shift your car into neutral. Then release the brake. The car will roll uphill for 100 feet or so. (The same thing happens to balls placed on the road surface, as well as rain runoff.)

Killjoys claim it is nothing more than an optical illusion. These are the same folks who, as booger-eating schoolkids, ran around the playground telling the rest of the kids there was no such thing as the Tooth Fairy. Well, screw them. Come to Spook Hill and see if you don't roll away a believer!

Fifth St. & Wales Dr. N, Lake Wales, FL 33853

Contact: Lake Wales Chamber of Commerce, 340 W. Central Ave., PO Box 191, Lake
  Wales, FL 33859

(863) 676-3445

Hours: Always visible

Cost: Free

historiclakewales.com/spookhill/

Directions: At the foot of 5th St., at Wales Dr., east of Rte. 27.

Edward's beauty parlor is gone.

Lakeland and Worthington Gardens
Edward Scissorhands Towns

When Tim Burton set out to make *Edward Scissorhands* in 1989, he needed a freshly built, cookie-cutter subdivision for the exterior shots. What he found was the Carpenter's Run development northeast of Tampa. The film crew painted the homes in pastel shades, trimmed the newly sodded lawns, and added a topiary here and there—instant movie set! Of course, the homes in Carpenter's Run have long since been repainted, and the twig-sized trees and shrubs that you see in the movie have all but camouflaged this piece of cinematic history. But you can almost imagine you're back on the set if you squint reeeeeeal hard.

Carpenter's Run, Worthington Gardens, FL 32697
No phone
Hours: Always visible
Cost: Free
Directions: Just southwest of the intersection of Rte. 54 and Cypress Creek Rd.

The 1950s-era strip mall where Edward hopes to establish a beauty parlor, on the other hand, looks pretty much the way it did in the movie. The Southgate Shopping Center is located in Lakeland, the hometown of Publix, the retail chain that was the flagship in many art deco and googie-style malls throughout the south. This mall is one of the few that retains its original architectural features.

Southgate Shopping Center, 2500 S. Florida Ave., Lakeland, FL 33803
No phone
Hours: Always visible
Cost: Free
Directions: Four blocks south of Beacon Rd. on Rte. 37 (Florida Ave.).

Leesburg
Ozzy Crash Site

You probably know that before he became America's doddering rock 'n' roll grampa, Ozzy Osbourne was a party animal. So was the rest of his band, particularly guitarist Randy Rhoads. On March 19, 1982, these rockers were headed for the Tangerine Bowl where they were to play in the Rock Superbowl XIV. They had stopped west of Leesburg at a private airfield community named Flying Baron Estates. The 25-year-old Rhoads got the wacky idea to buzz their touring bus from the sky, so he and the group's hairdresser, Rachel Youngblood, hired local pilot Andrew Aycock to take them up for a spin. After circling the airport three times, Aycock dove toward Ozzy's customized behemoth. The Beechcraft Bonanza's wing clipped the bus, the plane spun out of control, and slammed into the two-story home of Voncile Calhoun.

Cleanup crews didn't find any pieces "larger than a telephone" in the burning rubble. Ozzy and three others on the bus escaped injury, but were understandably rattled. They checked into Leesburg's Hilco Inn and canceled their Rock Superbowl appearance. Fans had to be satisfied with seeing Foreigner, UFO, and Bryan Adams, which only compounded the tragedy.

Casteen & Airway Rds., Leesburg, FL 34748

No phone

Hours: Always visible, view from road

Cost: Free

Directions: Head west of town on Rte. 44, turn south on Flatwoods Rd., west on Casteen Rd., then south on Airway Rd. to the gated entrance to the community.

Naples
The Teddy Bear Museum

Teddy bears are not just for kids anymore; they're a serious business. Collectors will salivate at the 5,000+ bears in this massive collection, which is why most of them are safely behind drool-repelling glass. They've got versions of Paddington, Lone Star, Corduroy, Rupert, Smokey, and Pooh with a signed first edition of *The House at Pooh Corner*. There are displays featuring a Teddy Bear Wedding, a Teddy Bear Picnic, a Teddy Bear Parade, and the Three-Bear Cottage before Goldilocks busts in and starts trashing the place. While most of the museum's bears are made of fabric, some are sculpted from marble, crystal, bronze, and wood.

At the center of the museum is a larger-than-life-size hollow bear tree that acts as a "li-beary" for young readers. Teddy-filled balloons hover overhead, just out of the tots' reach. If kids want to get their hands on a bear, there are plenty for sale in the Paws Gift Shop. If you've got an old, tattered bear left over from childhood, the museum has a Mend a Friend service where expert craftspersons can restore your fluffy buddy.

2511 Pine Ridge Rd., Naples, FL 34109

(866) 365-BEAR or (941) 598-2711

E-mail: info@teddymuseum.com

Hours: Tuesday–Saturday 10 A.M.–5 P.M.; expanded hours during the holidays

Cost: Adults $8, Seniors $6, Kids $3

www.teddymuseum.com

Directions: Just northeast of the intersection of Rte. 31 (Airport Pulling Rd.) and Rte. 896 (Pine Ridge Rd.).

New Port Richey
Leverock's Altar Stone

A face from the past.

Talk about a stroke of good luck. When the owners of this establishment broke ground for the building, they unearthed a 2,000-year-old altar stone with two faces carved on the side. The state's archeological commission verified its authenticity, but rather than cart it off to a musty museum, allowed it to be displayed in front of the Leverock Restaurant. Unfortunately, few patrons of this eatery even know it's there, which is understandable; where it's placed, it looks almost like a traffic barrier.

In addition to the faces, the rock has a hollowed-out orifice for sacrificial offerings. Fruit? Animals?? *People*??? In truth, not much is known about exactly what was offered up to the gods by the people who carved this boulder. Let your imagination run wild.

Leverock Restaurant, 4927 Rte. 19 South, New Port Richey, FL 34652

(727) 849-8000

Hours: Always visible

Cost: Free

www.leverocks.com/newportrichey.html

Directions: One block north of Trouble Creek Rd.

This shell suit will set you back a few clams.
Photo by author, courtesy Shell Factory

North Fort Myers
Shell Factory

Don't even bother loading up your suitcase with souvenirs if you're
planning on stopping by the Shell Factory during your Florida sojourn.

This place will have everything you need and a few things you don't, and all at great prices. Google-eyed frogs made from clams? Got 'em. Shellacked alligator heads? Any size you want. Coconut monkeys? Pirate, sailor, or hula girl—they've got all three.

And don't forget the Shell Factory's massive shell selection—the world's largest—and all of them are for sale. Why spend hours combing a beach, hoping for the best and finding the worst, and straining your back in the process? The Shell Factory's got bin after bin after bin of bulk shells from Florida and the rest of the world—take your pick. But be sure to remove the price tags before you bring them home to show your friends.

If you're the type who finds loose shells impractical, perhaps you'd be interested in some of the housewares the Shell Factory has to offer: shell-encrusted mirrors and picture frames, shell-covered paperweights and desk sets, shell night lights, shell ties and suits, and best of all, shell toilet seats.

2787 N. Tamiami Trail, Ft. Myers, FL 33903

(239) 995-2141

Hours: Daily 9 A.M.–9 P.M.

Cost: Free

www.shellfactory.com

Directions: Just south of the northern merge of Rte. 41 and Business Rte. 41 (Tamiami Tr.).

HOMOSASSA SPRINGS

Replicas of the British crown jewels can be found in the lobby of the Crown Hotel (109 N. Seminole Avenue, (342) 344-5555) in Homosassa Springs.

What a dragster!
Photo by author, courtesy Don Garlits Museum of Drag Racing

Ocala
The Don Garlits Museum of Drag Racing

They didn't always call him Big Daddy Garlits; he had to work his way up from Garbage Don, racing his Swamp Rat on the Bakersfield circuit back in the 1950s. But heck, you probably already know that . . . if you're a *true* drag racing fan.

Garlits is to drag racing what Henry Ford was to automobiles: the biggest name around. With each Swamp Rat, from I to XXX, he made another breakthrough. Port injection . . . hypoid tires on the back . . . bicycle tires on the front . . . and when his 1969 Slingshot blew up in Long Beach, California, on March 8, 1970, tearing off half of his right foot in the process, Garlits built the first rear-engine dragster. (The museum has some of the fateful shrapnel on display.)

You'll see most of the Swamp Rats here in the museum, but so much more, too. Check out the famous Little Red Wagon and Shirley Muldowney's 1980 Attebury. Step into the Engine Museum and see a few motors that would never fit under your hood. Admire cabinets filled with household artifacts from the Garlits family. And be sure to buy the combination ticket that'll get you into the adjoining classic car museum. They've got a 1956 Chrysler Imperial sedan that Mamie Eisenhower bought for Ike's birthday, custom fitted with a 45 RPM record player. There's also a 1950 Mercury that was driven by the Fonz on *Happy Days*.

One thing is for sure: despite the name, this place is not a drag.

13700 SW 16th Ave., Ocala, FL 34473

(352) 245-8661

Hours: Daily 9 A.M.–5 P.M.

Cost: Drag Racing Museum, Adults $8, Seniors (55+) $6, Teens (13–18) $6, Kids (5–12)
  $3; Combination, Adults $12, Seniors (55+) $10, Teens (13–18) $10, Kids (5–12) $3

www.garlits.com

Directions: Exit 67 from I-75, 10 miles south of town, head east on Rte. 484, then south
  on 16th St.

Ocklawaha
Ma Barker's Death Site

When the FBI cornered what was left of Ma Barker's gang at a lakefront retreat, there was only one thing to do: kill 'em all! The gang had been on the run after kidnapping millionaire Edward George Bremer (one of FDR's close friends), as well as pulling off a string of bank robberies and other assorted antisocial behavior.

Most of Ma's sons were dead or incarcerated when the FBI came knocking on her door on January 16, 1935. Only she and Freddy were inside. Informed that they were going to be placed under arrest, Ma told the agent, "Let's see what Freddy says." Freddy was a man of few words—he fired a machine gun at the G-man instead.

The FBI launched tear gas into the house to blind the outlaws. A gun battle raged for 45 minutes, but then the shooting decreased. Every once in a while a breeze would blow a drape inside the house and the agents would begin firing again. This went on for another five *hours*, so long that local citizens had time to gather picnic baskets and bring them over to watch the events unfold. Finally, the feds got the courage to send the Barker's frightened hired cook into the house. He found Ma dead in a front room and Freddy on the stairs. In all, about 3,000 rounds of ammunition had been emptied into the building—4 bullets had hit Ma and 11 hit Freddy. The remaining 2,985 were in the walls, floors, furniture, stairs, cabinets, doors, trees, and God knows where else.

Both Ma and Freddy were taken to the Pyle Mortuary in Ocala where anyone and everyone could come by and take a look . . . until that autumn. They were finally returned to Oklahoma for burial.

Ocklawaha reenacts the Barker Gang Shoot-Out each January, though the current owners of the death home want no part of it. They've got their own problems, mostly from gangster-loving lookie-loos. Some say their house is also haunted by Ma's ghost; she's seen from time to time combing her hair.

Old Bradford House, Rte. 25, Ocklawaha, FL 32179

Private phone

Hours: Private residence; view from street

Cost: Free

Directions: Turn west at the Methodist Church, and drive to the end of the road; on the shores of Lake Weir.

INVERNESS

Inverness Police Chief Joseph Elizarde arrested the short-order cook at the Happy Dayz Diner (441 S. Route 41) in 2002 when the two hamburgers he'd ordered didn't arrive promptly.

LAKE PLACID

Lake Placid claims to be the Caladium Capital of the World.

Lake Placid is known as the Town of Murals.

This man's castle is his home.
Photo by author, courtesy Solomon's Castle

Ona
Solomon's Castle

Howard Solomon, the da Vinci of Debris, broke ground on his dream castle in 1972 in swampland unsuitable for typical development. He had no choice—he'd bought the land in the winter before he realized it flooded every summer. To date, he has built more than 12,000 square feet of a structure that is part bed-and-breakfast, part restaurant, part studio, part art gallery, and part what-have-you, all out of recycled material. The castle's walls shimmer like Camelot's, covered in aluminum printing plates discarded by a local newspaper. Solomon's Castle also has a moat, a dungeon, and a bell tower.

Lucky for you, it's all open to the public. Solomon's guided tour is not for the pun-phobic. The castle is filled with more than 200 sculptures, each one a different visual joke and punctuated with Solomon's cornball commentary delivered at the speed of Henny Youngman. Don't worry if you miss one of his gags every so often, another will follow momentarily and you don't want to slow down the tour. The castle contains more than 80 stained-glass windows, some containing Biblical scenes, others fairy tales, and a few both, just to see if you're paying attention.

When you're done, the Boat in the Moat is docked alongside the castle for your dining enjoyment. It's a full-size galleon-shaped restaurant that serves a surf and turf menu.

4533 Solomon Rd., Ona, FL 33865

(863) 494-6077

E-mail: castle@cyberstreet.com

Hours: October–June, Tuesday–Sunday 11 A.M.–4 P.M.

Cost: Adults $10, Kids (Under 12) $4

www.solomonscastle.com

Directions: Head west out of Zolfo Springs on Rte. 64, turn south on Rte. 665, then left on Solomon Rd.

Just put it in reverse and slowly back away.

Plant City
Dinosaur World

Something must have been brewing in the swamps of Gator Jungle. That old reptile attraction closed its door a few years back, but reopened a year later . . . as Dinosaur World! Could these enormous reptiles be mutations from the earlier park? Not to fear—they're just fiberglass.

Visitors enter Dinosaur World between the legs of an enormous *T. rex* whose body is the gift shop. The gift shop isn't really shaped like a dinosaur, it's the other way around. The park has more than 150 full-size prehistoric creatures shoehorned into a relatively small space. The dense plant life and swampy ponds give the impression that you've stepped back in time, and because the park is so new, the sculptures are fairly accurate by scientific standards. Dinosaur World has also a boneyard, a fossil dig, and a picnic area if you want to throw a cool kid's (or nerdy adult's) birthday party.

5145 Harvey Tew Rd., Plant City, FL 33565

(813) 717-9865

E-mail: info@dinoworld.net

Hours: Daily 9 A.M.–Sundown

Cost: Adults $9.75, Seniors (60+) $8.95, Kids (3–12) $7.75

www.dinoworld.net/florida.htm

Directions: Exit Branch Forbes Rd. north from I-4, turn left onto Harvey Tew Rd.

Not *my* fantasy.

Polk City
Fantasy of Flight

First-time drivers along I-4 are often shocked to see an airplane, nose down, crashed on the north side of the highway with a skydiver hanging from its tail section. But as they draw closer, they realize the plane is an advertisement for a local air museum: Fantasy of Flight.

Because of its fair weather, Florida is filled with aircraft museums. What makes this museum unique is that virtually all of the 40-some planes in its collection are still airworthy. Most have been restored (and all have been flown) by Kermit Weeks, Fantasy of Flight's creator and founder. They include a B-17 Flying Fortress, a B-24 Liberator, a Short Sunderland, a Star Constellation, an F3F Flying Barrel, a P-51C Mustang, and a Ford Tri-Motor used in the opening scenes of *Indiana Jones and the Temple of Doom*—the one Indy jumped out of using an inflatable lifeboat as a parachute.

Though you could take these old planes into the sky, if you want the experience of being a pilot you're just going to have to settle for the simulators of Fightertown. Hop into the cockpit of a Corsair Fighter and you'll be shooting down Japanese Zeros before you know it.

1400 Broadway Blvd. SE, Polk City, FL 33868

(863) 984-3500

Hours: Daily 9 A.M.–5 P.M.

Cost: Adults $24.95, Seniors (60+) $22.95, Kids (5–12) $13.95

www.fantasyofflight.com

Directions: Exit 44 from I-4, head north and follow the signs.

PUNTA GORDA

Every Halloween, Punta Gorda children are given ice cream purchased by a trust established for that purpose by the late Florida governor Albert Gilchrist.

Hundred of golf balls rained down on Punta Gorda on September 3, 1969. Police investigated local courses, only to find even more balls!

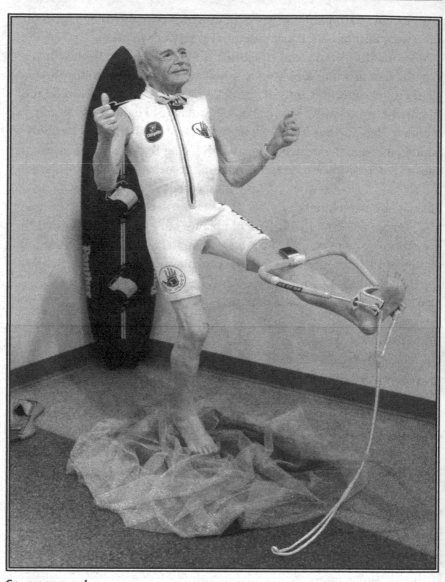

Go, gramps, go!
Photo by author, courtesy Water Ski Hall of Fame

Water Ski Hall of Fame and Museum

When Minnesota teenager Ralph Samuelson strapped two boards on his feet and asked a boat-driving friend to pull him around Lake Pepin on July 22, 1922, he didn't know he was launching an international sport.

But that is what he did, and waterskiing has grown steadily in popularity ever since. For many years, Samuelson was not given credit for the invention. That honor was sometimes bestowed on Richard Pope, the "Swami of the Swamp" who started Cypress Gardens, or Fred Waller, who introduced Akwa-Skees to the American public in 1925.

It took the work of the American Water Ski Educational Foundation (AWSEF) to set the record straight. Pope and Waller certainly did their part, but it's Samuelson's bronze bust that rightfully belongs in the entryway of this new and expanded museum. Follow the advancements in the sport, such as barefooting, swivel skiing, jumping, pyramids, and other stunts, along its informative photographic time line. Read the biographies of inductees such as "Banana George" Blair, "Jumpin Joe" Cash, and Fred Wiley, best known by the unimaginative nickname "Mr. Boat Driver." And check out the variety of skis over the years; hundreds are mounted on a high display circling the exhibits.

The Hall of Fame is more than just a museum. It is also the repository of the Chuck Sligh Water Ski Library, and has a video archive of every national competition since the first event back in 1939. The AWSEF offers scholarships to individuals and grants for water ski teams, and is developing a lake behind the museum to be used for future competitions.

AWSEF Water Ski Experience Hall of Fame/Museum, 1251 Holy Cow Rd., Polk City, FL 33868

(863) 324-2472

E-mail: awsefhalloffame@cs.com

Hours: Monday–Friday 10 A.M.–5 P.M.

Cost: Adults $5, Kids $3

www.waterskihalloffame.com

Directions: Take Exit 44 (Rte. 559) from I-4, go north to the first stop, then east to Holy Cow Rd.

SARASOTA
By law, you cannot sing while wearing a bikini in Sarasota.

Port Charlotte
She-inal

Some ideas arrive long before the world is ready for them. Others are just dumb, like the She-inal.

The She-inal was designed by Kathie Jones in the early 1990s for Urinette, a porcelain fixtures company. The goal was to use no more floor space than a standard male urinal, but still meet the wee-wee needs of the typical female. The solution? A small funnel that could be maneuvered between the legs using a long, curved handle. The funnel was

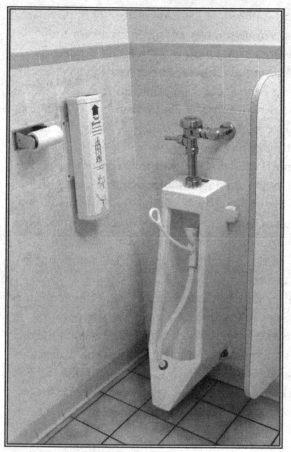

An idea ahead of its time.

attached to a hose that drained into a basin—how simple and easy!

Well, not so fast. During its entire development, nobody questioned whether the average woman wanted to be ... you know ... *intimate* with the same crotch funnel as hundreds of strangers. About 700 She-inals were built before Urinette sold the manufacturing rights to a third party. Few She-inals survive today, the most famous being this little-used device at an interstate-exit Dairy Queen.

Because the She-inal is located in a single-user rest room, men are allowed to view the device from the open door when the room is empty. Men seem more fascinated with the device than women, but then again, they're more entertained by urination in general.

You need not make an ice-cream purchase to look at it. (Just ask the clerks—on any given day there are as many folks interested in the She-inal as the Dilly Bars.) But in all fairness, you should pick up at least a dipped cone to reward this fast-food joint for preserving a unique artifact of bathroom history. And please, do everyone a favor: wash your hands.

Dairy Queen, 909-C Kings Hwy, Port Charlotte, FL 33980

(941) 743-8665

Hours: Daily 10 A.M.–10 P.M.

Cost: Free; Ice cream extra

www.urinal.net/dairy_queen

Directions: Exit 170 from I-75, heading west, just ahead on the right in the same
  building as the Amoco gas station.

Sanibel
Bailey-Matthews Shell Museum

Because of Sanibel Island's unique geology—the shallow waters off its western and southern shores extend for some distance—the town has long been a favorite destination for shell hunters. There's even a medical term for the hunchback posture of folks looking for shells on the beaches here: the Sanibel Stoop.

Writer Anne Morrow Lindbergh came to Sanibel Island for a week following the death of her mother in 1955. She, too, combed the shores and what she came back with inspired her to write the bestselling *Gift from the Sea*, a series of saccharine meditations on life, love, and death, each tied to a different shell.

Today, the island has a museum for the stooped to visit when the weather's bad. The Bailey-Matthews Shell Museum has not only specimens from the Gulf Coast, but shells from around the world, from Argonautas to channeled whelks, from chestnut turbans to cowries, this place has them all.

3075 Sanibel–Captiva Rd., Sanibel, FL 33957

(239) 395-2233

Hours: Tuesday–Sunday 10 A.M.–4 P.M.

Cost: Adults $5, Kids (6–18) $3

www.shellmuseum.org

Directions: Just west of Locke Ave. heading west out of town on Rte. 867 (Sanibel–
  Captiva Rd.).

Sarasota
Circus Museum

When Ringling Brothers moved its winter headquarters to Sarasota in 1929, the town was changed forever. Not only did the circus bring money into the local economy, the Ringlings brought high culture, including one of the most impressive art museums on the Gulf Coast. You can read about that in some other guidebook—in this one we'll stick to the strange.

Your ticket at the Ringling Museum pays for admission to see the Rubens and the Rembrandts, but wait on all that until after you've seen the Circus Museum. Located on the path to John Ringling's Moorish palace Cà d'Zan (its tower taken from the old Madison Square Garden), the museum contains artifacts going back to the days when the circus was called the Ringling Brothers Moral, Elevating, Instructive & Fascinating Concert and Variety Performance. You'll see Emmett Kelly's Wearie Willie costume, covered in safety pins, and the broom he used to sweep up spotlights; the Super-Repeating Cannon that blasted Bruno Zacchini skyward performance after performance; the tiny clown car driven by the immortal Lou Jacobs; and creepy life casts of the faces of famous Ringling clowns. Circus wagons, sideshow banners, lion tamers' chairs, gigantic clown props, sequin-covered trapeze outfits, and train models from the movie *The Greatest Show on Earth*—they're all here.

5401 Bay Shore Rd., Sarasota, FL 34243

(941) 359-5700 or (941) 351-1660

Hours: Daily 10 A.M.–5:30 P.M.

Cost: Adults $15, Seniors (55+) $12, Kids (12 and under) Free

www.ringling.org

Directions: Just west of Rte. 41 (Tamiami Trail) at DeSoto Rd.

DEAD CARNIES

With so many circuses wintering in Sarasota, it's little wonder that some of the world's most famous carnies are buried near here. Tightrope walker **Karl Wallenda** and two other members of his family who died in high-wire accidents are buried at the Manasota Memorial Park (1221 53rd Avenue E) in Bradenton. And after animal trainer **Gunther Gebel-Williams** died of brain cancer on July 19, 2001, he was interred at Venice Memorial Gardens (950 Center Road) in Venice Gardens.

Jackson 5 Mobile

Long before Michael Jackson started the massive remodeling job on his face, his father, Joe Jackson, was doing the same thing on a couple of Cadillacs. He used the back end of a 1971 Cadillac station wagon and the front end of a Cadillac sedan to make the ultimate touring car for the Jackson 5, and included a color television mounted on the center fold-down armrest. This green behemoth is just one vehicle in this impressive collection of automobiles, arcade games, musical instruments, and more.

What else does the Sarasota Classic Car Museum have? John Lennon's 1965 Mercedes. A Magic Vibra-Massage Chair. The guitar collection of Bad Company's Mike Ralph. Not one but *two* DeLoreans. An antique arm-wrestling machine. And a bunch of outboard motors, ice skates, barber chairs, and Beanie Babies.

Sadly, one pop culture artifact they once had, but don't any longer, is the 1948 Plymouth from the movie *Christine*. That evil-mobile is no doubt out there somewhere, attacking unsuspecting teenagers.

Sarasota Classic Car Museum, 5500 N. Tamiami Trail, Sarasota, FL 34243

(941) 355-6228

Hours: Daily 9 A.M.–6 P.M.

Cost: Adults $8.50, Seniors (65+) $7.65, Teens (13–17) $5.75, Kids (5–12) $4

www.sarasotacarmuseum.org

Directions: At the corner of Rte. 41 and University Pkwy.

SARASOTA

Sarasota news anchor Christine Chubbock shot herself with a .38 revolver, live, on WXLT-TV's *Suncoast Digest* on July 15, 1974. Before she did, she announced, "In keeping with Channel 40's policy of bringing you the latest in blood and guts in living color, you are going to see another first: attempted suicide." The attempt was successful.

Modern prehistoric service

Spring Hill
A Prehistoric Mechanic

Just south of Weeki Wachee Springs is an auto repair shop that looks like it belongs in Bedrock, not Florida. Three auto-bays of this former Sinclair station fit between this crudely formed brontosaurus's six—yes, six—legs. Its head and neck form the office and the tail is used for storage. The building is 110 feet long, and its head rises 48 feet into the air. Once billed as "The Only Dinosaur Station of Its Kind in the World," Harold's no longer pumps gas. Today, it's strictly mechanical.

Harold's Auto Center, 5299 Commercial Way, Spring Hill, FL 34606

(352) 596-7755

Hours: Always visible

Cost: Free

Directions: South of Rte. 50 on Rte. 19 (Commercial Way).

Tarpon Springs
A Fine Way to Treat a Relic

Every January 6 on the Feast of the Epiphany (commemorating Jesus Christ's baptism), the Greek Orthodox Archbishop of Tarpon Springs hauls a holy cross down to Spring Bayou and chucks it into the water. A fine way to treat a relic? Not so fast—it's part of the religious ceremony! Dozens of young divers are swimming in the bayou when the cross sinks, and the first one to bring it back to the surface will have good luck for the coming year.

One Greek Orthodox item that *won't* be tossed into the local waters any time soon is the cathedral's statue of St. Nicholas. A replica of an older statue at the St. Sophia Cathedral in Kiev, Ukraine, this saint has been spotted weeping on Christmas Day in 1969, 1973, and 1989. Water was also seen oozing from its halo.

St. Nicholas Greek Orthodox Cathedral, 36 N. Pinellas Ave., Tarpon Springs, FL 33589

(727) 937-3540

Hours: Monday–Friday 9 A.M.–5 P.M.

Cost: Free

www.ci.tarpon-springs.fl.us

Directions: At the intersection of Rte. 19 (Pinellas Ave.) and Tarpon Ave.

BUT WAIT, THERE'S MORE . . .

Still looking for miracles? In 1939, Steve Tsalichis fell ill with a mysterious fever. More than a dozen doctors could do nothing to cure the slowly cookin' kid. Then, while in a coma, the 11-year-old had a vision of St. Michael who told him that he would be cured, but that he had to build a shrine in the saint's honor. The boy recovered, and the shrine went up next door. The Shrine of St. Michael (113 Hope Street) is still popular with those seeking cures.

WEEKI WACHEE

Aliens from outer space left footprints around Weeki Wachee Springs on March 3, 1965, according to witness John Reeves, who also claimed they took a picture with a glass box.

Rub-a-dub-dubbed out.

Spongeorama

California had its Gold Rush, Oklahoma had its Land Rush, and Tarpon Springs had its Sponge Rush. Following the discovery of massive natural sponge beds off Tarpon Springs in 1905, the region saw a boom in Greek immigration. Sponges, sponges, sponges—they were a thriving local industry until the Red Tide swept through in 1939. No, not Commies, but a bloom of microscopic plankton that wiped out the beds during the 1940s. American consumers, desperate for absorbent, squishy cleaning tools turned to synthetic sponges, which signaled the demise of old world sponge diving in the New World.

To be honest, after walking through Spongeorama's museum in the rear of the Sponge Factory Store, you might agree that the Red Tide was a blessing in disguise. A diorama of the Sponge Diver's Nightmare says it all: "Sponge Diving: Probably the most dangerous occupation in the United States." No kidding! A dead mannequin lies on the dock, blood oozing from his nose, mouth, eyes, and ears, another tragic victim of the bends. Other scenes show happier times, such as Romans bathing (the first culture to use sponges), and local kids diving for the cross the archbishop keeps tossing in the bay. But it's the image of the bloody diver that will haunt you for tub times to come.

510 Dodecanese Blvd., Tarpon Springs, FL 33589

(727) 942-3771

Hours: Daily 9 A.M.–6 P.M.

Cost: Free; Film $1

www.tarponsprings.com

Directions: One block west of Rte. 19 (Pinellas Ave.), at the docks.

Wauchula
Sorry, Wrong Baby!

It must have been a busy day at Hardee Memorial's maternity ward on December 2, 1978. Two newborns, looking very much alike, were somehow switched and went home with the wrong families. (Sure, blame the hospital if you want, but none of the *parents* spotted the difference.)

Skip ahead nine years when one of the switchees, Arlena Twigg, died of congestive heart failure. During the postmortem, doctors noticed something odd: the girl's blood type could not have come from either of her parents, Ernest and Regina. So if Arlena wasn't their biological daughter, whose was she?

As it turns out, she was the offspring of Barbara and Robert Mays. Their daughter, Kimberly Mays, was biologically a Twigg.

Enter the lawyers, and talk TV. The Twiggs sued the hospital for switching the babies, and sued the Mays to have Kimberly . . . or the *real* Arlena . . . returned. In a 1993 court battle, Robert Mays (by then a widower) retained custody of the girl he raised, and even prevented the

Twiggs from home visits. Kimberly's insistence in court that she wanted to stay with Mays was crucial in the ruling.

But then Kimberly became a teenager, and in 1994 decided she no longer wanted her court-determined father and ran off to live with the Twiggs. Then, in 1996, when she was tired of the Twiggs, she returned to her father in North Carolina.

Kids these days. . . .

Florida Hospital Wauchula (former Hardee Memorial Hospital), 533 Carlton St., Wauchula, FL 33973

No phone

Hours: Always visible; view from street

Cost: Free

Directions: Two blocks west of Rte. 35/17 (6th Ave.), six blocks south of Rte. 636 (Main St.).

I told you they were real!
Photo by author, courtesy Weeki Wachee Springs

Weeki Wachee
Weeki Wachee Springs

Contrary to popular belief, mermaids are not born or bred, but *transformed*. The fish-tailed maidens you'll see at Weeki Wachee Springs were humans at one time, just like the rest of us. But a year of training in skills ranging from breath control to hose sucking to underwater costume changes separates the mermaids from the mermortals.

And is it ever worth it—the underwater Weeki Wachee show is a sight to behold! The plots change from year to year, but most intersect with Hans Christian Andersen's fairy tale at some point. One year the Little Mermaid partied at Carnival in Rio. In another show, she was off to Never Never Land with Peter Pan. And recently she hung out with Pocahontas, no doubt swapping horror stories about working for the Man. The Disney Man, that is.

The Weeki Wachee formula—bathing beauties underwater and behind glass—has been basically the same since the springs first opened in 1947. The park and mermaid show were the brainchild of Navy frogman Newton Perry, who perfected the hookah lines and the hokey stories. When you sit in the Underwater Theater, you're not just looking out into a crystal clear lagoon, you're looking back into Florida roadside history.

6131 Commercial Way, Weeki Wachee, FL 34606

(352) 596-2062

E-mail: wwachee@hotmail.com

Hours: Daily 9:30 A.M.–5:30 P.M.

Cost: Adults $12.95, Seniors (55+) $12.95, Kids (3–10) $9.95

www.weekiwachee.com

Directions: At the intersection of Rtes. 19 and 50.

ANOTHER MERMAID!

A woman was pulled from the Atlantic Ocean two miles off the coast of Fort Lauderdale on September 12, 1996. She was wearing a T-shirt, tan slacks, and sneakers, and claimed to have just come up for air when she was spotted by a fisherman. She also said she'd developed incredible powers after eating seaweed, and had been out there three days visiting her underwater family while "in transition." She was put under psychiatric observation at Memorial Regional Hospital in Hollywood.

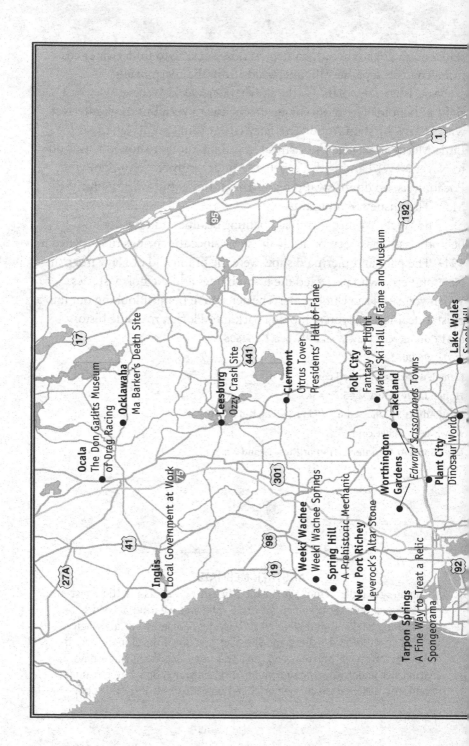

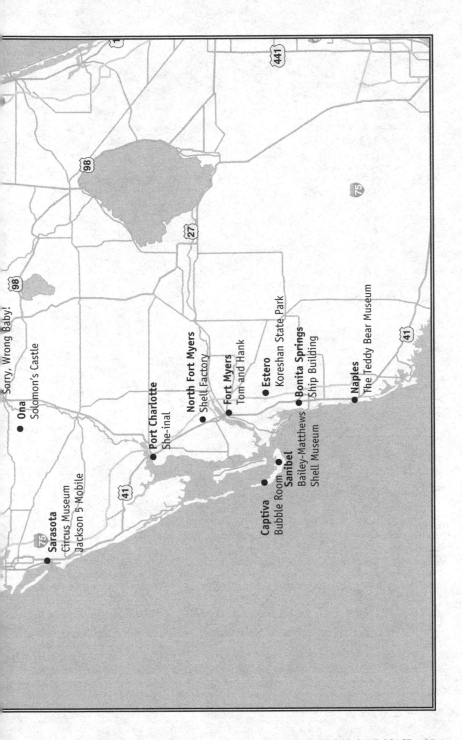

Sorry, Wrong Baby!

● **Ona**
Solomon's Castle

● **Sarasota**
Circus Museum
Jackson 5-Mobile

● **Port Charlotte**
She-inal

North Fort Myers
Shell Factory

Fort Myers
Tom and Hank

● **Estero**
Koreshan State Park

● **Bonita Springs**
Ship Building

Captiva
Bubble Room

Sanibel
Bailey-Matthews
Shell Museum

● **Naples**
The Teddy Bear Museum

4

Tampa/St. Petersburg Area

*B*ack in 1885, a report from the American Medical Association declared Pinellas Point (part of present-day St. Petersburg) to be the healthiest spot in the United States, at least as far as disease was concerned. Word got around and the region grew into a Mecca for retirees. Maybe it's the weather—the sun shines on St. Pete an average of 361 days each year—or the local diet—in 1992 St. Pete received a $1,000 grant from the California Prune Board because the city's per capita prune consumption was 89 percent higher than the national norm—but this much is clear: retirees live about one year longer if they move to the area.

That's not to say Tampa/St. Pete doesn't have hazards. In 1985, 87-year-old tourist Jack Comiskey and his wife Winifred drove their rental car onto a runway at St. Petersburg's Albert Whitted Municipal Airport, thinking it was an interstate. The pair shot over the seawall at 50 MPH into Tampa Bay, but at least they didn't hit a plane. (Neither was seriously injured.) Three years later, in 1998, aging daredevil Evel Knievel took a spill on a Tampa golf course . . . and broke his hip.

So beware, travelers! Though you'll soon learn that Jesus, the Virgin Mary, and Elvis have risen from the dead in this Gulf Coast wonderland, your fate could just as easily go the way of Jack Kerouac, Mary "The Cinder Lady" Reeser, or the Lobster Boy. And believe me, none of them faded into quiet, peaceful retirement.

Yeah, there's a resemblance.
Photo by author, courtesy South Forida Museum

Bradenton
Snooty

Folklorists have traced the mermaid myth back to early sightings of manatees, and it's easy to see why—these things are *adorable*! They may not have shapely curves and long, flowing hair to conveniently cover their naughty bits, but to a sailor who has spent months at sea, they must have seemed heaven-sent.

If there is a world's best-known manatee, it's Snooty, the first manatee born in captivity. His original name was Stinky, and he was born in the Miami Seaquarium on July 21, 1948. When he moved to Bradenton a year later, his name was changed so as not to scare away the tourists. Snooty resides in the Parker Aquarium's 600,000-gallon tank at the South Florida Museum. He doesn't do much more than swim in circles, eat pounds and pounds of food, and paddle around some more. This might seem boring, but it's a lot better than trying to get by in a real world filled with speedboats, the manatee's only unnatural enemy.

South Florida Museum, 201 10th St., Bradenton, FL 34205

(941) 746-4131

E-mail: info@southfloridamuseum.org

Hours: July and January–April, Monday–Saturday 10 A.M.–5 P.M., Sunday Noon–5 P.M.;
   August–December and May–June, Tuesday–Saturday 10 A.M.–5 P.M., Sunday Noon–5 P.M.

Cost: Adults $9.50, Seniors (60+) $7.50, Students $6, Kids (7–12) $5

www.southfloridamuseum.org

Directions: Two blocks north of Manatee Ave. (Rte. 62), two blocks west of Rte. 41.

CLEARWATER

A 15-foot-tall penguin was reported to be wandering the beaches of Clearwater in February 1948. One of 24 separate witnesses described it as having "a head like a rhinoceros, but with no neck. . . . It was gray and covered with short thick fur. . . . It didn't run into the water, or dive in; it sort of slid in half sideways." It was also reported to have overturned a lifeguard platform near the Everingham Pavilion. Its 18-inch tracks were spotted on the beach again in 1966. A local auto salesman later admitted that he had perpetrated the hoax using a pair of fake concrete feet.

Just add water.

Wet Jesus

A few years back, maintenance workers at the Palma Sola Presbyterian Church got a surprise while doing a routine pressure washing of the building's brick exterior; they found themselves face-to-face with Jesus. This sort of thing happens all the time at Catholic churches but rarely at

Protestant denominations. The beard, the halo, the spooky stare . . . there was no mistaking it. *That* was Jesus.

But what to do about it? Was it a miracle? Or had the church perhaps forgotten they'd painted over a mural that was now bleeding through its cream-colored exterior? Word got around, and hundreds of folks started dropping by to see the mysterious but familiar face. Most were convinced it was a message from God.

Soon, the church realized it had a problem. Jesus only showed up when the wall was wet, and the church caretaker was getting tired of dragging out the hose every time a carload of pilgrims showed up. So the church installed a sprinkler system to spray the eastern wall twice a day, and the miracle became almost routine. Today, few people wait in the parking lot for the twice-daily apparitions, but that's the good news: you get a front row seat!

Palma Sola Presbyterian Church, 6510 W. 3rd Ave., Bradenton, FL 34209

(941) 792-3141

Hours: Rewettings at noon and 4 P.M.

Cost: Free

Directions: One block north of Manatee Ave. (Rte. 62) on 67th St., turn east on 3rd Ave. and the church is on the right; image on the east side of the building, just above the air conditioning unit.

Clearwater
Aye Aye, Captain!

What would cause a mild-mannered insurance agent and a teacher for the hearing impaired to turn to a life of piracy? Well, can you think of a better way to retire? When they left the workaday world, Captain Memo and Panama Pam had visions of traveling around the Caribbean. Unfortunately, they ran out of cash. Coaxed back to Clearwater by a group of Canadian investors hoping to open a pirate cruise ship, the pair were surprised to discover they'd been hornswaggled—neither they nor the Canadians had any more money.

But the couple did have a boat. Panama Pam went to work as a cocktail waitress and Captain Memo transformed their sailing ship into the *Pirate's Ransom*. A pair of pantaloons and a bandanna later, the Pirate Cruise was launched!

The cruise today is much more elaborate than its humble beginnings. The current pirate vessel holds up to 125 swashbucklers and a crew that includes Gangplank Gary, Mutiny Michael, Tricky Tracey, and Jewel Thief Julie. During your two-hour cruise you'll be outfitted with a pirate's hat, dance the limbo, search for treasure, fire tiny cannons, look for dolphins, and come ashore at Dunedin where you will run the residents through with your swords and burn the town to the ground. Wait . . . strike that last bit . . . this is a *friendly* pirate cruise.

Aaarrrrrgh, plunderin' ain't what it used to be!

Captain Memo's Pirate Cruise, Clearwater Municipal Marina #3, 25 Causeway Blvd.,
  Clearwater, FL 33767

(727) 446-2587

E-mail: info@captainmemo.com

Hours: Daytime Cruise daily 10 A.M.–2 P.M.; Call for other cruises (Champagne, Sunset, etc.)

Cost: Adults $28, Seniors (65+) $22, Juniors (13–17) $22, Kids $18

www.captainmemo.com

Directions: Just south of Rte. 60 (Memorial Causeway) off Mandalay Ave., on the
  harbor side.

LARGO
A fire at Largo's Littlefield Nursing Home on March 29, 1953, killed 32 residents and the owner, Mrs. Littlefield.

PALMETTO
In 1955, the CIA secretly released the whooping cough virus in Palmetto, killing as many as a dozen children and sickening hundreds more.

She does do windows.

Don't Wash That Window!

Though the water stains had been building up for some time, it wasn't until December 17, 1996, that a woman noticed that the streaks on the window of a Clearwater bank looked familiar. Omigod—the Virgin Mary! And who could argue? The rainbow-hued image filled nine large windowpanes and combined to form a portrait of Mary, her head bowed slightly to the left.

Before long, thousands of folks were flocking to see her. A local radio DJ offered a video game console to anyone willing to toss a brick through the window, but got no takers. Later, in May, vandals threw a substance that stained the stains. But was the virgin defiled? Hardly! Two rainstorms later their sin had been washed away.

Science-loving infidels have tried to explain away the image as hard water deposits from the sprinkler system, and true enough, you can see similar rainbow patterns around the entire building.

The building, Virgin Mary and all, has been sold to a religious group out of Ohio called the Shepherds of Christ Ministries. The bank is now used as a gift shop and devotional area. They are also involved in fundraising to keep the image protected for future generations.

Shepherds of Christ Ministries, 21649 U.S. Highway 19N, Clearwater, FL 33765

(888) 221-3041 or (727) 725-9312

Hours: Always visible

Cost: Free

www.SofC.org

Directions: At the northeast corner of Drew St. and Rte. 19.

JESUS STAYS CLEAN

Linda Martin of New Port Richey left a pan of oil on her burning stove in 1997, igniting a small kitchen fire. After the fire department put out the blaze, they noticed that soot covered everything in the room *except* a mail-order statue of Christ's resurrection. Martin and the firefighters proclaimed the lily-white figure a miracle.

RUSKIN

Ruskin claims to be the Salad Bowl of America.

ST. PETERSBURG

St. Petersburg has been called both the City of the Unburied Dead and God's Waiting Room.

A King collection.

Dunedin
Elvis Has Never Left the Building

Memphis Gold would be an otherwise typical Elvis collectibles shop were it not for its owner, Jerry Theriault. This diehard fan saw the King of Rock 'n' Roll 85 times, starting in 1957. Little by little Elvis's aura rubbed off on him, to the point where Theriault now looks like the singer. You'll know you really have struck Memphis gold when you step through the front door and spot the owner with his cool sideburns and rockabilly pompadour.

Theriault has amassed a large collection of Elvis-abilia, and most of it is for sale. Elvis concert programs, Elvis photos, Elvis beer steins, Elvis mouse pads, Elvis books, Elvis Christmas ornaments, Elvis HO-scale trains, Elvis buttons, Elvis mugs, Elvis umbrellas, Elvis collector plates, Elvis magazines, Elvis dolls, Elvis jewelry, Elvis salt and pepper shakers, and Elvis sunglasses with sideburns attached. You never know what you'll find here, but you can be sure of one thing: whatever you find will have Elvis on it.

Memphis Gold, Inc., 1143 Main St., Dunedin, FL 34698

(727) 738-8412

Hours: Tuesday–Saturday 11 A.M.–5 P.M., Sunday Noon–5 P.M.

Cost: Free

www.memphisgold.com

Directions: One block east of Pinehurst Rd. on Rte. 580 (Main St.).

. . . AND IN AN UNRELATED STORY

An Elvis impersonator reportedly abducted an 18-year-old Tampa woman in 1988, and forced her to drive him 10 hours to the airport in Birmingham, Alabama. She was released unharmed.

TAMPA

Actress **Thelma "Butterfly" McQueen** was born in Tampa on January 8, 1911.

Billy Graham started his evangelical crusades in a Tampa storefront in 1939 while attending the Florida Bible Institute.

Gibsonton
The Murder of the Lobster Boy

Every town has its bad apples, and in Gibsonton there was a whole bushel called the Stiles clan. Grady Stiles, Jr.—the Lobster Boy—was a violent drunk who ruled over his family with an iron claw. His wife, Mary Teresa Stiles, was a grifter who first performed in sideshows as the Blade Box Girl and the Electrified Girl. Over many years and two marriages, the couple had three children: Donna, whose fiancé Grady murdered in Pittsburgh; Cathy, who, with her husband Tyrill Berry, ran an animal freak show that featured a two-headed raccoon; and Little Grady, who also exhibited the genetic abnormality called ectrodactyly. The couple's family also included Glenn Newman, Jr., the Human Blockhead, a young man with a low IQ who could pound three-penny nails and ice picks up his nose. Newman was the offspring of Mary Teresa and Glenn Newman, Sr., the Midget Man, whom she had wed between her first divorce and second marriage to Stiles.

Confused?

It's a story that could only happen in Gibsonton, better known as Freaktown USA. Years ago this small, tightly knit community became a popular home base for circus performers when they weren't on the road. Carnies and freaks were attracted to Gibsonton because of its loose zoning laws that allowed circus animals to graze on private property. It was also the home of Giant's Camp, a restaurant and collection of efficiency cabins run by 8'6" Al Tomaini and his diminutive wife, Jeanie, the World's Only Living Half Girl (she had no body below the waist).

Stiles and his crew lived in a cluster of trailer homes on the southeast side of town along Bull Frog Creek. When Stiles wasn't drinking at the nearby Showman's Tavern, he was drinking at home. Though both his hands were fused into claws, and his legs were more like flippers, Stiles was certainly not disabled. In 1978 he shot his daughter's fiancé Jack Layne in the back, then claimed self-defense. During his trial, Paul Fishbaugh (the Fat Man) and Percilla Bejano (the Bearded Lady) testified as character witnesses. The jury and judge must have felt pity for Stiles, for though he was found guilty of third-degree murder, he was sentenced to only 15 years *probation*.

Getting away with murder must have emboldened the Lobster Boy, because his abuse of the family grew worse. In late 1992, Mary Teresa and Glenn Newman, Jr., hired 17-year-old Chris Wyant to shoot Stiles. For his effort, Wyant would receive $1,500 in cash that Mary Teresa had skimmed from the sideshow till while on the road. On November 29, 1992, Wyant did it, shooting Stiles multiple times in the back of the head while he watched television. Police unraveled the plot in short order, and the trio was brought to trial.

Mary Teresa never denied taking out the contract on her husband, but claimed she was not guilty of first-degree murder, using a battered wife syndrome defense. The jury was unsympathetic to that argument. She was found guilty of conspiracy to commit first-degree murder and manslaughter with a firearm, and was sentenced to 12 years in prison and 5 years probation. Glenn Newman, Jr., was found guilty of conspiracy to commit first-degree murder and murder in the first degree, and got life in prison. The trigger man, Wyant, was found guilty of conspiracy to commit first-degree murder and murder in the second degree with a firearm. He was given 27 years.

The Lobster Boy is buried in the International Independent Showmen Gardens of Memorials cemetery in Thonotosassa.

Stiles Home, 11117 Inglewood Dr., Gibsonton, FL 33534

Private phone

Hours: Always visible, view from the street

Cost: Free

Directions: East off Rte. 41 on Symmes Rd., north on North St., west on Lovegren Ln., and north on Inglewood Dr.

Safety Harbor
Whimsy: The Bowling Ball Art Museum

Three cheers for Kiaralinda (no last name, like Cher) and Todd Ramquist! When they set out to landscape their yard, they didn't lift a design out of *Better Homes and Gardens*. They had better ideas, and they came up with them all by themselves.

Decorate with bowling balls? Sure! But not just any bowling balls, but more than 500 *painted* bowling balls. They were so inspired by their collection they began requesting artistic balls from their friends. To date, they've got about 80, all enshrined in their evolving Bowling Ball Art Museum.

But the garden didn't stop there. They built trees out of blue and green bottles. They arranged thousands of broken tiles into elaborate sidewalk mosaics. They painted the house bright purple and ornamented it with multicolored gingerbread scrollwork. They collected discarded items and assembled them into funky sculptures. And they're still at it.

What's the result? A fabulous studio, garden, and living space they call Whimsy, a home fit for a publication that doesn't exist, but should: *BEST Homes and Gardens.*

Bowling Ball Art Museum, 1206 N. 3rd St., Safety Harbor, FL 34695

Private phone

Hours: Always visible

Cost: Free

www.kiaralinda.com

Directions: One block north of Main St. (Rte. 576), four blocks east of McMullen Booth Rd. (Rte. 611).

St. Petersburg
Bridge Trouble

If you weren't around to see St. Petersburg's Bay Bridge the morning of May 9, 1980, you're lucky. During a torrential rainstorm, a freighter slammed into one of the bridge's supports, knocking out a 1,200-foot section of the roadbed. Drivers on the bridge couldn't see any better than the freighter pilot, and a truck, several cars, and a Greyhound bus with 26 passengers

Skyway to hell.

aboard plunged into the chasm. In all, 35 died, and the vital transportation artery was out of commission.

Rather than repair the old structure, a new bridge was constructed alongside it to the tune of $244 million. The new Sunshine Skyway Bridge rises much higher than the one it replaced, which is used today as a fishing pier.

This soaring, elegant display of modern civil engineering has tempted more than a few suicide victims; so many, in fact, that operators have installed a suicide hotline phone at its highest point. The Skyway Bridge Jumper Pool (www.jumperpool.com), a twisted Web site that charts the death toll, also logs bets on future jumpees.

One person who could have used the phone was a teenage girl some believe jumped off the big bridge shortly after it opened. Her ghost still haunts the bridge, hitchhiking on approaches to the 4.1-mile tollway. Unsuspecting drivers, some admitting they were tempted by her tight T-shirt, pick up the victim along the way. For some reason, they always comply when she asks them to stop at the summit. Here she hops out of the car, runs to the edge, and leaps over the railing to yet another death.

Sunshine Skyway Toll Bridge, I-275/Rte. 19, St. Petersburg, FL 33711
(727) 893-2786
Hours: Always visible
Cost: $1/car
Directions: The bridge connects St. Petersburg to Palmetto.

The Cinder Lady

Mary Hardy Reeser went out with a bang. Or at least with a flash. This 67-year-old widow had led a quiet, unassuming life, but her death attracted considerable attention. Why? SHC. Spontaneous human combustion. One evening she retired to her apartment, all 175 pounds of her, and the next morning she was 10 pounds of ashes.

It happened the night of July 1–2, 1951. Landlord Pansy Carpenter was the last to see her alive the night before. Reeser had been talking of returning to her native Pennsylvania to get away from, get this, *the heat.* Carpenter came by to drop off a telegram the next morning and found the doorknob too hot to touch. With the help of two handymen she entered the apartment and discovered a grisly scene: Reeser's lounge chair was burned down to its coils, but the nearby drapes and a pile of newspaper were untouched. Lying just outside the contained, charred area was a left foot, still wearing a bedroom slipper. On closer inspection, they found a singed liver, part of a backbone, and Mary's skull, shrunken to the size of a baseball.

Arson investigators could not explain what had caused Reeser to ignite, nor why the fire had contained itself. The case of the "Cinder Lady" was chalked up to SHC, at least by those who believe in the phenomenon. Scientists dismiss the notion that people burst into flames unexpectedly as absurd—what causes the ignition?—and others point to it as an urban myth created by none other than Charles Dickens in *Bleak House*, a warning against the hazards of alcohol consumption. Some evidence seems to suggest that a fat human body can burn like a candle under the right (or wrong) circumstances, when lit by a cigarette, for example. Mary Reeser was a heavy smoker, and not exactly petite.

Whatever the cause of SHC, one thing's for certain: it's a nasty way to shed this mortal coil. Still, there could be worse ways to go. At least you save on cremation.

1200 Cherry St., St. Petersburg, FL 33701

No phone

Hours: Private property; view from street

Cost: Free

Directions: One block west of Beach Dr. NE, at 12th Ave.

TAMPA

Colonel Tom Parker, Elvis's manager, was Tampa's dogcatcher during World War II.

Yodeling singer **Slim Whitman** was born Otis Dewey Whitman in Tampa on January 20, 1924.

Ah, the good ol' days!
Photo by author, courtesy of Florida International Museum

Cuban Missile Crisis

There are few museum exhibits that capture a moment in history as well as the Florida International Museum has captured the frightening 13-day standoff known as the Cuban Missile Crisis. To start, visitors are ushered into an early 1960s living room and asked to have a seat on the couch—the president is about to speak. It appears that the Soviet Union has placed offensive missiles on Cuban soil, barely 90 miles from U.S. soil. The president has decided to "quarantine" the island.

Uh-oh.

After receiving the news, you pass through a groovy cocktail lounge where those worried about the end of the world could have found solace in a bottle, followed by a classroom where kids were taught to "Duck and cover!" You'll see a high-altitude pressure-suit worn by one of the CIA's U-2 pilots, a Soviet military uniform and packet of cigarettes, a B-52's nuclear security alarm, and a genuine (unarmed) cruise missile. They've even got an Acme Fallout Shelter, probably donated to the museum by Wile E. Coyote. The shelter was never used because of the

Nuclear Test Ban Treaty of October 7, 1963; you'll see one of the pens JFK used to sign that important document.

If all this fun wasn't enough, the Florida International Museum is also the repository of the most impressive collection of Kennedy-abilia outside of his presidential library in Boston. Items on display run the gamut from the familiar to the mundane: JFK's rocking chair from Evelyn Lincoln's office; the president's combs, nail clippers, file, and brush (with hairs); Jackie's gold lamé jacket and matching earrings; Joe Kennedy's tennis socks; the hand grip from the Zapruder camera; a jack from the trunk of Kennedy's fateful Dallas limousine; JFK Jr.'s sun suit; the last electric bill from Kennedy's Georgetown apartment; the uniform police officer Maurice "Nick" McDonald was wearing when he arrested Lee Harvey Oswald at the Texas Theater; Kennedy's hometown ballot box from New Bedford, Massachusetts; Jack Ruby's black jacket from Neiman Marcus; and a cardboard model of Dealey Plaza used to assist the press at the release of the Warren Commission Report.

Florida International Museum, 100 Second St. N, St. Petersburg, FL 33701

(800) 777-9882

Hours: Monday–Saturday 9 A.M.–6 P.M., Sunday Noon–6 P.M.

Cost: Adults $12, Seniors (55+) $11, Kids (6–18) $6

www.floridamuseum.org

Directions: East of I-275 between I-175 and I-375.

Jack Kerouac Runs Off the Road

Jack Kerouac was a bastard, plain and simple. The drunken lout and author of the classic American roadtrip novel *On the Road* was run out of Lowell, Massachusetts, and eventually landed in St. Petersburg at his mom's place. Long past his prime and dismissed by his peers (Truman Capote criticized his stream-of-consciousness prose by observing, "That isn't writing, that's typing"), Kerouac would stumble from bar to bar in St. Pete and, if the notion struck him, Tampa, all the while screaming that he was King of the Beats, dammit!

He was in his late 40s and still living with his mother, Gabrielle, in a home on St. Petersburg's 10th Avenue North when he got into a brawl at a local bar—nothing new for Jack. But this time his body said, "Enough!" On October 20, 1969, he was admitted to St. Anthony's

Hospital after he began vomiting blood. Doctors used 30 pints of blood while trying to correct several broken ribs, an untreated hernia, and a liver that looked like Swiss cheese. He died the next day.

St. Anthony's Hospital, 1200 7th Ave. N, St. Petersburg, FL 33705
(727) 825-1100
Hours: Always visible
Cost: Free
www.bsahealth.org
Directions: Just north of I-375, between 11th and 14th Sts.

Salvador Dalí Museum

St. Pete's slow shuffleboard-loving lifestyle might seem surreal to anyone under, say, 70 years old, but you haven't seen how surreal it can be until you visit a former marine storage warehouse near downtown's Bayboro Harbor. Inside you'll find the Salvador Dalí Museum, which claims to be the most comprehensive collection of the artist's work. The museum is home to 95 oils, more than 100 watercolors, and more than 1,300 prints, spanning the years 1917 to 1980, shortly before the artist's death.

The museum opened in 1982, started with the collection of millionaires A. Reynolds Morse and Eleanor Reese. The pair had been purchasing Dalí pieces since the 1940s, and wanted their collection to remain intact. St. Petersburg came forth with an attractive offer and a large hurricane-proof vault, and the museum was born. Today, you can wander the galleries with other confused and amused art lovers staring at melting clocks. The museum has works from Dalí's Early, Transitional, Surreal, and Classical Periods, including works such as *Eggs on a Plate Without a Plate, The Hallucinogenic Toreador, The Ghost of Vermeer of Delft Which Can Be Used as a Table*, and *Big Thumb, Beach, Moon, and Decaying Bird*.

1000 3rd St. S, St. Petersburg, FL 33701
(800) 442-3254 or (727) 823-3767
E-mail: info@salvadordalimuseum.org
Hours: Monday–Wednesday and Friday–Saturday 9:30 A.M.–5:30 P.M., Thursday 9:30 A.M.–
   8 P.M., Sunday Noon–5:30 P.M.
Cost: Adults $12.50, Seniors (65+) $10, Students $6, Kids (5–9) $3
www.salvadordalimuseum.org
Directions: One block east of 4th St. S, at 11th Ave.

There's no such thing as too much Christmas spirit.

'Tis the Season

Christmas in America means never having to say "Enough is enough."
Just ask Ted Kresge. Each holiday season since 1977 he, with a dozen
helper elves, has erected a light display to celebrate the season called (no
surprise) the Christmas Display. The yard is filled with plastic illuminated characters, many of which are animated. The walls of Kresge's
home are mounted with robotic scenes of Yuletide cheer, from traditional scenes from *A Christmas Carol* to more obscure dioramas, such as
the Flintstones driving through Jurassic Park. And every square inch is
covered in lights, lights, and more lights.

Sound terrific? Not to two Grinchy neighbors who moved into the
neighborhood in 2001. These ingrates sued to have the Christmas Display unplugged. Though Kresge had been working at his creation for a
quarter century with no complaints, and though those morons had
bought homes that they knew were adjacent to the most popular drive-
by holiday site in St. Pete, they still felt he had done them wrong, and

took him to court. In a settlement, Kresge agreed to scale back his display from a 600,000-light extravaganza to a scant 110,000 bulbs, dropping his electric bill to a manageable $1,200. A fraction of its former self, it's still an impressive show. You should see it before the Scrooges try to ruin what little merriment is left.

2719 Oakdale St. S, St. Petersburg, FL 33705

Private phone

Hours: December, after dark

Cost: Free

www.christmasdisplay.org

Directions: Take 4th St. (Rte. 92) south to Lakeview Ave. (22nd Ave.), then take the next glancing left onto Oakdale St.; drive two blocks to the T at Bethel Ave., turn right, and the home is on the left.

Tampa
Kids Do the Darndest Things!

The flight of 15-year-old Charles Bishop on January 5, 2002, was unsettling on a variety of levels. On a 12-minute journey, this kid flew a Cessna 172R over restricted airspace at McDill Air Force Base (the headquarters of the then-ongoing war in Afghanistan), came within 1,000 feet of a Southwest Airlines 737 near the Tampa International Airport, and slammed into the 28th floor of the Bank of America Plaza in downtown Tampa. A suicide note on his body expressed sympathy for Osama bin Laden.

How did this happen? Bishop had been training for his pilot's license at National Aviation (5700 Roosevelt Boulevard), but while his instructor thought Bishop was performing his preflight checks at St. Petersburg–Clearwater International Airport, he was actually taxiing to a runway for an unapproved takeoff. Bishop's indulgent mother claimed her son would never, ever, ever have done this of his own free will, and said Charles suffered from depression brought on by the acne medication Accutane. To drive home her point, she filed a $40 million lawsuit against the drug's manufacturer, Hoffmann–La Roche. The case has yet to be settled.

Bank of America Plaza, 101 E. Kennedy Blvd., Tampa, FL 33602

(813) 225-8153

Hours: Always visible

Cost: Free

www.bankofamerica.com

Directions: Downtown, surrounded by Kennedy Blvd. (Rte. 60), Jackson St., Ashley Dr., and Tampa St.

World's Longest Continuous Sidewalk

If you're the jogging type, but aren't crazy about being run over at intersections, has Tampa got a sidewalk for you! Running along the western shore of Hillsborough Bay, from Ballast Point to the mouth of the Hillsborough River, the concrete pathway is completely unbroken for six and a half miles, the World's Longest Continuous Sidewalk. Think of it this way: if you jog from one end to the other four times, you've more than run a marathon, and never crossed a street.

Bayshore Blvd., Tampa, FL 33606

No phone

Hours: Always visible

Cost: Free

Directions: Along Hillsborough Bay running roughly parallel to the Lee Roy Selman Expressway (Rte. 92/618).

5

ORLANDO AREA

Have you ever noticed how most Orlando guidebooks offer multipage strategies on how to avoid long lines at the major theme parks? Go to this ride early. Go to that ride late. Go to that other ride after the fireworks show. Some even go so far as to suggest the optimum route through a park that minimizes the walking distances between the ride exits and entrances.

Well, here's a bit of news: *you're on vacation*. A trip to Orlando should not turn into just another job. Relax—you don't get enough time off as it is. Enjoy yourself! And if you want to avoid the long lines, don't go to the big parks in the first place; that's where the long lines are.

Sure, if the Orlando area didn't have anything else to offer, Disney World might be worth the trouble. But Mr. Toad's Wild Ride is a pathetic fender-bender compared to the figure-8 School Bus Demolition Derby in Bithlo, Skull Kingdom is much scarier than the Haunted Mansion, and the Peabody's Parade of the Ducks beats the Main Street Parade any old day . . . and it's free!

Every parent's nightmare. Every child's fantasy.

Bithlo
School Bus Demolition Derby

The scene is something out of *Mad Max*: a dozen school buses careening around a racetrack, banging fenders while jockeying for position, narrowly avoiding broadside collisions on a figure-8 track. In the end, only one bus will be the winner, while all the others will be overturned, ignited, or split in half. It's the grand finale of Orlando Speed World's semiannual Crash-a-Rama, and it's every child's not-so-secret fantasy.

Racetrack owner Bucky Buckman knows a crowd-pleaser when he sees it, and quite simply, the standard rust-bucket demolition derby doesn't cut it with today's reality-TV, carnage-savvy fans. Let's be honest, it just isn't as exciting watching a Caprice Classic get rammed as it is a 60-seater Blue Bird with screaming tots painted in its windows. Depending on the Crash-a-Rama show, you might also see a Boat 'n' Trailer Race, each car pulling an aluminum bass boat (some containing fishermen mannequins), or an RV Demolition Derby. The Winnebagos are modified to disintegrate into a million splinters on impact, no doubt unnerving a few visiting campers.

Unfortunately, there isn't an endless supply of old school buses and recreational vehicles to go around, so check out the racetrack's Web site for the next big Crash-a-Rama event. (Races, however, run every weekend.) Then mark your calendar, put in for those vacation days, and head on down to Bithlo. Do not miss this show.

Orlando Speed World, Rtes. 50 & 520, Bithlo, FL 32709

Contact: PO Box 1500, New Smyrna Beach, FL 32170

(407) 568-1367

E-mail: fastcar@totcon.com

Hours: Call for schedule

Cost: Adults (Frontage) $10–$15, Adults (Pit) $15–$20, Kids (11 and under) Free

www.newsmyrnaspeedway.com/osw/oswindex.html

Directions: West of the intersection of Rtes. 50 and 520.

Celebration
Disney's Planned Community

When Walt Disney first envisioned his Experimental Prototype Community of Tomorrow—EPCOT—he described it as "like the city of tomorrow ought to be, a city that caters to the people as a service function. It will be a planned, controlled community. . . . In EPCOT there will be no landowners and therefore no voting control. People will rent houses instead of buying them. . . . There will be no retirees. Everyone must be employed." The whole thing was to be located under a massive glass dome, which would be temperature controlled.

But before Uncle Walt's vision of a voterless, work-until-you're-dead community came to pass, he dropped dead. EPCOT was eventually built, but its original concept was chucked to make way for a theme park arm of the Magic Kingdom. Disney's town of tomorrow had to wait until the 1990s: Celebration. Luckily, it's nothing like Walt's vision, which is not to say that it hasn't had its problems.

When the town of Celebration broke ground, it already had 5,000 families waiting in a lottery pool for the first 350 homes, even though real estate experts claimed the dwellings were priced 20 to 40 percent higher than similar homes in nearby communities. But Disney had the trust factor going for it—would Mickey Mouse screw buyers over? Never! And Celebration offered something other developments didn't: New Urbanism. In a nutshell, the idea was/is to re-create the perfect small-town atmosphere of the 1920s (which is essentially a myth) and inject it with modern conveniences. Garages and automobiles take a backseat to wide sidewalks, front porches, and shopping districts within walking distance.

The schools were to be different, too. Rather than traditional letter grades, children were given only "Not yet" or "Achieving" marks. Instead of classrooms, kids were organized across grade levels in "neighborhoods" of 100 students managed by four-member teaching teams. The schools turned out to be a focus of disillusionment in Celebration's early years; parents felt that their children weren't getting the education they expected from a multinational entertainment empire, and some pulled their kids in favor of private schools.

And then there was the unanticipated shock of living in an experimental suburban fishbowl. Because Celebration is not a gated community, tourists cruised through the streets, gawking at residents as if they were actors or robots. Imagine going out to get your newspaper in your bathrobe, and having a busload of Germans snapping photos of you. Don't let this discourage you from visiting Celebration, however. The town is worth a look, but don't harass the locals.

Celebration Hotel, 700 Bloom St., Celebration, FL 34747

(407) 566-6000

E-mail: sales@celebrationhotel.com

Hours: Always visible

Cost: Free; Rooms $199/night and up

www.celebrationhotel.com

Directions: Turn south on Celebration Ave., off Rte. 192 just east of I-4, and follow signs through town.

EATONVILLE

Writer **Zora Neale Hurston** was born in Eatonville on January 7, 1903.

Eatonville is the nation's oldest incorporated "all-black city."

The way things ought to be.

Kissimmee
Big Bamboo Lounge

Long before Disney World, there was the Big Bamboo Lounge. The original owner, Bruce Muir, dressed up his shack of a bar with South Seas World War II decor, then erected a fake watchtower to attract motorists along Route 192. Some of those motorists were a mysterious team of land-grabbers who were gobbling up real estate west of Kissimmee at $200 an acre. That land was later used for Walt Disney's eastern theme park. While the attraction was being built in the late 1960s, the Big Bamboo was the bar of choice for construction workers, imagineers, and artists, many of whom left sketches of characters on the walls and cocktail napkins as thanks. Some of these are still framed behind the bar.

Since those early days of Disney World, it has become a tradition for employees to leave their park badges with the Big Bamboo after they leave the park for the last time. Hundreds—no, *thousands*—of big-eared badges cover the walls, as do badges from Red Lobster, Hooters, and other high-falutin' chains. There are also business cards, newspaper clippings, stuffed animals, and other junk, much of it covered in cobwebs and decades of grime. (The Big Bamboo doesn't seem to be big on feather dusters.)

A while back, Muir went to that Big Tiki Bar in the Sky. His will stipulated that the Big Bamboo be closed for good three years after his death, and it was. But then it reopened, and it's a good thing for Orlando. For all Disney's efforts at building the world's perfect tourist attraction, it's hard to avoid one undeniable fact: the Big Bamboo has more character and more heart in its cinder block walls than all the pre-fabricated "atmosphere" in the Magic Kingdom.

4849 W. Irlo Bronson Hwy., Kissimmee, FL 34746

(407) 396-2777

Hours: Daily 3 P.M.–2 A.M.

Cost: Free; Booze extra

Directions: Just east of Vineland Blvd. on Rte. 192 (Irlo Bronson Hwy.).

The gator gets revenge.

Big Gator

Jungleland Zoo closed its cage doors for good in October 2002, and not a moment too soon. Originally started as a haven for abandoned and injured wild animals, the conditions there eventually became as bad as, or worse than, where the animals originally lived. Even the humans at Jungleland Zoo suffered; several slow-footed gator wrestlers were maimed. The attraction got a fair amount of unwanted publicity in 1998 when Nala, a lioness named for the Disney cartoon character, escaped from her pen and went AWOL for three days. Before she mauled any tourists, she was discovered barely 150 yards from the compound, hiding under a palmetto bush.

Prodded by a local television station, state wildlife authorities stepped in. Nala and friends are now long gone, adopted by other parks. What Jungleland Zoo left behind, however, is an enormous concrete alligator in its former parking lot, adjacent to the appropriately named Gator Motel. The 126-foot-long gator has a crushed land cruiser between its jaws, and a safari guide hanging on for dear life.

Gator Motel, 4576 W. Irlo Bronson Hwy., Kissimmee, FL 34746

(407) 396-0127

Hours: Always visible

Cost: Free

www.gatormotel.com

Directions: Just west of the Gator Motel on Rte. 192 (Irlo Bronson Hwy.).

KISSIMMEE

Airplanes passing over Kissimmee may not, by law, fly faster than 25 MPH if lower than 100 feet. The law was enacted after the first airplane to take off from Kissimmee killed a cow.

Kissimmee is Calusa for "heaven's place."

Kissimmee was once known as Cow Town.

Who cares about Alaska and Hawaii?

Monument of the States

Dr. C. W. Bressler-Pettis had a great idea and a whole lot of concrete. In 1943, he wrote to all the state governors requesting that they send a representative stone or brick from each of their home states for him to embed into a monument. Every governor sent something, probably because the doctor also immortalized their names in the same edifice.

Sorry to say, it has not been updated since the admittance of Alaska and Hawaii. It does, however, have several meteorites from outer space.

The Monument of the States stands about 50 feet tall and is topped by a 562-pound concrete bald eagle. The tower bulges near the top, breaking the pointy pyramid, making it look like it's swallowing a grapefruit. The good folks of Kissimmee keep it decorated with Christmas lights during the holidays. It is also traditional to leave some type of home-state memento of your own. So go ahead, bring a rock.

Johnston St. & Monument Ave., Kissimmee, FL 34741

No phone

Hours: Always visible

Cost: Free

www.kissimmee.org/departments/cd/histour/monument.htm

Directions: One block northwest of Tohopekaliga Lake on Monument Ave., across the street from the library.

Nudist Hall of Fame

The Kissimmee area has long been known for one thing. No, not cows. No, not Disney. Nudism! OK, it was mostly just nudists who knew that, but they count. So when somebody suggested establishing a Nudist Hall of Fame, it only seemed natural, au natural, to do it in Kissimmee.

The family-oriented Cypress Cove Nudist Resort was already home to the American Nudist Research Library. Why not establish the Hall of Fame there? So it came to be that men and women who have furthered the cause of living free of society's lingering Victorian prudishness are honored in this club's small library. Members would spend more time learning about these visionaries, if they weren't so busy playing volleyball.

Though Cypress Cove is a private club, they do have a Villa Hotel open to nonmembers. They've also got a restaurant called Cheeks Bar & Grill, and a sandal and suntan lotion shop called the Fig Leaf Boutique. There are some restrictions on who can visit the resort. After all, they're not looking for a bunch of lookie-loos to ruin their fun in the sun. However, each year they do throw open their doors for the Celebration for the Not So Clothes Minded. Check the Web site for details.

Cypress Cove Nudist Resort, 4425 Pleasant Hill Rd., Kissimmee, FL 34746

(407) 933-5870

Hours: Visitors by appointment

Cost: $85–$135/night

www.cypresscoveresort.com

Directions: Just north of the intersection of Rte. 531 (Pleasant Hill Rd.) and Poinciana
Rd., south of Kissimmee.

Splendid China

When you arrive at Splendid China, you pass through acres of empty lots, park your car within a few feet of the front gate, and march right up to the ticket booth. Though the *real* China may have a billion-something citizens, Splendid China has barely enough to field a baseball team. What's going on here?

The attraction has had trouble from its inception. After opening its gates in 1993, it was picketed daily by the Citizens Against Communist Chinese Propaganda who said it was a not-so-clever front for the People's Republic of China. Acrobats and entertainers, brought over from the mainland and dropped into the vortex of consumer America, kept defecting. And then the kiss of death: no tourists showed up.

Not that there isn't plenty to see here. The park has no fewer than 60 historic Chinese landmarks re-created in miniature, spread over 76 acres. You may know the Forbidden City, the Great Wall (rebuilt here with 6 million tiny bricks), and the 8,000 Terra Cotta Warriors of Xian. But what about the Wind and Rain Bridge, the Mogao Grottoes, the Tengwang Pavillion, and the Jin Gang Bao Zuo Pagoda? They're here, too, and more.

Splendid China will likely survive as long as the Chinese government wants it to, whether it makes money or not. Standard economic rules just don't apply. Still, the park could take a hint from Disney's success: if you want to run a tight ship, hire a bunch of shameless money-grubbers.

3000 Splendid China Blvd., Kissimmee, FL 34747

(800) 244-6226 or (407) 396-7111

E-mail: schina@earthlink.net

Hours: Daily 9:30 A.M.–7 P.M.

Cost: Adults $28.88, Seniors (55+) $25.99, Kids (5–12) $18.18

www.floridasplendidchina.com

Directions: Three miles west of I-4, turn south off Rte. 192 (Irlo Bronson Hwy.) at the
large dragon near Mile Marker 5, and follow the signs.

Squeeze this.

World's Largest Half Orange

There are plenty of roadside emporiums willing to ship boxes of Florida
citrus to your family and friends, but none as impressive as Eli's Orange
World, housed inside the World's Largest Half Orange. This bright
orange hollow hemisphere is 92 feet in diameter and weighs almost 18
tons. In addition to fresh-picked fruit, it offers a wide selection of T-
shirts, Disney and Florida souvenirs, and orange-flavored candy, mar-
malade, and snacks. If you don't want to lug it all back on the plane,
they'll mail your purchases to your home in the cold, cold North.

Eli's Orange World, 5395 W. Irlo Bronson Hwy., Kissimmee 34746

(800) 531-3182 or (407) 396-1306

E-mail: orangeworld@earthlink.net

Hours: Daily 8 A.M.–11 P.M.

Cost: Free

www.orangeworld192.com

Directions: On Rte. 192 (Irlo Bronson Hwy.) at Polynesian Isle Blvd.

The future that never was.

Xanadidn't

It's a vision of the future that never happened and probably never will, a home so energy efficient it was actually *made* of insulation: Xanadu, the House of the Future. Builder J. Thomas Gussel came up with the unique method of construction: inflate a large balloon, coat it with a thick layer of polyurethane, and let dry. Once it hardens, cut out a doorway and deflate the balloon. Ta da! Instant home.

Xanadu is filled with groovy features James Bond and Hugh Hefner might envy: televisions set into the walls, a hi-fi stereo, and round, velour-covered beds. But by the mid-1980s, the House of the Future already seemed hopelessly out of date. Where was the personal computer? The CD player? And by the 1990s, what kind of futuristic domicile doesn't have a two-SUV garage?

Time has Xanadu's number, and time is running out. Only two other Xanadus were ever built, one in Gatlinburg, Tennessee, and the other in the Wisconsin Dells, and both of them have already met the wrecking ball. Against the odds of unbridled Orlando-area development, the Kissimmee location survives. Though it is no longer open to the public, this big pile of oversized marshmallows is up for sale. If you're willing to purchase the land beneath it, this House of the Future of the past is all yours.

Xanadu, 4800 W. Irlo Bronson Hwy., Kissimmee, FL 34746

(407) 438-4575

Hours: Always visible; view from road

Cost: Free

Directions: Just east of Vineland Blvd., next to the Key Motel.

Lake Buena Vista
Disaster at Disney World

So you think Disney World is perfect, right? Welllllll, almost. The park has had its share of troubles, which is understandable considering the millions of guests that pass through its gates each year. And since you're not likely to hear about these problems in the standard travel guides, they're offered here:

- Not long after the park opened in 1971, the Mark Twain Paddleboat rammed a raft on the River of America, dumping several dozen guests into the water.
- The clean, blue water of Disney World's Bay Lake was achieved by draining the water, ripping out all the cypress trees (which will turn the water brown), and lining the lake bottom with beach sand.
- Three rocket ships on Space Mountain crashed into one another a month after the attraction opened in 1975. The computer glitch injured 41 riders.
- About 200 passengers aboard the Monorail had to be evacuated in 1985 after the ride caught fire.
- The world's last dusky seaside sparrow perished at Disney World on May 16, 1987.
- In 1991, a wardrobe assistant was caught secretly videotaping the women's dressing room in Cinderella's Castle. Six members of the Kids of the Kingdom chorus sued Disney for $37.5 million, but the case was settled out of court.
- Disney World received $57.7 million from Orange County tax coffers in 1989 to upgrade its sewer system. Meanwhile, the county canceled plans for low-income housing because it had "run out of money."

- The crown jewel of the Disney cruise line, Castaway Cay in the Bahamas, was named Gorda Cay until the corporation purchased it in the 1990s. Before that, it was long known to be a popular refueling stopover for drug dealers en route from South America with marijuana, cocaine, and Quaaludes.
- Disney's Splash Mountain ride has an unofficial Web site named Flash Mountain (www.flashmountain.com/spl.html) that documents the efforts of park guests to expose themselves to the souvenir cameras on the ride's final drop.
- Disney established a $75,000 trust fund with the Audubon Society after it was learned that a few "cast members" may have been involved in the extermination of several endangered black vultures who had roosted atop the Contemporary Resort, and had been attacking tortoises on Discovery Island.
- A baby was born in the women's bathroom outside Space Mountain on November 8, 1997.
- Several months before Disney's Animal Kingdom opened in 1998, its endangered black rhino died unexpectedly. An autopsy revealed that it died from a massive lung infection brought on by a 2-foot-long sharpened branch inserted into its lower intestine sometime *before* the animal was purchased. Also dead during the park's first few months was a hippopotamus, four cheetah cubs, and a pair of West African crowned cranes.
- Costumed cast members revolted in the 1990s after years of being forced to wear communal underwear provided to them by the park. Many claimed the garments often weren't adequately laundered. Labor negotiations included the right to take the underwear home at night to wash it.
- After Disney threatened to sue three Hallandale preschools over Disney-themed murals painted on their buildings, Universal Studios came in and painted them over . . . with the Flintstones, Scooby Doo, and Yogi Bear.
- An employee of BET Soundstage filed a complaint with the Orange County Sheriff on October 5, 1998, stating that basketball star Shaquille O'Neal had assaulted her near Pleasure Island's Bridge 3. She only did so after she reported the incident to Disney Security, but they failed to file a report.

- The park recently halted the release of pigeons during the daily "Cinderella's Surprise Wedding Show" because local hawks were timing their hunts for the event.
- Disney World and its surrounding parks sell 170,000 gallons of ice cream each year, enough to fill 12 average swimming pools.
- A divorced father held his son and a waiter hostage at Disney's Boardwalk Inn on June 30, 2000, in a dispute over visitation rights. Both hostages were later freed.

Hang on—it's going to be a bumpy ride!
Courtesy Jeffrey Glover

Disney World, Lake Buena Vista, FL 32830

(407) W-DISNEY

Hours: Times vary; check Web site

Cost: Prices vary

disneyworld.disney.go.com/waltdisneyworld/index

Directions: West of I-4 on Rte. 192 (Irlo Bronson Hwy.), then north on World Dr.

EXTERMINATE MICKEY?

If you see a bright yellow car with big, black ears racing along a Florida highway, know this: it has nothing to do with Walt Disney. The car is one of a fleet of vehicles modified for Truly Nolan, the Sunshine State's biggest exterminator (www.trulynolan.com, (800) GO-TRULY). They don't just kill rodents, but bugs, too. Why didn't Truly Nolan design a car that looks like a giant cockroach? C'mon, this is Florida—mice *sell*.

LAKE BUENA VISTA

Lake Buena Vista was named for the California street on which the Disney studios are located.

Lots of lobster lovin'.

Orlando
Frisky Lobster

Lobsters aren't known for their keen eyesight. The evidence is parked outside one of three Orlando area eateries: a 15-foot lobster is mating with a red Volkswagen Beetle belonging to the Boston Lobster Feast. This copulating crustacean covers most of the bug's roof, but not so much that it prevents the car from being driven from restaurant to restaurant.

Somehow this unnatural union between machine and marine life is supposed to attract customers. Maybe they've got a point. What restaurants without hokey gimmicks do you see listed in this guide?

Boston Lobster Feast, 8204 Crystal Clean Lane, Orlando, FL 32809

(407) 438-0607

Boston Lobster Feast, 8731 International Dr., Orlando, FL 32819

(407) 248-8606

Boston Lobster Feast, 6071 W. Irlo Bronson Hwy., Kissimmee, FL 34746

(407) 396-2606

Hours: Daily 4–10 P.M.

Cost: Free; Meals $7–$30

www.bostonlobsterfeast.com

Directions: The lobster car is parked most often outside the Kissimmee location, just
west of I-4 on Rte. 192 (Irlo Bronson Hwy.).

THE LOBSTER'S NOT THE ONLY FRISKY ONE . . .

On July 6, 1999, a 27-year-old Miami man was found nude and dead in
the killer whale holding tank behind Shamu Stadium at Orlando's Sea
World (7007 Sea World Drive, (407) 351-3600, www.seaworld.com).
Police believe the victim snuck into the off-limits area after hours to
swim with the orca Tillikum, and drowned. The orca then played with
his dead body, somehow pulling off his trunks.

LONGWOOD

The Senator, a cypress in Longwood, is estimated to be 3,500 years
old. It was 165 feet tall until shortened to 127 feet by a hurricane,
but it's s still the largest tree in the eastern United States.

ORLANDO

On September 26, 1953, it rained dime-sized toads during two different thunderstorms in Orlando.

Jaws 3-D was filmed at Orlando's Sea World.

Goodbye, dear chicken.

Photo by author, courtesy Gatorland

Gatorland

If all Florida attractions were as fabulous as Gatorland, Disney World would be strapped for Mickey Money. You know you're in for something special when you enter Gatorland through the open jaws of an oversized alligator head, the first of 5,000+ alligators on the premises, and one of the few that isn't alive and snapping. Just past the main entrance, stop for some Gator Chow (hot dogs), to feed the reptiles. Follow the trail to the right and you'll eventually find the 800-seat gator-wrestling arena. Though it looks dangerous, the wranglers here are well trained in how to snag a big one. The secret? Approach the gator from behind, being careful to remain in its blind spot. Don't try this at home, kids!

But *do* try it at the next stop: Up Close Encounters. After an educational lecture, the little tykes are invited to pose astride a small gator for $5. Its jaws are taped shut, just to be safe.

Gators who aren't lucky enough to lounge around while tourists chuck hot dogs at them end up as wallets in the gift shop, and on the menu at Pearl's Smoke House. Pearl serves gator nuggets and barbecued gator ribs. A word of warning: gator ribs aren't like baby back ribs, they're smaller and more fish-like, and kind of "knuckly."

If you need to walk off them swamp vittles, head over to the observation tower overlooking the breeding marsh. A trail winds through various habitats where red flags mark the gators' nests, often near the walkway. Well-placed native plants, crashed planes, and sunken boats give the illusion that you're strolling through an open swamp, and it's easy to imagine danger lurks just beneath the palm fronds. Better stay on the path . . .

Finally, you're invited to Gatorland's signature show: the Gator Jumparoo. Full, raw chickens are suspended from a clothesline over a gator pen, a juicy meal for the first gator willing to jump for it. The chicken can disappear in a single lunging snap, but if you visit Gatorland on a day when the reptiles aren't frisky (usually in cooler weather), the show's emcee will lean out from the platform, chicken in hand, and coax a gator to take a bite. Keep that camcorder running—you never know when you'll get some great footage for Fox-TV's *When Animals Attack!*

14501 S. Orange Blossom Trail, Orlando, FL 32837

(800) 393-JAWS or (407) 855-5496

E-mail: customerservice@gatorland.com

Hours: Daily 9 A.M.–6 P.M.

Cost: Adults $17.93, Kids (3–12) $8.48

www.gatorland.com

Directions: On Rte. 17/92/ 441 (Orange Blossom Tr.) south of Rte. 417 (Central Florida Greenway).

ALLIGATOR FACTS

Alligators are a generally misunderstood species, so it's time for a few facts:

★ The word *alligator* is a bastardization of "el lagarto," Spanish for "the lizard."

★ To "hypnotize" a gator, simply turn it on its back. Blood will rush to its teeny brain, causing it to pass out momentarily.

★ An alligator's jaw can exert 2,000 pounds of force per square inch.

★ An alligator will grow as many as 6,000 teeth during its lifetime.

★ Florida logs between 16 and 20 gator-on-human attacks each year, but only nine people have been *killed* by alligators since 1948 when record-keeping began.

The Holy Land Experience

Look around Orlando and what do you see? Water slides. Miniature golf courses. Gator wrestlers. T-shirt shops. Tattoo parlors. Now tell me what you *don't* see. Urban planning. Inexpensive hotels. And God. That's right, the closest you're likely to come to a cautionary religious message is watching Mickey Mouse get in a heap of trouble after dabbling in the black arts in *The Sorcerer's Apprentice*.

Well, no more. Enter, stage *waaaay* right, The Holy Land Experience. Founded by Reverend Marvin Rosenthal in 2001, this Christian-themed amusement park puts the Jesus back in "Jesus, how much is it to get in here?" Covering roughly the years 1450 B.C. to A.D. 66, the park has a wide selection of Biblical attractions in an authentic Middle Eastern setting. Step into the Theater of Life in the Temple of the Great King to see *The Seed of Promise*, where God plays macho head games with Abraham, and heaven looks like a foggy Wal-Mart parking lot filled with cheerful zombies. See the world's largest scale model of Jerusalem's old city. Check out the ancient artifacts in the Scriptorium, the Center for Biblical Antiquities. Take in a little evangelizing at Calvary's Garden Tomb next to the pungent Dromedary Depot. And be sure to see the multimedia presentation at the Wilderness Tabernacle: a golden Ark of the

Covenant erupts with a blinding column of light and smoke, the Pillar of Cloud, though nobody's head melts à la *Raiders of the Lost Ark*. Could Hollywood have lied to us?

The Holy Land Experience is not all fun and games. The daily program outlines a strict behavioral policy, setting it apart from secular attractions, including a dress code (no halter-tops, short-shorts, bathing suits, or Spandex), behavior code (no drunkenness or lewd and lascivious conduct), and worship code (no unapproved "religious activity . . . deemed by the staff to be causing a disturbance"). So take those Daisy Dukes, pentagram amulets, and beer can sippy hats somewhere secular!

4655 Vineland Rd., Orlando, FL 32811

(866) USA-HOLYLAND

Hours: Times vary; call ahead or check online schedule

Cost: Adults $29.75, Kids (6–12) $19.75

www.holylandexperience.com

Directions: Just west of I-4 at Conroy Rd. (Exit 78).

ANOTHER HOLY AMUSEMENT PARK?

The Holy Land Experience isn't the first religious theme park proposed for Orlando, just the first to get off the ground. The now-late magician **Doug Henning** and the **Maharishi Mahesh Yogi** once drew up plans for a 480-acre park named Vedaland. It was to have 38 rides based upon enlightenment and mystical understanding through transcendental meditation. One ride would be a trip over a fake rainbow, and another was to a building that appeared to hover over a pond. Though the original goal was to open in 1993, it never got off the ground.

ORLANDO

Orlando's old City Hall, the Soreno Building, was blown up for the movie *Lethal Weapon III* as a way to save the city the demolition expense.

Actor **Wesley Snipes** was born in Orlando on August 4, 1963.

Only ducks may crap in the fountain.
Photo by author, courtesy of Peabody Hotel

March of the Ducks

Every morning at 11 A.M., five ducks living on the roof of the Peabody Hotel waddle onto the elevator, ride down to the lobby, and hop into the fountain, all to the tune of John Philip Sousa's "King Cotton March." In the afternoon, at 5 P.M., they get out of the fountain, waddle back over to the elevator, and return to the roof.

Does this all sound vaguely familiar? It should, because the Peabody Hotel in Memphis, Tennessee, has been parading its ducks since the 1930s. The original ducks, which were a hunter's live decoys, were first left in its lobby as a joke. But the birds decided to stay. Soon folks were gathering to watch the twice-daily March of the Ducks, and the Peabody knew it had a great PR gimmick on its hands.

When the Peabody opened a new hotel in Orlando, it bought a new bunch of quackers. The ducks are now part of its corporate logo, and out of respect for its mascots, no duck is ever served in any Peabody restaurant.

Peabody Orlando, 9801 International Dr., Orlando, FL 32819

(800) PEABODY or (407) 352-4000

Hours: Daily 11 A.M. and 5 P.M.

Cost: Free

www.peabody-orlando.com

Directions: Just across the street from the Convention Center on International Dr.,
north of Rte. 528 (Beeline Expressway).

Pirate's Dinner Adventure

Aaaaaargh, mateys, did the Pirates of the Caribbean leave you wanting
more pillagin' and plunderin'? Then crack open your treasure chests and
head on over to the Pirate's Dinner Adventure!

You're told to arrive early for the King's Feast, a chance for some
predinner snacks in a courtyard ringed with tacky souvenir emporiums,
a tarot card reader, and a maritime "museum." *Ta-ta-ta-daaah!* the
trumpets blare and a crew of swashbuckling servers marches out for the
presentation of the hors d'oeuvres. Never have nachos, pretzels, and car-
rot sticks been given such a fanfare!

About the time the pretzels run out the preshow begins. It seems the
peaceful folk of Port Santa Cruz de Timucuan are having a Freedom Festival, and you're invited. And what better way to celebrate freedom than
to bow down in subservience to the stunning Princess Anita? Please,
Your Highness, take a seat on the throne! Next, a belly dancer undulates
with a python and a scantily clad gypsy girl sways overhead on a trapeze.
Let freedom swing!

But the preshow doesn't last forever. Captain Sebastian the Black
and his band of pirates (the flotsam and jetsam of Orlando's boy band
puppy mill) raid the party, kidnap Princess Anita, and kick open the
doors to the main performance arena.

Inside, six color-coded sections surround a 300,000-gallon lagoon
that holds a three-masted Spanish galleon. You soon learn that between
bites of Buccaneer Beef and Walk-the-Plank Mixed Vegetables you're to
cheer for your section's assigned pirate as he performs daring stunts such
as swinging back and forth on a rope, jumping on a trampoline, and getting kicked in the crotch for the kids to laugh at. Cirque du Soleil it ain't.

There is a story line to the show, but it's rather difficult to follow, not because it's complex but because the panting performers are hard to hear over all the cheering. Just remember this: you'll know it's over when the kids are sworn in as crew members, handed muskets, and told to surround the ship. The princess is freed, having won the heart of a reformed pirate lad, and the audience jumps up and sings "YMCA." Now *that's* entertainment.

6400 Carrier Dr., Orlando, FL 32819

(800) 866-2469 or (407) 248-0590

Hours: 8 or 8:30 P.M.; Occasional 11:30 A.M. matinee

Cost: Adults $43.95, Kids (3–11) $26.95

www.piratesdinneradventure.com

Directions: North of Sand Lake Rd. (Rte. 482), west of Universal Blvd.

NOT THE REGULAR EATERIES

Apparently it isn't enough to enjoy a quiet meal with the family in Orlando. No sirree, even the simple task of eating has evolved into an opportunity to multitask; why just eat when you can eat and watch a show at the same time?

"Show" in Orlando doesn't mean dinner theater with *The Fantasticks*, but medieval warriors on horseback, interactive murder mysteries, and kitschy vaudeville revues. Several of these shows have debuted and then mercifully disappeared: American Gladiators, Buffalo Bill's Wild West Dinner Extravaganza, and Blazing Pianos. But there are more where they came from. Here's a sampling:

★ **Arabian Nights** (6225 W. Irlo Bronson Highway, Kissimmee, (407) 239-9223, www.arabian-nights.com) If the kids love Lipizzaner horses and unicorns, this is the place. Treat them to an evening of equine entertainment and nary a hint of Middle East unrest.

★ **Capone's Dinner and Show** (4740 W. Irlo Bronson Highway, Kissimmee, (407) 397-2378, www.alcapones.com) Unlimited alcoholic beverages make this rat-a-tat revue popular with those decompressing from a day at Disney. To enter this speakeasy, find the secret door in the adjoining ice cream parlor.

★ **Medieval Times Dinner and Tournament** (4510 W. Irlo Bronson Highway, Kissimmee, (407) 396-2900, www.medievaltimes.com) Medieval Times transports you back to 1092 when folks dined with their bare hands and wore color-coded paper crowns. You will, too, while watching horseback riders joust, swordfight, and juggle. Contrary to the eatery's literature, the knights do not really "battle to the death." Too bad.

Ripley's Believe It or Not! Odditorium

Anyone attracted to oddballs (and that means *you*) should have a statue
of Robert Ripley on the dashboard. He was and is the Patron Saint of
Bizarre and Mysterious Artifacts. Though he's long dead, you'll get a
chance to meet him just inside the entrance of this Orlando Odditorium
built to resemble a museum tipping into a Florida sinkhole. A hologram
of Ripley sits behind the desk in his study and tells you the story of his
quest for the curious through 192 foreign countries.

The Odditorium's artifacts are loosely grouped by subject, though
some items are placed at random. First, a banana mailed to Ripley with
no more than a stamp and address on the peel. Beside it, a hunk of the
original transatlantic cable. And next, a penis sheath from New Guinea;
the plaque states it was used less for ornamentation and more to protect
against insect bites. Just remember *that* when the conversation starts to
drag at your next cocktail party.

The collection demonstrates that Ripley was clearly a champion of the
fine arts. You'll see a replica of the Mona Lisa made from burnt toast, an
Elvis painting containing the hidden images of 600 other Elvi, and two
portraits of Abraham Lincoln, one done with pennies and the other with
human hair. At the center of one gallery is a full-size replica of a Rolls Royce
made from a million matchsticks by Reg Pollard of Manchester, England.

If you're squeamish, you might want to pass through the animal
oddities exhibit quickly. Here you'll find the stuffed and pickled remains

of a six-toed pig, a two-headed calf, a Siamese piglet, and Mike the Headless Chicken. The Odditorium's Torture Chamber doesn't have the remains of those killed in the Crusades, but it does have the instruments that got the job done: flesh pinchers, bone crushers, and the Iron Maiden of Nuremberg. Those were the days!

Though there seems to be no end to the wonders . . . Tom Thumb's tuxedo, a collection of antique bedpans, a vampire-killing kit, the Petrified Man . . . there's even more in the Ripley collection than you know. Somewhere in an Orlando office park, in a warehouse known only as Building 34, is the balance of the company's treasure trove. Time for a new wing on the Odditorium, Ripley's—we weirdos await!

8201 International Dr., Orlando, FL 32819

(800) 998-4418 or (407) 363-4418

Hours: Daily 9 A.M.–1 A.M.

Cost: Adults $15.95, Kids (4–12) $10.95

www.ripleysorlando.com

Directions: South of Sand Lake Rd. (Rte. 482) on International Dr.

BELIEVE IT OR NOT, YOU'RE PREGNANT

An African fertility statue at Ripley's Orlando headquarters was credited with helping 13 women become pregnant in 1995 whether they wanted it or not. Most were employees who handled the statue and weren't expecting the by-product. Word got around. Soon, barren couples were showing up unannounced to touch the statue. The figure of a woman and a child has since made a Fertility Tour of the United States. Hey, the Rolling Stones can't keep it up forever.

ORLANDO

Orlando was once named Jernigan.

Actress **Delta Burke** was born in Orlando on July 30, 1956. She was crowned Miss Florida in 1974.

Gather, Goths.

Skull Kingdom

So, Goths, were you expecting the Magic Kingdom to be more occult-oriented than it turned out to be? Well then, get your anemic corpses-to-be over to Skull Kingdom where the bloody bacchanalia really begins!

A cashier with black fingernail polish hands you a ticket and informs you of the attraction's only rule, which is more of a vague threat: Don't touch anything, and it won't touch you. This is good advice. Your group is asked to choose a leader, which is important—the last half of this walk-through spook house is unguided, and you'll be grabbing the belt loop of the person in front of you.

The tour begins innocently enough with a scene of a winged skeleton flying over what looks like a glowing torture chamber, or hell, or hell's torture chamber. "Beware of what lies ahead!" a booming voice warns. And what lies ahead? A fluorescent room filled with evil clowns—a Toon Town of Terror! Beyond that, the guide abandons you in a library where the furniture moves of its own accord. A secret passageway opens, and just about the time you're wondering whether to proceed, a masked Michael Meyers enters by the only other exit, arm upraised, butcher knife in hand.

On second thought, maybe you *will* go thataway—fast. The rest of your journey is a blur of dark hallways and horrific scenes. If you slow down to take a closer look, Mr. Meyers reappears and silently but effectively encourages you to move along. Eventually you stumble onto what appears to be a toxic spill or radioactive meltdown where mannequin workers vomit bright green liquid into 50-gallon drums. Amid the flashing yellow lights and the wail of the sirens you hear the whir of a chainsaw drawing closer. A red "Exit" sign appears and the tour quickly ends with your group stumbling and screaming into the gift shop with a psychotic maniac at your heels.

5933 American Way, Orlando, FL 32819

(407) 354-1564

E-mail: info@skullkingdom.com

Hours: Monday–Thursday 6–11 P.M., Friday–Sunday Noon–Midnight

Cost: Adults $12.50, Not recommended for kids under age 8 (but for them it's free!)

www.skullkingdom.com

Directions: On the northeast corner of International Dr. and Republic Dr., across from Wet 'n' Wild.

WINTER PARK
Richard Manuel, pianist for The Band, hung himself in his Winter Park hotel bathroom on March 4, 1986.

Up, up, and hopefully not away.
Courtesy SkyVenture

SkyVenture and SkyCoaster

Have you ever wanted to skydive, but the thought of throwing yourself out of an airplane seemed a little stupid? Then drop on by SkyVenture where instead of you falling *down*, the air goes *up*. The facility is essentially a vertical wind tunnel that blows 120 MPH winds upward through a Plexiglass chamber. Decked out in a helmet and jumpsuit, you step through a narrow door and onto the grating where you're blasted into the air by the powerful wind. Don't worry, there's always an instructor in the chamber who will teach you the basic skydiving moves, and prevent you from being tossed around like a cow in a tornado.

If you're not entirely sure this is your type of fun, why not stop by the visitor's gallery? It's free! And because there's often a skydiving club training, you're likely to see acrobatic maneuvers that are much more graceful than you're likely to do on your first ride, which is to bob up and down in the air about six feet off the floor.

6805 Visitors Circle, Orlando, FL 32819

(407) 903-1150

Hours: Monday–Friday 2 p.m.–Midnight, Saturday–Sunday Noon–Midnight

Cost: Adults $38.50, Kids (3–12) $33.50

www.skyventure.com

Directions: Across from Wet 'n' Wild off International Dr.

So, after visiting SkyVenture, you're intrigued by the idea of skydiving, but you're still not ready to jump out of a plane? How about SkyCoaster? It's the World's Tallest Swing at 300 feet, and the only restriction on riding it is that you be 42 inches or taller.

One, two, or three riders are strapped into a harness and suspended face down, Superman-style, from two very long cables. A third cable clamps to the foot of the harness and pulls riders upward and back until it seems they can't go any higher, then releases them. By the time they roar past the crowds at the bottom of the arc, they're cruising at 85 MPH and screaming as if they're looking death in the face, and they're not amused. But the bystanders sure are.

2850 Florida Plaza Blvd., Kissimmee, FL 34746

(407) 397-2509

Hours: Daily Noon–Midnight

Cost: One flyer $37, Two flyers $64, Three flyers $81

www.skycoaster.cc

Directions: Next to Old Town on Rte. 192 (Irlo Bronson Hwy.), behind Burger King.

Tiki Island Adventure Golf

Miniature golf courses are as thick as T-shirt emporiums in Orlando, but one deserves singling out: Tiki Island Adventure Golf. Its two 18-hole courses wind their way past tiki gods and waterfalls and tropical critters—all very run-of-the-mill—but it's the last holes that are the showstoppers. Like most putt-putt establishments, Tiki Island offers an incentive to hit a hole-in-one on either of the last greens, but if you make the shot here, the four-story volcano at the center of the park erupts *and* you win a free game. And if you 10-putt the last hole? They just might toss you into the burning lava.

7460 International Dr., Orlando, FL 32819

(407) 248-8180

Hours: Daily 10 A.M.–11:30 P.M.

Cost: 18 holes, Adults $8.99, Kids (12 and under) $7.99; 36 holes, Adults $12.99, Kids $11.99

Directions: One block north of Rte. 482 (Sand Lake Rd.) on International Dr.

Time to rearrange?
Photo by author, courtesy *Titanic: The Exhibition*

Titanic: The Exhibition

All aboard, vacationers! Have no fear, this trip aboard the *Titanic* promises to come out much better than its maiden voyage. The journey begins when you buy your ticket and are assigned the name of a passenger or crew member aboard the bottom-bound ocean liner. Keep that ticket handy to learn your fate from the exhibit's Memorial Wall just before you exit.

But that's getting ahead of the tour. First you're going to learn from a costumed guide with a thick Irish brogue (or, depending on the guide, another annoying accent) how the "unsinkable" *Titanic* was designed and constructed. You'll see replicas of the gangway into steerage, the first-class accommodations, and the gilded grand staircase. Throughout the museum are items recovered from the North Atlantic, including life jackets, tableware, and deck chairs, mixed in with props from the movie about the disaster. As your tour moves closer and closer to the iceberg, the rooms get progressively colder and the Enya music reaches a crescendo. Feel the chill on the deck beneath the stars and imagine jumping into the icy waters below. You'll be spared the agonizing plunge, but suffer a fate almost as painful: the exit through the Titanic-sized gift shop.

The Mercado, 8445 International Dr., Suite 202, Orlando, FL 32819

(877) 410-1912 or (407) 248-1166

Hours: Daily 10 A.M.–8 P.M.

Cost: Adults $16.95, Kids (6–11) $11.95

www.titanicshipofdreams.com

Directions: South of Sand Lake Rd. (Rte. 482) on International Dr.

Texas has the most pricks.
Photo by author, courtesy Cactus World, Inc.

Plymouth
Florida Cactus, Inc.

Here's one greenhouse where you should look twice, maybe three times, before sitting down to soak in the greenery. As is probably obvious from its name, Florida Cactus, Inc., specializes in prickly succulents, and they're *everywhere*. What is less obvious, before you see them all in one location, is the amazing variety among cacti. They're round, flat, tall, squat, fuzzy, purple, flowery, spiky, wrinkled . . . you name it . . . there's a cactus to fit any decor, unless you decorate with balloons. And they're all for sale.

This greenhouse/living museum has cacti species from every state in the union and most foreign countries. It has also arranged 50 unique species into a living, 24-by-12-foot cactus map of the United States where each state is covered with a different variety. Until recently, they also had a working Cactus Clock that was 24 feet in diameter. It has been replaced with a smaller, but still impressive, version that's five feet wide.

2542 S. Peterson Rd., Plymouth, FL 32703

Contact: PO Box 2900, Apopka, FL 32704

(407) 886-1833

Hours: Monday–Friday 7 A.M.–5 P.M.., Saturday 7 A.M.–11:30 P.M.

Cost: Free

Directions: North on Rte. 441, left on Boy Scout Blvd., right on Rte. 437, left onto Peterson Rd., then drive to the end.

A slithering superstar.
Photo by author, courtesy Reptile World Serpentarium

St. Cloud
Reptile World Serpentarium

Unlike the majority of snake-themed roadside attractions, the Reptile World Serpentarium is a genuine research facility. It was started in 1972 to collect and distribute poisonous venom for medical research, and in 1976 opened its doors to the public. Today, at noon and 3 P.M., you can watch handlers farm venom from cobras, vipers, mambas, and rattlesnakes by having them chomp on empty vials capped with rubber membranes.

One wing of the Serpentarium houses its research facilities, while the other is filled with snake pens. Reptile attractions are notorious for smelling like urine, but the Serpentarium, while hardly glamorous, is clean and well maintained. Apparently, if you want to handle these deadly snakes on a daily basis, you've got to treat them with respect. Lots of it. Lots, lots, lots, lots, lots.

5705 E. Irlo Bronson Hwy., St. Cloud, FL 34771

(407) 892-6905

Hours: Tuesday–Sunday 9 A.M.–5:30 P.M.

Cost: Adults $5.50, Teens (6–17) $4.50, Kids (3–5) $3.50

Directions: Just east of the Rte. 532 turnoff on Rte. 192 (Irlo Bronson Hwy.).

Winter Park
Rocks of the Rich and Famous

You may never get the chance to tour the world and see the former homes of the world's rich and famous, but you can see pieces of their homes in a unique walk of fame at Rollins College. The idea came from Hamilton Holt, who served as college president from 1925 to 1949. He collected more than 800 stones and bricks from the homes and birthplaces of famous individuals and placed them in a semicircular walkway on campus.

The elements have all but erased some of the inscriptions, and others are obscured by the grass growing between them, but hundreds of names are clearly visible: Harry S Truman, Louisa May Alcott, Jack London, Mr. Fred Rogers (a Rollins alum), Charles Dickens, Cleopatra, Lillian Gish, Abe Lincoln, Teddy Roosevelt, Martin Luther King, Maya Angelou, Will Rogers, Booker T. Washington, Socrates, George Washington, Charles Darwin, Mary Baker Eddy, and P. T. Barnum. There are also plenty from the college's benefactors, people you've never heard of and likely never will again.

Rollins College Walk of Fame, 1000 Holt Ave., Winter Park, FL 32789

(407) 646-2000

E-mail: contact@rollins.edu

Hours: Always visible

Cost: Free

www.rollins.edu/walk

Directions: On the east side of Carnegie Hall at Mills Lawn.

Sinkhole!

Florida might not seem prone to cataclysmic geologic events such as earthquakes and volcanoes, but it does have something you're not likely to find anywhere else: sinkholes. The by-product of the state's active underground aquifers, sinkholes can open up just about anywhere, and when the people above least expect it. (They do, however, open up most often during full and new moons.)

Take, for example, the German Car Service, a Porsche repair shop in Winter Park. One night in 1981 it disappeared into a 350-foot wide, 100-foot deep sinkhole, along with a home, a laundry, an Olympic swimming pool, and a printing company. An entire city block—gone!

The hole has since been filled, mostly, but you can still see where it happened from the south end of the ballpark north of Fairbanks Avenue. And if you're lucky, another hole might open up during your visit!

900 block of W. Fairbanks Ave., Winter Park, FL 32789

No phone

Hours: Always visible

Cost: Free

Directions: Ten blocks east of I-4 on Fairbanks Ave., between Denning and Harper Sts.

THAT SINKHOLE FEELING

About 350 new sinkholes are reported around Florida every year. And while these new holes are interesting, a few of the old holes are even better:

★ **Devil's Millhopper** (4732 Millhopper Road, (352) 955-2008) in Gainesville is the state's oldest sinkhole attraction. Visitors march 221 steps down into the 117-foot-deep hole, passing plants that are only found in the Appalachians.

★ **Sunken Gardens** (1825 4th Street N, (727) 551-3100) in St. Petersburg was rescued from demolition by the city and reopened in 2002. Talk of turning it into a nudist colony got the city to cough up the dough.

★ **The Ravine Gardens** (1600 Twigg Street, (386) 329-3721) in Palatka is three miles in diameter that has been landscaped with terraces, swinging bridges, and water features.

6

THE ATLANTIC COAST

T hose folks in Miami think they're so cool. But let me ask you, did they ever send a man to the moon? Do they host the state's fastest, loudest, and deadliest sporting event? Do they have the original Batmobile, hmmmmmmmmm?

No, no, and no. For all of these things you have to go to Florida's coolest coast, the Atlantic coast—not too far north, not too far south, and not too far inland. In this region you'll find the Daytona International Speedway, the navy's UDT-SEAL Museum, the International Hamburger Hall of Fame, and the world's vortex of cool: the Kennedy Space Center.

But that's not all! If you plan it right, in a single day you can stand inside the open jaws of the World's Largest Alligator Statue; visit Kit, the talking car from *Knight Rider*; and swing a mallet at the Liberty Bell. And if you feel you absolutely, positively, have to go to church, why not do it in Daytona Beach where you never have to leave your car? Now *that's* cool.

When you're headed to the moon, size definitely matters.

Cape Canaveral
Kennedy Space Center

OK, OK, the Kennedy Space Center is hardly an out-of-the-way, little-known tourist attraction. But it is, without a doubt, the *coolest* place on the planet. In a world obsessed with moronic, self-satisfied celebrities, it's comforting to know there's a place where the nerds with pocket protectors, the ones who push the boundaries of human exploration, are given the respect they deserve.

Your tour starts at the Visitor's Center Complex. There are plenty of things to see here—the *Explorer*, a full-size, walk-through Space Shuttle model; the Rocket Garden; the Launch Status Center, where you can get briefings on present and upcoming Shuttle flights; the massive Space Shop; the Astronaut Encounter, where you'll meet an actual space traveler; and the Astronaut Memorial—but please listen to this advice: head for the buses. The best stuff isn't even at the Visitor's Center.

Your bus tour takes you past the massive Vehicle Assembly Building, or VAB, where the rockets and shuttles are prepared for launch before being rolled out to the pads. You'll be allowed to get off the bus at the Launch Complex 39 Observation Gantry to get a long-distance view of the Shuttle pad and, if you're lucky, one will be waiting to launch.

The Apollo/Saturn V Center is the next stop on the tour, and it's by far the most interesting. You enter the museum through the Firing Room Theater where you'll see the actual command center computers from the Apollo program counting down to a moonshot launch. After blastoff, you exit to find yourself facing the five engines at the back end of a *Saturn V* rocket, one of the three still in existence. This 30-story-tall baby is able to deliver 7.5 *million* pounds of thrust on liftoff. Scattered around the museum are artifacts from NASA's Apollo years: Jim Lovell's *Apollo 13* space suit, the Astronaut Van used to transport the crews to the pad, the 1975 *Apollo-Soyuz* space capsule, the mothballed lunar lander from the canceled *Apollo 18* mission, and the launch and landing simulators used during astronaut training. Be sure to take in the show at the Lunar Theater where you'll witness the first moon landing on a re-created lunarscape.

In light of NASA's recent tragedy of the Space Shuttle *Columbia*, some have questioned whether the exploration of space is worth the risk. Those who have doubts have obviously never visited the Kennedy Space Center, because if they had they'd walk away with an answer: Hell yes, it is!

Kennedy Space Center, FL 32899

(321) 449-4444

Hours: Daily 9 A.M.–5:30 P.M.

Cost: Adults $26, Kids (3–11) $16; Maximum Access (includes Astronaut Hall of Fame, see page 173), Adults $33, Kids (3–11) $23

www.KennedySpaceCenter.com

Directions: Off Rte. 3 north from Merritt Island, or Rte. 405 east from Titusville.

CAPE CANAVERAL

The ill-conceived New Vietnam Amusement Park was to be constructed near Cape Canaveral in the mid-1970s, but it never got off the ground. In one "ride," designers had planned to simulate a firefight with an unseen enemy in the underbrush.

Séance central.

Cassadaga
The Cassadaga Spiritualists

Even the deceased head south for the winter. Although this community of Spiritualists is open year-round, the winter brings the greatest influx. Three hundred and fifty mediums and New Age followers live in this town founded by George Colby, a man guided to Florida in 1875 by four spirits: Seneca (an Indian), the Philosopher (a German), Wandah (a healer), and Professor Huffman (a public relations specialist). Once established, the Spiritualist Camp was eventually incorporated in 1894.

The town today looks pretty much the way it did in the 1920s when the cabins were constructed: spooky. The streets in Cassadaga are narrow and covered by a canopy of trees draped with Spanish moss. All of the mediums and healers here have been certified by the National Spiritualists Association of Churches, which means you won't find anyone using crystal balls, tarot cards, or hypnosis here—they're strictly forbidden. But you will find the souls of your dead loved ones . . . for a price. Appointments with mediums, spiritual advisors, and healers can be made through the Cassadaga Bookstore or the Cassadaga Hotel.

Cassadaga Spiritualist Camp, 1112 Davis St., PO Box 319, Cassadaga, FL 32706

(386) 228-2880

Hours: Always visible; call for appointments; Church services Sunday 10:30 A.M.

Cost: Free; Negotiate readings and healing in advance

www.cassadaga.org

Directions: Exit 54 from I-4, head north on Rte. 472, then east on Rte. 4101 (Cassadaga Rd.).

Cassadaga Hotel, 355 Cassadaga Rd., Cassadaga, FL 32706

(386) 228-2323

Hours: Always visible; call for appointment; Church services, Sunday 10:30 A.M.

Cost: Rooms $55–$80

www.cassadagahotel.com

Directions: Exit 54 from I-4, head north on Rte. 472, then east on Rte. 4101 (Cassadaga Rd.).

Christmas
Christmas in Florida

If Santa Claus ever retires, Christmas, Florida, is where he'll probably end up—they'd probably elect him mayor! The town was founded around the ruins of Fort Christmas, established here on December 25, 1837. Though the fort was abandoned three months after it was built, its name remained. As a town grew on the site, residents named streets with the holiday theme in mind: Frosty, Antler, Sleighbell, Candycane; and Santa's reindeer: Dasher, Dancer, Matthew, Luke, Comet, Cupid, and Blitzen.

For 11 months a year the town's post office is fairly quiet, but in December, look out! Thousands of cards and packages arrive to be sent back out with the town's official holiday postmark. The tradition was started by postmaster Juanita Tucker in the 1930s with an embossment reading "Glory to God in the Highest / CHRISTMAS / Orange County,

Florida." Bowing to the Constitution, the post office today offers your choice of a religious or secular embossment.

For the remainder of the year, the post office retains its holiday theme with a display of items sent to Santa by youngsters and adults who should know better.

Christmas Post Office, 23580 E. Colonial Dr., Christmas, FL 32709

(407) 568-2941

Hours: Always visible

Cost: Free

Directions: On the south side of Rte. 50 (Colonial Dr.).

Bite me? Bite *you*!

Swampy the Giant

Have no fear, the enormous alligator in the parking lot at Jungle Adventures is not a *real* alligator, but a cleverly disguised ticket booth and gift shop. His name is Swampy the Giant, and he's the World's Longest Alligator Statue at 220 feet from snout to tail. Those who want to give folks back home the impression that they live dangerously can pose inside his open mouth.

Swampy was constructed years ago when this attraction was less interested in education and more interested in gator wrestlin'. Now under new management, Jungle Adventures focuses on a wider swamp-life experience, including jungle cruises, and re-creations of an Indian village and the Spanish Fort Mees. It's also got a wildlife show with monkeys, parrots, snakes, possums, bears, raccoons, turtles, and the endangered Florida panther, plus guest appearances by a big cat that has never lived in these parts, a Bengal tiger.

Jungle Adventures, 26205 E. Highway 50, Christmas, FL 32709

(877) 4-A-GATOR or (407) 568-2885

E-mail: jungleadv@aol.com

Hours: Always visible; Park, daily 9:30 A.M.–5:30 P.M.

Cost: Adults $16, Seniors (60+) $12.50, Kids (3–11) $8.50

www.jungleadventures.com

Directions: On the north side of Rte. 50.

Cocoa Beach
I Dream of Jeannie

Though the characters in *I Dream of Jeannie* were entirely fictitious, you wouldn't know it from the way they were once treated in their very real hometown. In fact, when Major Anthony Nelson married Jeannie in 1969, the Mayor of Cocoa Beach hosted a four-day celebration that included a mock marriage license issued to Larry Hagman and Barbara Eden at City Hall.

Sadly, little enthusiasm for the 1964–1970 sitcom remains in this city. The nine rockets that stood outside Major Nelson's office at the Technology Laboratory on Patrick AFB rusted to the point where they had to be taken down. The couple's address was never revealed, so there's no home to drive by. About all that remains is a tiny street named in the show's honor, and that ain't much.

Johnnie Johnson Nature Center, Lori Wilson Park, 1320 N. Atlantic Ave., Cocoa Beach, FL 32952

(321) 868-1123

E-mail: info1@cocoabeachchamber.com

Hours: Always visible

Cost: Free

www.brevardparks.com/nature/loriwilson.htm

Directions: *I Dream of Jeannie* Lane leads north off Rte. A1A (Atlantic Ave.), two miles south of Rte. 520.

Daytona Beach
Dale Earnhardt's Last Lap

It's the story NASCAR fans know all too well. On February 18, 2001, Dale Earnhardt was in a dead heat for third place in the final lap of the Daytona 500. Rounding Turn Four, the Intimidator's number 3 black Chevy Monte Carlo spun sideways and slammed into the retaining wall, breaking Earnhardt's neck. He was rushed to Halifax Medical Center (303 N. Clyde Morris Boulevard), where he was pronounced dead. He was just short of his 50th birthday.

A sad story . . . yes . . . but the race goes on! If Earnhart's was a cautionary tale, it's that you should enjoy auto racing while you can. And what better place than the museum located mere steps from the track where he crashed? Step on over to the Velocitorium to see how car technology keeps improving. Try your hand at changing a tire in a mock-up of a Daytona pit—the pros do it in 16 seconds. Can you? Track tours leave from just beyond the gift shop. Regardless of the raceway's schedule, you'll get an up-close tram tour of the infield, but if you're lucky (and there are no time trials in progress) they'll ride up onto the 31-degree banking turns.

Daytona USA, Daytona International Speedway, 1801 W. International Speedway Blvd., Daytona, FL 32114

(386) 947-6800

Hours: Daily 9 A.M.–7 P.M., but extended for special events

Cost: Adults $20, Seniors (60+) $17, Kids (6–12) $14

www.daytonausa.com

Directions: East of I-95 on Rte. 92 (International Speedway Blvd.).

LI'L DALE, THE INTIMIDATING GOAT

While it may reflect poorly on Dale Earnhardt's karma, some NASCAR fans think the Intimidator was reincarnated as a pygmy goat. Why? On April 4, 2002, a kid bearing Earnhart's signature number 3 was born at Keuka Kids Champion Meat and Dairy Nubians (305 Keuka Road, (386) 684-6655, community-2.webtv.net/pierson1/KeukaKidsNubianFarm/) in Interlachen. Owners Jerry and Laura Pierson are proud of their famous goat, though they have no immediate plans to let it drive their car.

No place to neck.

Drive-In Services

Think of it as a drive-in movie, but with Jesus at the end instead of a car chase. The Drive-In Christian Church looks like an old drive-in theater, because that's exactly what it once was. Knowing how much Daytona folks love their cars, the church's founders converted this old theater to a driver-friendly house (or garage?) of worship. Just tune your car radio to 88.5 FM for the sermon broadcast twice each Sunday morning. Feel like singing along to the hymns? A lot of parishioners just honk their horns. I bet the neighbors love that.

Now just because the Bible says "Be fruitful and multiply" doesn't mean making out in your backseat during services is acceptable behavior. And don't expect to receive communion in the concession stand either.

Drive-In Christian Church, 3140 S. Atlantic Ave., Daytona Beach, FL 32118

No phone

Hours: Sunday 8:30 A.M. and 11 A.M.

Cost: Free

Directions: One block south of Rte. 7865 on Rte. A1A (Atlantic Ave.).

Hamburger Harry on the Hamburger-Harley.
Hamburger-Harley© Hamburger Harry Sperl, photo ©Harrod Blank, www.artcaragency.com

International Hamburger Hall of Fame

Few people are as crazy about hamburgers as Harry Sperl. This guy is *obsessed* with hamburgers. He's converted his motorcycle into the Hamburger-Harley, a mouthwatering three-wheeler with fiberglass catsup, lettuce, cheese, tomato, and all-beef patty wedged between two toasted buns as the seat. It's even rigged to emit steam from its patty while a stereo system plays the sound of sizzling meat.

Harry also purchased the Good Burger Mobile, a converted AMC Pacer with a sesame seed bun for a hood, from the movie *Good Burger*. And Harry sleeps on a round waterbed shaped like a ... do I need to tell you? If it has anything to do with hamburgers, Harry's probably got it:

banks, posters, glasses, magnets, music boxes, cookie jars, hats, toys, puppets . . . he's even been spotted in a catsup-red cape and boots, the superhero of burgerdom.

And like all dreamers, Hamburger Harry has set his sights even higher. He's commissioned architect Eugene Tsui to design the International Hamburger Hall of Fame building, a structure that has classic Greek columns and a classic sesame seed bun for a roof (a drawing is on his Web site). Harry's looking for a corporate sponsor to fund the construction, but until then, his enormous burger-abilia collection will remain in his basement. For now, the museum is only open during a once-a-year Open House. Drop him an e-mail and find out when the next event is scheduled.

Contact: Hamburger Harry, 1000 N. Beach St., Daytona Beach, FL 32117

(386) 254-8753

E-mail: harry@burgerweb.com

Hours: Once a year at the Open House

Cost: Free

www.burgerweb.com

Directions: You'll get them from Harry.

DAYTONA BEACH

Author **Stephen Crane** was trapped in a lifeboat for 30 hours after the ship he was on, the *Commodore*, sank off Daytona Beach in 1897. He turned the experience into his short story, "The Open Boat."

It is illegal to molest trash cans in Daytona Beach.

The dance floor at the Dayton Beach Pier (1200 Main Street) is the largest in the world.

Educator **Mary McLeod Bethune** lived at 640 Second Avenue in Daytona Beach where, in 1904, she founded the Daytona Normal and Industrial Institute for Negro Girls, later to become Bethune-Cookman College. She is buried on campus.

Klassix Auto Attraction

There are classic cars, and there are Klassix. This Daytona Beach auto museum has plenty of beautiful old cars, but it's the one-of-a-kind models that bring in the crowds. Front and center is a Batmobile rescued from a cave just outside Gotham City. It no doubt could outperform the Flintmobile in the adjoining room, even though this stone-age car has been upgraded from its foot-powered days—it appears to have been made from a modern golf cart. Klassix also has Dragula, a coffin-shaped dragster from the B-movie *Munster Go Home*; Grease Lightning, from the customizing dream sequence in *Grease*; the Green Hornet's machine-gun-modified limo once chauffeured by Bruce Lee; and one of the few noncrashed Bluesmobiles from the forgettable *Blues Brothers 2000*.

And then there's Kitt. You remember Kitt, right? David Hasselhoff's talking car on *Knight Rider*? Of course you do—don't deny it. Sorry to be the one to break the news, but Kitt no longer talks. He's probably bitter that Hasselhoff tossed him aside for a *Baywatch* dune buggy. A sign taped to Kitt's steering wheel warns visitors, "Please look, dream, and enjoy this classic part of American history, but DO NOT TOUCH." How could we, when we're so paralyzed with excitement?

2909 W. International Speedway Blvd., Daytona Beach, FL 32124

(904) 252-3800

E-mail: klassix@totcon.com

Hours: Daily 9 A.M.–6 P.M.

Cost: Adults $14, Seniors (55+) $12.93, Kids (7–12) $7

www.klassixauto.com

Directions: Just west of I-95 on Rte. 92 (International Speedway Blvd.).

FORT PIERCE

Writer **Zora Neale Hurston** lived the final years of her life at 1734 School Court Street in Fort Pierce. After dying of a stroke in 1959, she was buried in an unmarked grave in the Garden of Heavenly Rest (Avenue S and 17th Street). Years later, writer **Alice Walker** bought a marker for her plot that reads, in part, "A Genius of the South."

G.I. Uh-oh.

Fort Pierce
UDT-SEAL Museum

Each of the nation's armed forces has a special-forces component, and for the navy they're the UDTs and SEALs. Started in 1943 as the NCDUs (Naval Combat Demolition Units), these frogman forces were trained in setting underwater mines and defusing those of the enemy. The NCDUs were eventually renamed the UDTs (Underwater Demolition Teams) as another elite group, the SEALs (Sea, Air, and Land units), evolved to walk on land and fly through the air.

The UDT-SEAL Museum is a collection of both the tools of their trade and the souvenirs of their efforts. Outside, on the lawn around the building, are minisubmarines, helicopters, and speedboats. Inside you'll find knives, guns, and no-nonsense killing tools, such as the piano wire tool used for "silent takedowns of enemy guards and sentries." (What, you think these guys are choirboys?)

To get a little hint of the UDT-SEAL attitude toward its targets, check out the motto on the photograph of a burning Iranian oil platform, destroyed by SEAL Team 2 during Operation Ernest Will in the Persian Gulf: "To err is human, to forgive is not our policy." The same sentiment is expressed less eloquently on a roll of Jane Fonda toilet paper on display.

One of the museum's prime pieces of UDT-SEAL booty is a throne used by Panamanian strongman Manuel Noriega before his 1990 capture. The throne is taken out from time to time, but there's no guarantee when it'll show up next. (You certainly will *never* see the 100 pounds of tamales wrapped in corn stalks that U.S. forces confiscated during the invasion. They told the world they were bundles of cocaine.)

UDT-SEAL Museum, Hutchinson Island, 3300 N. Rte. A1A, Fort Pierce, FL 34949
(561) 595-5845
Hours: May–December, Tuesday–Saturday 10 A.M.–4 P.M., Sunday Noon–4 P.M.;
 January–April, Monday–Saturday 10 A.M.–4 P.M., Sunday Noon–4 P.M.
Cost: Adults $5, Kids (6–12) $2
www.navysealteams.com/options.htm
Directions: North of the North Beach Causeway on Rte. A1A.

HOBE ISLAND
President Bill Clinton slipped on a step at the Hobe Island home of golfer **Greg Norman** on March 14, 1997, tearing the cartilage attached to his kneecap.

JENSEN BEACH
Jensen Beach is the Sea Turtle Capital of the World.

What a ding dong.

Melbourne
The Liberty Bell

What is it about the Liberty Bell? That clumsy clanger is accident-prone! Everyone knows about the crack in the original bell, but what about some of its ding-a-ling offspring? Just before 1976, in preparation for the nation's 200th anniversary of independence, 30 new Liberty Bells were cast at the same Whitechapel Bell Foundry that made the original. One of the bells was purchased by the schoolchildren of Brevard County and turned over to a local veterans group that planned to get a little more mileage out of it. Sometime after the Bicentennial, while it was being towed by a truck in a local parade, the driver made a tight turn and dumped the kids' bell off the float and onto the roadway.

Well, you can hardly notice the flattened edge today. Unlike the original bell, the damage did not render it unringable. In fact, volunteers will hand you a rubber mallet to do the honors—see what freedom ringing really sounds like! The 2,080-pound bell sits in a museum housed in Melbourne's old domed water tank (which helps amplify the sound), along with other patriotic artifacts. They also have replicas of 32 important documents from our nation's history, from the Mayflower Compact to the Instrument of Surrender in the Pacific signed by the Japanese to end World War II. They're guarded by a green Statue of Liberty made from an old store mannequin, and surrounded by firearms and souvenirs from all our nation's wars, and both a Lincoln Memorial and Capitol Building constructed with pennies.

Honor America, 1601 Oak St., PO Box 1776, Melbourne, FL 32902

(321) 727-1776

E-mail: America@worldnet.att.net

Hours: Monday–Friday 10 A.M.–4 P.M., Saturday 10 A.M.–2 P.M.

Cost: Donations accepted

home.att.net/~honor

Directions: Six blocks west of Rte. 1, three blocks north of Rte. 192, in Wells Park.

Rest in peace?

New Smyrna Beach
Dead Dummett in the Middle of the Road
Charles Dummett was a bit of a klutz. On April 23, 1860, he was hunting with a friend when he tripped on a root and fell on his rifle, which fired. His

grief-stricken father, Douglas, buried him at the spot where his son drew his last breath, and covered the plot with a 30-square-foot concrete slab.

Fast forward about 100 years. New Smyrna Beach was in the midst of a land boom. Developers were platting a street that they soon discovered would plow right through the tomb of the former teenage resident. When nobody could come up with an easy solution to relocate the luckless lad, they fell back on Plan B: route the road around the grave—on both sides.

Dummett's plot today looks more like a suburban carrefour designed to slow speeding traffic, but if you're willing to pull aside the vines and weeds you'll see the inscription on the slab.

Canova Dr., New Smyrna Beach, FL 32169

No phone

Hours: Always visible

Cost: Free

Directions: Take Flagler Ave. east over the North Causeway, turn right on Peninsula Ave. (the first light), then right on Canova, following it around to the left.

LAKE MARY
Lake Mary calls itself the Village Not for Tourists, Not for Excitement, but for Modest, Tranquil, Healthful Living.

MELBOURNE
The Doors' **Jim Morrison** was born in Melbourne on December 8, 1943.

ORMOND BEACH
Multimillionaire **John D. Rockefeller** often handed out dimes to children in front of the Ormond Union Church, then gave lectures to his captive audience about the virtues of thrift. He died at the age of 98 at his home at 15 E. Granada Street.

ST. LUCIA
Jellyfish have been known to clog the cooling vents of St. Lucia's nuclear reactor, causing shutdowns.

SANFORD
Sanford is often called Celery City.

Port Orange
Seven Dwarfs' House

Snow White and the Seven Dwarfs was only a movie to most people, but to Alfred Nippert, it became an obsession. For some reason, Alfred decided he had to re-create the dwarfs' house in exact detail. He sent his carpenter, Ernie Whidmeir, to the animated movie as many times as he needed to get every detail exactly right, and within three months of the movie's premiere, the fake house (meaning the *real* house) was completed.

Nippert then invited Walt Disney to visit, which he did. Those who were there claimed Disney was very impressed. This was 1939, long before Disney even thought about breaking ground for Disneyland. In fact, some believe that Nippert's creation was the spark that ignited Disney's theme park flame. Too bad that inferno is now burning up the whole Sunshine State.

Museum Center at Spruce Creek, 1819 Taylor Rd., Port Orange, FL 32128

(904) 255-0285

Hours: By appointment only

Cost: Donations encouraged

Directions: 1.5 miles west of I-95 on Taylor Rd., behind Gamble House, along Spruce Creek.

Titusville
American Police Hall of Fame & Museum

In early 2003, the American Police Hall of Fame & Museum began its move from downtown Miami to Titusville. The move won't be cheap, and it'll be difficult, so it may take some time before it reopens its doors. In other words, check out the Web site before you load all the kids in the minivan and head for Titusville.

Oh, but what a museum it'll be! In Miami, the museum didn't shy away from the grittier aspects of law enforcement and the penal system. They had an electric chair in which visitors could take shocking gag photos, a gas chamber, bricks from the St. Valentine's Day Massacre wall with a re-creation of the Chicago crime scene, the police car from *Blade Runner*, skulls showing gunshot wounds, a blood-spattered guillotine on wheels (it even worked!), and lots and lots of crime scene photos.

The museum's new facility will be even larger. It will include a 9,000-square-foot gun range, a virtual courtroom, a crime lab, and simulators to teach tactical driving and shooting. Golly, who needs Disney World?

Vectorspace Blvd. & Rte. 1, Titusville, FL 32780

(305) 573-0070 (Miami office)

E-mail: policeinfo@aphf.org

Hours: Call ahead

Cost: Call ahead

www.aphf.org

Directions: Just southeast of the intersection of Rte. 1 and Rte. 406 (Columbia Blvd.).

FLORIDA LAWS

Of course, police would have nothing to do without laws, and Florida has a lot of them. Here are a few of the Sunshine State's statutes:

★ You cannot hire away your neighbor's cook.

★ Swearing is a second-degree misdemeanor.

★ It is illegal to shower naked; you must wear a bathing suit or clothes.

★ By law, you cannot fart after 6 P.M. on Thursdays.

★ School buses may not transport livestock.

★ If you see a horse approaching while driving a car, you must stop, dismantle your vehicle, and hide it in the bushes.

★ You may not have sex with a porcupine.

★ Your bike can be impounded for driving it while drunk.

★ You cannot kill deer while you are swimming.

★ It is against the law to break more than three plates, or chip more than four cups, during any one day.

★ If you hide under a sidewalk, you can be charged with disorderly conduct.

Astronaut Hall of Fame

In the fall of 2002, the Astronaut Hall of Fame closed its doors due to financial difficulties. It was a sad day, for this private museum was the world's largest treasure-trove of astro-junk. They had display cases crammed with such strange and wonderful personal artifacts as Alan Shepherd's toothbrush, a roll of dimes carried into orbit by Gus Grissom, Buzz Aldrin's grade school report card . . . you get the idea. Everything was donated by astronauts, their families, and friends.

Luckily, the Kennedy Space Center has stepped forward to purchase the facility, and it is now undergoing a face-lift. What will it look like when it reopens its doors in 2003? Cleaner, larger, and with an expanded display of training simulators to be used by the adjoining Space Camp. But let's hope they don't go overboard trying to make it educational—they've already got the Kennedy Space Center Visitor's Center Complex for that. Somewhere there needs to be a place for all the random garbage left over in NASA's attic.

6225 Vectorspace Blvd., Titusville, 72780

(321) 449-4444

Hours: Daily 9 A.M.–5:30 P.M.

Cost: Adults $13.95, Kids (3–11) $9.95; Maximum Access (includes Kennedy Space Center, see page 156), Adults $33, Kids (3–11) $23

Directions: Just southeast of the intersection of Rte. 1 and Rte. 406 (Columbia Blvd.).

U.S. Space Walk of Fame

If you can't get an up-close ticket to a Shuttle launch at Kennedy Space Center, the next best viewing site is from the U.S. Space Walk of Fame in neighboring Titusville. The riverside park offers a clear view to the east. The park is divided into two walkways, one honoring the Mercury program and the other the Gemini missions. Each flight is marked with its own plaque listing the astronaut(s) and explaining the goal of the mission. (By the way, the fact that this region's area code is 3-2-1 is no accident.)

Of course, if you're really a space nut, there are other sites in the area that are also worth visiting: the favorite hangouts of the early astronauts. In Melbourne, Fat Boys Barbecue (1941 N. Wickham Road) was a favorite eatery, and has the pictures and autographs on the wall prove it. Alma's Seafood and Italian Restaurant (306 N. Orlando Avenue) in Cocoa Beach was also popular with the spacemen; Alan Bean, the first person to eat spaghetti on the moon, claimed the NASA pasta he ate wasn't nearly as good as Alma's. Try to beat *that* endorsement!

Space View Park, Indian River Ave. & Broad St., Titusville, FL 32796

Contact: Space Walk of Fame Foundation, PO Box 6385, Titusville, FL 32782

(321) 264-0434

E-mail: president@spacewalkoffame.com

Hours: Always visible

Cost: Free

www.spacewalkoffame.com

Directions: Along the Indian River, two blocks south of the Rte. 406 bridge, and two blocks east of Rte. 1 (Washington Ave.).

Vero Beach
Indian River Citrus Museum

Don't let anyone fool you; if your citrus isn't from the Indian River district of Florida, it's just not worth the trouble to squeeze. Well, at least that's what folks in this part of the state will tell you. And boy, are they citrus *snobs*. Florida orange growers from the wrong side of the tracks are not welcome to put the Indian River label on their produce . . . Orlando . . . Sarasota . . . Tampa . . . take a hike!

The disturbing tale of citrus redlining is just part of what you'll learn at this industry museum. On a lighter note, they've also got a nifty collection of old farm tools and harvesting equipment, though they don't have the classic Man-on-Ladder. The favorite exhibit, however, seems to be the extensive collection of antique citrus crate labels from the region's many groves.

2140 14th Ave., Vero Beach, FL 32960

(561) 770-2263

Hours: Monday–Saturday 10 A.M.–5 P.M.

Cost: Free

Directions: Two blocks west of Rte. 1, one block north of Osceola Blvd. (20th St.).

ORANGE YOU GLAD YOU KNOW?

Do you know these citrus statistics?

★ The orange is not native to Florida; it was brought here during the 1500s by the Spanish.

★ Each year, more orange trees are killed by lightning in Florida than by disease.

★ About 79 percent of the nation's grapefruit and 73 percent of the nation's oranges are grown in Florida.

★ Most Americans receive their daily allowance of vitamin C from Florida orange juice.

★ Most Florida orange trees are grafted onto lemon tree roots.

★ Most California lemon trees are grafted onto orange tree roots.

★ Orange juice is the Florida State Beverage.

★ Nothing rhymes with the word *orange*.

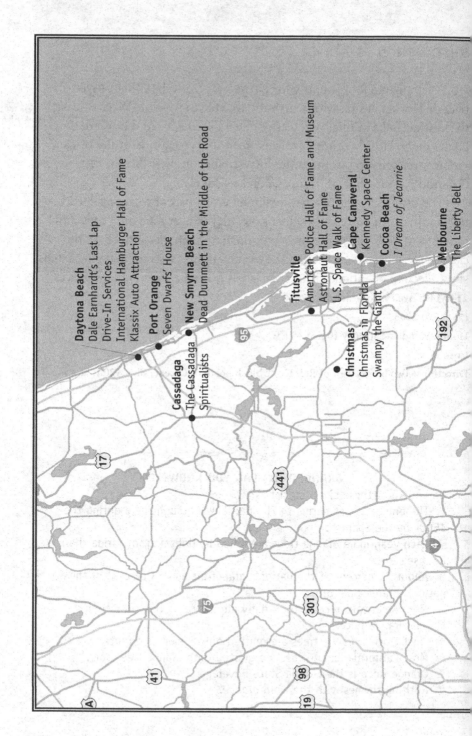

Daytona Beach
Dale Earnhardt's Last Lap
Drive-In Services
International Hamburger Hall of Fame
Klassix Auto Attraction

Port Orange
Seven Dwarfs' House

New Smyrna Beach
Dead Dummett in the Middle of the Road

Cassadaga
The Cassadaga Spiritualists

Titusville
American Police Hall of Fame and Museum
Astronaut Hall of Fame
U.S. Space Walk of Fame

Cape Canaveral
Kennedy Space Center

Cocoa Beach
I Dream of Jeannie

Christmas
Christmas in Florida
Swampy the Giant

Melbourne
The Liberty Bell

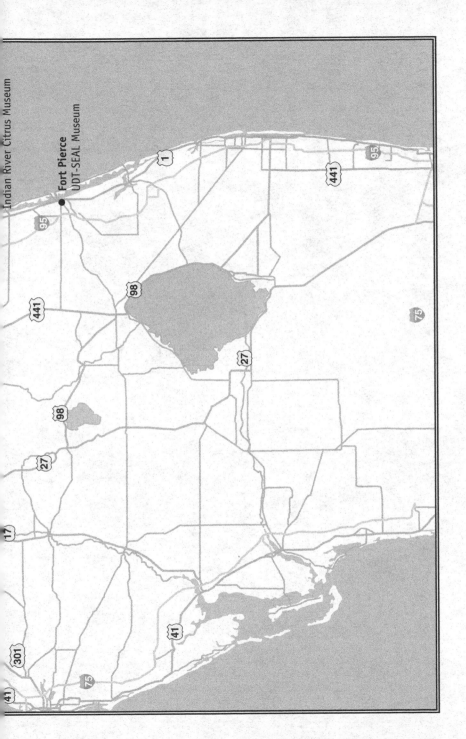

7

THE SOUTH

*W*hen making your final approach into any of southern Florida's airports, you'll look out the window and see one of two things: acres and acres of uninhabitable swamps, or blocks and blocks of uninhabitable housing developments—take your pick.

Well, perhaps it's not as bad as all that. On closer inspection, there are a few places worth visiting, wedged between the golf courses and the strip malls and the gated communities. In southern Florida you can find boats that fly like planes, planes that cruise like boats, and blimps that don't move much at all. What's more, the region is also home to some of Florida's most enduring mysteries, like the Bermuda Triangle, the Ghost of Flight 401, human cloning (maybe), and the Coral Castle.

On second thought, maybe it *is* worth a look around. . . .

Coconut Creek
Butterfly World

Let's face it, the trouble with butterflies is that they're too jumpy and too fragile to grab on to. So what's a lepidopteran lover to do? Well, you could drive out into the country and sit in a field all day hoping for the best, or you could come to Butterfly World, where thousands of exotic butterflies and moths live in a three-acre simulated rain forest.

This specialized aviary is filled with blooming plants to attract these beautiful insects, not that these butterflies have the opportunity to search for nectar elsewhere. If you wear a bright yellow or Hawaiian-print shirt, they just might think you're a flower as well and flutter around you. This living natural history museum has more than 80 species on free-range display. Butterfly World has recently added another environment to the facility, the Jewels of the Sky Hummingbird Aviary, where these tiny, hyperactive birds buzz around your head.

Please remember that when walking through the aviaries, you should take care to stay on the path. If you wander off the trail and step on a butterfly, you could change the trajectory of Earth's history. Sci-fi movies have shown this to be true.

Tradewinds Park, 3600 W. Sample Rd., Coconut Creek, FL 33073

(954) 977-4400

E-mail: gardens@butterflyworld.com

Hours: Monday–Saturday 9 A.M.–5 P.M.; Sunday 1–5 P.M.

Cost: Adults $14.95, Seniors $9.95, Kids (4–12) $9.95

www.butterflyworld.com

Directions One block west of Rte. 91 (Florida's Turnpike) on NW 36th St. (Sample Rd.).

BOCA RATON
Ultra-swanky Boca Raton's name translates from Spanish as "mouth of the mouse."

COCONUT CREEK
Wendy's founder **Dave Thomas** graduated from Coconut Creek High School (400 NW 44th Avenue), 45 years after he dropped out of school to go into the restaurant business.

Don't try this at home.

Everglades
Fan Boats

Going to the Everglades and not riding on a fan boat is like going to Vegas and not playing the slots—it just isn't done! Imagine an airplane propeller practically strapped to your back as you fly across the swamps, lower than any plane ever could or should, with nothing between you and the wild, hungry gators but the seat belt on your wire mesh chair. That's fan boating.

There is no way to list all the roadside attractions offering fan-boat tours, and there is no need to even try; you'll find them just about everywhere there's a swamp. Head west out of Miami until things get wet. Some of the more modern attractions offer rides in multiple-seat boats, but the best rides are to be had on the two-seaters, like the ones you used to see on *Gentle Ben*.

And before you hop aboard, you should resign yourself to one thing: you can kiss that hairdo good-bye.

The Everglades, FL

Various phones

Hours: Hours vary

Cost: Prices vary

Directions: Most fan-boat attractions are located along the Tamiami Trail (Rte. 41) or
   Alligator Alley (I-74/Rte. 84).

The Ghost of Flight 401

On December 29, 1972, Eastern Airlines Flight 401 went down in the Everglades on approach to Miami International, killing 101 passengers and crew. The pilot and copilot were so busy worrying about a front landing gear light that they failed to watch the falling altimeter, and flew head-on into the swamp. That's a spooky enough story, but it gets a lot spookier.

In an unprecedented display of corporate penny-pinching, Eastern Airlines pulled parts from the downed Lockheed L-1011 Tri-Star and reused them on other L-1011s, most notably on Plane 318. Nobody was any the wiser . . . until a couple ghosts showed up.

Both Captain Bob Loft and flight engineer Don Repo (played by Ernest Borgnine in a movie about the crash) started appearing on airplanes in which the parts had been reused, often warning the crew of an impending disaster. It would have been weird if they were alive and did this, but both had died in the first crash. Sometimes just their faces appeared—on the instrument panel, in an overhead bin, near the galley oven—but other times their voices came across the PA system. Eastern had to ground several flights when their still-living employees became unnerved by the dead stowaways.

When it came out that Eastern had reused parts, it proved to be a major embarrassment for the airline. Maintenance crews went back and removed all the haunted parts, and a superstitious pilot did an exorcism of Plane 318's galley. That seemed to do the trick. There have been no further reports of Loft or Repo.

In retrospect, this might have been a bad idea. Eastern, in effect, fired two perfectly capable safety inspectors. Wouldn't it have been better if they had placed a reused part in every plane in their fleet? Given the choice between dying in an airplane crash or having a ghost ride along in the luggage bin, which would you choose?

The Everglades, FL

No phone

Hours: Never visible

Cost: Free

Directions: Nineteen miles northwest of the airport, 8 miles north of the Tamiami Trail.

Fort Lauderdale
Cosmic Muffin

If you're driving around Fort Lauderdale and you spot a Boeing 307 Stratoliner jetting along one of the town's many waterways, don't be alarmed—it's only a boat! No, the *Cosmic Muffin* hasn't always been an oceangoing vessel. At one time it was Howard Hughes's private plane, but a 1964 hurricane ended its flying days. With its wings and tail removed, it was shipped to Florida. A decade later it was waterproofed and fitted with an inboard motor, then launched as the most unique houseboat around. Jimmy Buffet fans might know the *Cosmic Muffin* from its mention in the song "Desdemona's Building a Rocket Ship," and from his novel *Where Is Joe Merchant?*

Current owner Dave Drimmer is looking for a corporate sponsor for this one-bedroom houseboat. Until then, he often moors his plane/boat at such places as Fort Lauderdale's River Walk. Tourists can come aboard and take a closer look—and maybe buy a *Cosmic Muffin* T-shirt. There's no guarantee where it'll be, though, unless you drop Drimmer a line.

Contact: Dave Drimmer, Plane Boats, Inc., PO Box 7245, Fort Lauderdale, FL 33338
(954) 462-8676
Hours: By appointment
Cost: Free if on public display
www.captain-net.com/plane-boat.html
Directions: With appointment.

International Swimming Hall of Fame

You might think there wouldn't be a lot to see at this place, just a bunch of trophies, velour jumpsuits, and skimpy Speedos. Not so! Though it's a one-room museum, it has both the World's Largest Trophy and the World's Smallest Trophy (made from a thimble), as well as tributes to Esther Williams, Mark Spitz, Ronald Reagan, Greg Louganis, Johnny Weissmuller, and Buster Crabbe (including his leopard-skin Tarzan loincloth and Billy the Kid outfits).

The Hall of Fame honors every sport where water is involved, including diving, water polo, and synchronized swimming. If you want to take a dip, the museum is part of a huge aquatic complex that's open to the public for a minimal fee. And in an interesting bit of sports history, this is where Olympic diving champion Greg Louganis first learned to swim and dive.

One word of warning: the Hall of Fame has tentative plans to move the museum to Pompano Beach, so check the Web site before you put it on your travel itinerary.

501 Seabreeze Blvd., Fort Lauderdale, FL 33316

(954) 462-6536 (Museum); (954) 828-4580 (Pool)

Hours: Daily 9 A.M.–5 P.M. (Museum); 8 A.M.–8 P.M. (Pool)

Cost: Museum, Adults $3, Seniors $1, Kids $1; Pool, Adults $3, Seniors $2, Kids $2

www.ishof.org

Directions: Two blocks south of Las Olas Blvd. on Rte. A1A (Seabreeze Blvd.).

Lost in the Bermuda Triangle?

It was the case that launched the world's fascination with the Bermuda Triangle. On December 5, 1945, five TBF Grumman Avengers took off from Fort Lauderdale Naval Air Station with 14 aboard . . . and vanished. The pilots on Flight 19, on a torpedo training mission, apparently became confused by their spinning compasses and couldn't find their way back to the mainland. The U.S. Navy sent up a PBM Martin Mariner out of Cocoa Beach with 13 aboard to search for the downed planes. They all disappeared, too.

After a thorough but fruitless investigation, the Navy Board of Inquiry summed it up: "They vanished as completely as if they'd flown to Mars." This statement, coupled with a report from an amateur ham radio operator who claimed he'd heard a pilot warn, "Don't come after me . . . they look like they're from outer space," put the Bermuda Triangle scenario into full play.

Technically speaking, the Bermuda Triangle is a geographic region bounded by lines connecting Bermuda to the Florida Keys to Puerto Rico. Over the years, more than 100 planes and boats have vanished without a trace, taking more than 1,000 lives. Could they be victims of magnetic forces from the lost continent of Atlantis? (Psychic Edgar Cayce predicted the continent would be discovered near Bimini, and after he died, divers in 1968 discovered the Bimini Roads. Two "roads" made of square blocks of granite lie 19 feet beneath the surface of the ocean on the north side of the island, yet the closest granite source is Georgia.) Maybe they were swallowed up by huge methane bubbles rising unexpectedly out of the Hoodoo

Sea? Or stranger still, they could have been abducted by aliens, as was suggested in the final scenes of *Close Encounters of the Third Kind.* (One UFO researcher claims that one of the Grumman Avengers did reappear . . . orbiting earth in a photo taken by the *Apollo 11* crew!)

Well, it was actually none of the above. Navy crews searching for pieces of the *Challenger* Space Shuttle in 1986 came across an Avenger off New Smyrna Beach; it turned out to be the lead plane on the mission. Aviation experts now believe the pilots were simply disoriented in a rainstorm and ran out of gas. Case closed.

Or is that what the Men in Black *want* you to think?????

**Fort Lauderdale/Hollywood International Airport (former Fort Lauderdale NAS),
  320 Terminal Dr., Fort Lauderdale, FL 33315**

(954) 359-6100

Hours: Always visible

Cost: Free

www.broward.org/fll.htm

Directions: South of I-595 on Rte. 1 (Dixie Hwy.).

MORE BERMUDA TRIANGLE MYSTERIES?

The list of planes and ships missing in the Bermuda Triangle is a long one. Here are some of the most frequently cited cases. (For more, check out www.bermuda-triangle.org.)

★ The Cuban ship *Rubicon* was found floating in the Bermuda Triangle in October 1944. Its crew had vanished, but a dog was aboard, the lone survivor. Mutiny by mutt?

★ A DC-3 en route from San Juan to Miami in December 1948 disappeared with 30 passengers and crew.

★ Twenty-two crew were lost aboard the *Southern Districts* when it vanished near the Straits of Florida in December 1954.

★ The *Marine Sulphur Queen*, a freighter with 39 aboard, disappeared near the Dry Tortugas in February 1963.

★ Two KC-135 tanker planes based out of Homestead went off the radar screen 200 miles short of Bermuda. Eleven crew members were never seen again.

★ A cabin cruiser dubbed the *Witchcraft* vanished one mile off Miami in December 1967, taking two down with it.

A whole lotta shakin' goin' on!
Courtesy Mai-Kai

Mai-Kai

In recent years, tiki bars have become the hangout of choice for self-proclaimed hipsters, but don't let that scare you away from visiting the Mai-Kai, probably the world's (and certainly Florida's) greatest Polynesian restaurant/bar/revue. The Mai-Kai's food, or drinks, or performances alone would merit a five-star rating, but all three in one place? How do they do it?

The Mai-Kai first opened in 1956 and has been expanding and perfecting its operation ever since. Twice nightly in the restaurant's main room, a troupe of flame-throwing, hip-gyrating, ukulele-playing performers wow the well-fed, rum-soaked dinner crowd. From the undulating grass skirts to the Samoan fire knife dance, the Islander Revue is worth every penny of the additional $9.95 show fee.

Before or after the big show, visit the ship-shaped Molokai Bar where you can knock back a tropical drink or two, like a Deep Sea Diver, a Shark Bite, a Sidewinder's Fang, a Shrunken Skull, a Zombie, or the four-person Mystery Drink. Step outside into the Mai-Kai's tropical gardens where pathways and bridges pass waterfalls, flaming torches, orchids, and tiki god statues. This really is paradise.

3599 N. Federal Highway, Fort Lauderdale, FL 33308
(800) 262-4524 or (954) 563-3272
E-mail: info@maikai.com
Hours: Daily 5 p.m.–2 a.m.; Shows, Sunday–Thursday 7 and 9:30 p.m., Friday–Saturday 7 and 10 p.m.
Cost: Meals $16–$30; Tropical drinks $6.25–$13
www.maikai.com
Directions: On Rte. 1 (Federal Hwy.) north of Oakland Park Blvd. (31st St.).

More than enough.

Hollywood Beach
The Clones Are Here?

Maybe it was just a slow news day, but on December 27, 2002, a press conference in Hollywood Beach became the nation's lead story: scientists had cloned the first human, and her name was Eve. She had been born to an infertile American couple the day after Christmas. The announcement had been made by Brigitte Boisselier, chief executive officer of Clonaid (www.clonaid.com), a research institute set up by the Raëlians, a UFO cult that believes the human species was cloned from extraterrestrials and planted on earth as a colony.

Uh-huh.

What followed was a heated public debate on the morality of cloning, followed by calls for immediate congressional action. Nobody much discussed whether or not people should be paying any attention to a kooky UFO cult in the first place. Though Boisselier claimed that an independent geneticist would be allowed to test the DNA of the clone and the cloned, to see if they matched, the geneticist's results have never been released. Big surprise.

Holiday Inn, 2711 S. Ocean Dr., Hollywood Beach, FL 33019

(800) 237-4667 or (954) 923-8700

Hours: Always visible

Cost: Free

Directions: On Rte. A1A (Ocean Blvd.) south of Rte. 820 (Hollywood Blvd.).

FORT LAUDERDALE
Boxer **Rocky Marciano** lived at 2561 Del Lago Drive and 2700 N. Atlantic Boulevard in Fort Lauderdale. After dying in a plane crash, he was buried at Lauderdale Memorial Gardens (499 NW 27th Avenue, (954) 581-9033).

Tennis star **Chris Evert** was born in Fort Lauderdale on December 21, 1954.

HOMESTEAD
The tangelo was first developed at the University of Florida's Subtropical Experiment Station in Homestead.

Leedskalnin is Latvian for "a little over the top."
Photo by author, courtesy Coral Castle

Homestead
The Coral Castle, a.k.a. The Love Token of Edward Leedskalnin

Edward Leedskalnin was jilted by 16-year-old Agnes Skuffs the day before their planned wedding in Latvia. What did he do about it? What any strange person might: he moved to America and built a 1,100-ton monument to his heartbreaker out of enormous hunks of coral and automobile parts.

He called it Rock Gate Park. It was first located in Florida City, but Leedskalnin moved it to Homestead and this larger plot of land in 1936. He forever held out hope that his Sweet Sixteen would return to him, and the couple would live happily ever after in this home/astronomical observatory built of stone. Fat chance. He died of stomach cancer in 1951, still a virgin.

The story gets weirder. Leedskalnin never weighed more than 100 pounds his entire life, but the coral rock blocks he used were in the neighborhood of 5 tons each, with some as many as 30 tons. How did he do it? *Nobody knows.* He did all of his work alone, at night. Leedskalnin made vague references to tapping into the power of the ancient pyramids, wrote several rambling and indecipherable books about magnetism, and died with his secret. Did he master levitation? Some believe so. (There is, however, one oft-suppressed picture of Leedskalnin with a block and tackle.)

Check out the unique features of this site: a Florida-shaped dinner table, a fountain carved to look like a moon, an outdoor bathtub, two thrones for Leedskalnin and his betrothed, a lensless telescope aimed at Polaris, beds with stone pillows, a Repentance Corner complete with stocks for misbehaving children and wives, and two rock doors. One door weighs three tons and the other nine, each spin easily on single axles; they come within a quarter-inch of the wall on both sides, and can be turned by a small child.

When Hurricane Andrew all but blew Homestead off the map in 1992, the Coral Castle was virtually unscathed, though the gales ripped the roof off the adjacent gift shop. Must have been pyramid power.

28655 S. Dixie Highway, Homestead, FL 33030

(305) 248-6344

Hours: Daily 7 A.M.–9 P.M.

Cost: Adults $9.75, Seniors (62+) $6.50, Kids (7–12) $5

www.coralcastle.com

Directions: North of town on Rte. 1 (Dixie Hwy.) at 286th St.

Loxahatchee
Lion Country Safari

When it opened in 1967, Lion Country Safari was the first zoo of its kind: a drive-through game preserve. That's right, nothing but your thin car windows separates you from the man-eating, man-trampling, and man-biting critters in this 500-acre park. But don't worry, the 1,200-something animals here are well fed and cared for, so you don't have to worry that the lions are looking you over as if seeing a meatloaf with sunglasses.

Though you'd think it would be obvious to anyone with a shred of common sense, convertibles and pets are not allowed in the park. You can, however, rent a car at the main gate for $8 for an hour and a half. (The park also has kennel facilities.) Even if you don't have a convertible, you might want to rent a vehicle, especially if you don't want your new car covered in giraffe slobber.

Lion Country Safari's four-mile road wraps around a central park that is off-limits to the animals. The Safari World Walk-Through Adventure includes a miniature golf course, a petting zoo, and an animal theater. If you want to extend your stay, visit the adjacent KOA Campground where you will fall asleep to the sounds of roaring lions, trumpeting elephants, and chattering monkeys . . . if you fall asleep at all.

2003 Lion Country Safari Rd., Loxahatchee, FL 33470

(561) 793-1084; KOA (561) 793-9797

Hours: Daily 9:30 A.M.–5:30 P.M.; Last entry at 4:30 P.M.

Cost: Adults $14.95, Seniors $9.95, Kids (3–16) $9.95

www.lioncountrysafari.com

Directions: North of Southern Blvd. (Rte. 80), six blocks west of Seminole Rd.

LANTANA

A Boy Scout leader claimed he'd been attacked by a UFO while camping with his troop in a wooded area near Lantana in 1952. His uniform was burned in the incident. Several honest and upstanding scouts backed up his story.

The *National Enquirer* is headquartered in Lantana.

PAHOKEE

Singer **Mel Tillis** was born in Pahokee on August 8, 1932.

Postcards only?

Ochopee
World's Smallest Post Office

The folks who built this tiny building in 1934 had no idea that they were constructing what would become a historic structure. For the first 20 years it was used as a toolshed for the J. T. Gaunt Company, which ran a nearby tomato farm. But in 1953 the town's general store, which had been the local post office, burned to the ground. Ochopee's postmaster Sidney Brown needed someplace to put the mail, and the shed was pressed into service as the World's Smallest Post Office.

The building is 8' 4" wide by 7' 3" inches deep, and stands 10' 6" high. That's plenty big for this Everglades community's 400-some postal patrons. Every time there's talk of replacing it, the locals quash the idea—they like their puny postal claim to fame.

Tamiami Trail, Ochopee, FL 33943

No phone

Hours: Always visible

Cost: Free

Directions: East of Rte. 29 on Rte. 41 (Tamiami Trail), on the south side of the road.

Palm Beach
Henry Flagler Takes a Spill

In retrospect, millionaire Henry Flagler might have passed on installing pneumatic, automatic doors in the palatial Whitehall mansion he built in 1901. Sure, they seemed elegant and cutting-edge at the time, but little did he know that 12 years later they would fly open and murder him! One January day he was trying to enter a second-floor bathroom at the top of the grand staircase when the door burst open, knocking him down the steps to the first-floor landing. Flagler broke his hip in the fall, slipped into a coma, and died two months later.

Flagler is often called the Father of Florida for opening up the state to northern tourists via railroads and a series of enormous hotels along both coasts. Whitehall has been converted into a museum that honors his accomplishments. Some believe his ghost haunts the mansion; a maid once felt somebody slap her on the rump; when she turned around nobody was there. Others have found doors that couldn't be opened, and they credit the old man. (Can you blame him for wanting them to stay shut?)

1 Whitehall Way, PO Box 969, Palm Beach, FL 33480

(561) 655-2833

E-mail: flagler@paradista.net

Hours: Tuesday–Saturday 10 A.M.–5 P.M., Sunday Noon–5 P.M.

Cost: Adults $8, Kids (6–12) $3

www.flaglermuseum.us

Directions: South of Royal Poinciana Way at Cocoanut Row.

Palmdale
Cypress Kneeland

If you're looking for evidence that imagination and originality are being leeched from the roadside landscape, look no further than the crumbling Cypress Kneeland museum at a bend in the road south of Palmdale. There's little left of this magnificent attraction built by Tom Gaskins, just some funky old signs and an abandoned catwalk, but it's better than nothing.

You might look at a cypress knee (that stumpy protuberance growing up out of the water from the submerged root of cypress tree) and say, "Looks like a knot of wood to me," but Gaskins would have seen so much more. "There's Donald Duck. And Franklin Delano Roosevelt. Groucho

Marx, and the Mona Lisa. And yep, there's a lady hippo in a Carmen Miranda hat!" he'd say. And he was *right*.

Gaskins displayed his remarkable collection of familiar-looking knees in an open-air cinderblock structure south of Palmdale. Sometimes he would drag off his best pieces to *The Tonight Show* or *Sally Jesse Rafael*. And not one to just interpret nature, he also set out to alter it. Across the highway from his museum he built a catwalk through the swamp where his warped cypress experiments took place. He would coax knees to wrap themselves around Coke bottles and telephone receivers, while others he contorted with cables and heavy weights—Gaskins was a regular Dr. Frankenknee!

Sadly, Alzheimer's took Gaskins's life in 1998. His son, Tom Jr., kept the museum open, but it was a struggle. A few years back, somebody broke into the glass cases and ran off with some of the better pieces. Tom Jr. moved the remaining knees into storage, but is planning to reopen some day, probably in Venus (the town, not the planet). Until he does, you're just going to have to look at Gaskins's twisted old signs and rickety catwalk.

6870 Highway 27N, Palmdale, FL 33944
No phone
Hours: 8 A.M.–Sunset
Cost: Free
Directions: Just north of junction with Rte. 29.

Gatorama

Another gator park? Are these things everywhere?

Not quite. Gatorama happens to be one of the main alligator attractions on the backroads from Miami to Orlando, and it's a good spot to hop out, stretch your legs, and feed a few oversized reptiles. The park has covered walkways so you can visit even on a rainy day.

Gatorama's largest alligator is one mean sumbitch named Goliath. Back in 1999 this ornery cuss was gobbling up the other gators, so he had to be given a pen of his own. Take this as a warning not to let the kids dangle too far over the railing at his pen—Goliath's probably just waiting for a plump little human to drop in for dinner.

6180 U.S. Highway 27, Palmdale, FL 33944
(863) 675-0623
Hours: Monday–Saturday 8:30 A.M.–5:30 P.M., Sunday 10 A.M.–5:30 P.M.

Cost: Adults $9.95, "Critters" (Under 56 inches) $3.50

www.gatorama.com

Directions: Just east of the intersection of Rtes. 29 and 27, south of Palmdale.

Pompano Beach
Goodyear Blimp Base

If you want to see the Goodyear Blimp, you've got basically two options: attend a sporting event where it is scheduled to appear, or stop by one of its three home bases. There are actually three blimps: one in the company's hometown of Akron, Ohio; another in Carson, California; and this one in Pompano Beach. The Florida blimp is named the *Stars and Stripes*.

You can't miss its hangar on the southwest side of the airport—it's the one with the enormous Goodyear corporate logo on the side. Catching the 192-foot-long blimp is a little trickier, since it's often out at a game or, if not there, tied up inside.

The Goodyear folks used to give tours of the hangar, but since September 11 have canceled all unapproved visitations. Maybe they're thinking about the final scenes of *Black Sunday*, which was filmed in 1976 at Miami's Orange Bowl (1501 Third Street NW). The ever-creepy Bruce Dern pilots a bomb-laden blimp into the Super Bowl with the goal of wiping out all the spectators, included the president. While the idea of a slow-moving gasbag (maximum speed 50 MPH) as an instrument of terror seems ridiculous, even after the attacks in New York and Washington, they're not taking any chances; you're just going to have to see it from behind the fence.

1500 NE 5th Ave., Pompano Beach, FL 33060

(954) 946-8300

Hours: Always visible

Cost: Free

www.goodyearblimp.com/b_stars_stripes.html

Directions: Just east of Rte. 1 (Dixie Hwy.) at 15th St. N, east of the railroad tracks.

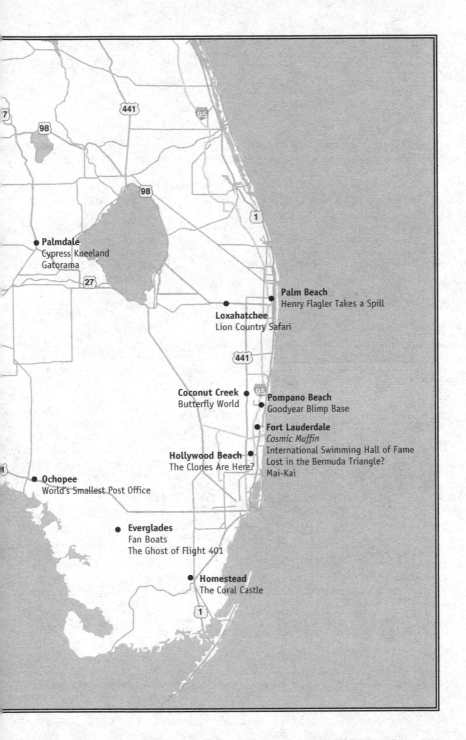

Palmdale
Cypress Kneeland
Gatorama

Palm Beach
Henry Flagler Takes a Spill

Loxahatchee
Lion Country Safari

Coconut Creek
Butterfly World

Pompano Beach
Goodyear Blimp Base

Fort Lauderdale
Cosmic Muffin
International Swimming Hall of Fame
Lost in the Bermuda Triangle?
Mai-Kai

Hollywood Beach
The Clones Are Here?

Ochopee
World's Smallest Post Office

Everglades
Fan Boats
The Ghost of Flight 401

Homestead
The Coral Castle

8

MiaMi Area

Things in Miami are not as they appear. . . . No, I'm not talking about the cosmetic enhancements that are all too obvious on South Beach. I'm talking about *places* like the Venetian Pool. You might get the feeling you're standing along the Grand Canal, waiting for a gondola, but you're really just hanging out in an abandoned rock quarry—a very nice rock quarry, but still a rock quarry. Or how about the Opa-Locka City Hall with its onion domes and minarets? Feels more like Casablanca than SoFlo.

And then there's Monkey Jungle. If you think you're headed for a zoo, you're right. But the only primates in cages at this place are the human customers. That's right, *you* are the one behind bars, and it's the *monkeys* who get to stare and point.

What's going on here? Better read on. . . .

That's a fancy rock quarry!
Photo by author, courtesy Venetian Pool

Coral Gables
Venetian Pool

The best face-lift you'll ever see in Coral Gables—and there are plenty to choose from—is the Venetian Pool. With its grottoes and barber-pole boat launches, waterfalls, and quaint little bridges, you'd never guess that it's a reclaimed rock quarry. The stone removed from this pit was used to build the surrounding community of Coral Gables, the first planned community in the United States. To cover his tracks, developer George Merrick hired Denman Fink in 1924 to transform the eyesore into a fake Italian-themed swimming pool. Fink had caves carved into the quarry walls and built a bathhouse villa beside it.

Today the Venetian Pool is used mostly as a restaurant and banquet facility. It is also a favorite filming location for movies shot in Miami.

2701 De Soto Blvd., Coral Gables, FL 33134

(305) 460-5356

E-mail: info@venetianpool.com

Hours: November–March, Tuesday–Sunday 10:30 A.M.–4:30 P.M.; April–June, Tuesday–Friday 11 A.M.–5:30 P.M., Saturday–Sunday 10 A.M.–4:30 P.M.; June–August, Monday–Friday 11 A.M.–7:30 P.M., Saturday–Sunday 10 A.M.–4:30 P.M.; September–

October, Tuesday–Friday 11 A.M.–5:30 P.M., Saturday–Sunday 10 A.M.–4:30 P.M.
Cost: April–October, Adults $9, Kids $5; November–March, Adults $6, Kids $3
www.venetianpool.com
Directions: One block east of Granada Blvd., three blocks south of Coral Way (Rte. 972).

Miami
Bob Marley Death Site
When Bob Marley checked into Miami's Cedars of Lebanon Medical Center, it was obvious that he wouldn't be checking out the preferred way. Two years earlier, he'd had a toe amputated (at a different hospital) and doctors informed him he had cancer. Marley ignored their advice to seek further treatment, and the cancer spread to his brain. On May 11, 1981, the 36-year-old musician passed away in this Miami hospital.

Cedars of Lebanon Medical Center, 1400 NW 12th Ave., Miami, FL 33136

(305) 325-5511

Hours: Always visible

Cost: Free

www.cedarsmed.com

Directions: On the northwest corner of 14th St. and 12th Ave.

THE MUSIC WORLD LOSES ANOTHER
The Bee Gee's **Maurice Gibb** died at Miami Beach's Mount Sinai Medical Center (4300 Alton Road) on January 11, 2003. The 53-year-old singer and paintball enthusiast had entered the hospital to undergo surgery for a blocked intestine. He died of a heart attack.

CORAL GABLES
The pool at the Biltmore Hotel (1200 Anastasia Avenue) in Coral Gables is said to be the largest in the continental United States. **Esther Williams** was often hired to perform here for guests, as was **Johnny Weissmuller**, to teach swimming lessons.

Janet Reno is not welcome.

Elian Gonzalez, International Pawn

Seldom have the American people been as polarized as they were about the five-month drama surrounding five-year-old Elian Gonzalez. The saga started on November 22, 1999, when Elian's mother, Elizabeth Brotons Rodriquez, and her boyfriend, Lazaro Munero, fled Cardenes, Cuba, on a makeshift boat. Munero and his brother had made the powered raft from aluminum irrigation pipes, inner tubes, and an outboard motor, and charged nonfamily members $2,000 a head to come along. Had either of the Munero brothers survived, they could have been charged with human smuggling when they reached U.S. soil. But their craft sank a day after they left for Florida, and all 14 passengers ended up in the shark-infested Atlantic.

Elizabeth wrapped Elian in a coat and lashed him to an inner tube. One by one the passengers drowned, including Elizabeth, until the final three survivors were spotted by a private fishing boat on November 25, Thanksgiving Day, three miles off the coast of Fort Lauderdale. The dehydrated Elian was taken to Joe DiMaggio Childrens Hospital (3501 Johnson Street), and was later released into the custody of his great-uncle, Lazaro Gonzalez.

Here is where the story took two completely different paths. To south Florida's anti-Castro Cuban American community, Elian was el Niño Milagro, the Miracle Child, rescued from an oppressed life under a communist dictatorship. Some even proclaimed him a modern-day Moses, set adrift by his mother, protected by dolphins and the Virgin Mary, and rescued by "The Fisherman," Donato Dalrymple.

Those who felt Elian should be returned to his father, most of whom were anti-Castro as well, were quick to point out the flaws in the Elian-as-Moses myth: the dolphins Elian saw were likely a school of mahi-mahi, and Dalrymple was not so much "The Fisherman" as he was "The Part-Time House Cleaner Who Went Fishing with His Cousin."

As the debate played out on cable television and in immigration court, the situation in Miami got even stranger. Each time the boy went out to play in the yard, dozens of camera crews and onlookers documented his every move. A rift developed in the family when great-uncle Manuel Gonzalez said during a hearing on Elian's fate that he believed the child should be returned to his father; Manuel was chased off afterward by an angry crowd screaming "Communist!" Marisleysis Gonzalez, a cousin who'd formed a stage mother–like bond with the boy, collapsed from exhaustion in a restaurant.

Wild rumors (believed by very few) circulated that a Santaria priestess had warned Castro he'd be overthrown by a child who was saved by dolphins, and that in order to stop it, he had to get him back and sacrifice him. A greasy smudge of the Virgin Mary appeared on a bank window in Little Havana, and the next day it also appeared on a mirror in Elian's bedroom.

The Miami relatives demanded Elian's case be heard in family court. Janet Reno said it was an immigration case, and that only his surviving parent could speak for the child. Court orders to return Elian to INS custody were all ignored. Miami-Dade Mayor Alex Penales announced city police would not assist federal authorities if they tried to return Elian by force. Reno ordered the child be delivered to authorities at the Opa-Locka Airport on April 13, but the relatives never showed. Nine days later, on the day before Easter, federal authorities burst into the home, seized Elian, and returned him to his father, who had come to the United States to pick his son up.

Miami erupted with street riots. Talk shows erupted as well. Almost everybody was shocked by the photograph of Elian screaming, at gunpoint, in the bedroom closet. Surprisingly, as divided as public opinion seemed to be, most observers agreed on two central facts. First, Juan Gonzalez was by all accounts a caring, loving father; and second, life in a country run by a communist megalomaniac is no picnic. Still, most Americans felt that Elian belonged with his father, no matter where he chose to live.

If you share that opinion, you might want to keep it to yourself if you plan to visit Unidos en Casa Elian, the United in Elian House. Elian's great-uncle Delfin Gonzalez bought the home where the raid took place and turned it into a museum. Unidos en Casa Elian is only open one day a week, and there's not a lot to see, just a simple four-room house that held the world's attention during the waning days of the Clinton administration.

2319 NW 2nd St., Miami, FL 33125

No phone

Hours: Sundays 10 A.M.–6 P.M.

Cost: Free

www.libertyforelian.org

Directions: One block west of 22nd Ave., two blocks north of Flagler St.

PLANNING TO PARTY

Miami's **Orange Bowl** (1501 Third Street NW, (305) 341-4700, www.orangebowl.org) has an open-ended reservation for a celebration marking Castro's fall from power, whenever that happens. It is also where President John F. Kennedy addressed a crowd of 35,000 disappointed Cuban Americans following the botched Bay of Pigs invasion in 1962. And it is the place where Miami Lawyer Stanford Cohen hosted his son Harvey's bar mitzvah. The $20,000 affair included a 68-piece marching band and wait staff dressed in costume.

FDR Near-Assassination Site

Chicago Mayor Anton Cermak went to Miami on February 15, 1933, to ask for President-elect Franklin Roosevelt's help in bailing him out of his city's teacher contract. But Roosevelt refused to see him because Cermak had supported Al Smith in the Democratic primary. So Cermak fell back on Plan B: ambush FDR at his car after the president-elect gave a speech in front of Bayview Park's bandshell.

But that also happened to be Plan A for Giuseppe Zangara, only this creepy little guy planned to ambush FDR with a *gun*. The self-proclaimed anarchist, who had been staying in a flophouse at 125 N.E. 5th Street, opened fire at FDR's car, wounding Cermak and four bystanders. Had his arm not been deflected by Mrs. Lillian Cross, he might have killed FDR. Roosevelt's motorcade transported Cermak to Jackson Memorial Hospital (1500 N.W. 12th Avenue). It also brought, strapped to a luggage rack, Zangara, who had been severely beaten by the crowd.

It only took five days to charge Zangara, hold a trial, and find him guilty of attempted murder. When Cermak died on March 6, Zangara was found guilty of murder. His motive made John Hinkley's Brooke Shields infatuation seem almost rational: Zangara had a tummy ache. He had been suffering from ulcers ever since he emigrated from Italy in 1923. He blamed his ulcers on his unsuccessful life in the United States. He clarified his motives at the trial: "I wanted to make it fifty-fifty since my stomach hurt. . . . My stomach hurt long time."

OK, Giuseppe, whatever you say.

Zangara went to the electric chair on March 20 at the state prison in Raiford. He screamed at the guards who were helping him toward the chair. "I go myself. . . . I no scared of electric chair!" After he was strapped in he shouted, "Filthy capitalists! Good-bye! Addio to all the world! Go ahead, push the button! Quick!" And they did.

Bayfront Park, 301 Biscayne Blvd. NE, Miami, FL 33132

No phone

Hours: Always visible

Cost: Free

Directions: Near the bandshell on Rte. 1 (Biscayne Blvd.) at 3rd St.

Jackie Gleason's Grave

Jackie Gleason will forever be remembered for threatening to send his *Honeymooner* wife Alice "to the moon" every week, but few people know that he might have meant that literally. Gleason was a UFO-aholic, and admitted he'd spotted flying saucers all over Florida. Friends of the Great One claimed he bragged that President Nixon took him to Homestead Air Force Base to view four embalmed aliens recovered by the government. The visit inspired Gleason to build a saucer-shaped home in Peekskill, New York, which he dubbed "the Mothership."

After Gleason died in Lauderhill on June 24, 1987, his will outlined that no expense should be spared to bury him in Miami, and that his mausoleum be inscribed with his famous line, "Away we go!" In retrospect, perhaps he meant on a space ship. Gleason's widow donated 1,700 volumes of his 3,700-book UFO and occult collection to the University of Miami library.

Our Lady of Mercy Cemetery, 11411 NW 25 St., Miami, FL 33172

(305) 592-0521

Hours: Daily 8 A.M.–5 P.M.

Cost: Free

Directions: Just east of the Florida Turnpike (Rte. 821) on 25th St. N.

SLY STALLONE'S FUTURE GRAVE

Nothing like planning ahead! **Sylvester Stallone**, one of Miami's über-celebrities, has already picked out his final resting place, and it's in one of the few cities that still take him seriously. Stallone moved to Coconut Grove in 1993 and gave his mansion's decorators very specific instructions: "Rococo me to the max." No doubt he has similar super-stylish instructions for his final interment in Our Lady of Mercy, the same cemetery that holds Jackie Gleason.

MIAMI

Singer **Debbie Harry** was born in Miami on July 1, 1945.

Monkey Jungle

Ever wonder what it's like to be a zoo animal? Then come to Monkey Jungle, "Where Humans Are Caged and the Monkeys Run Wild!" How is this possible? Well, the monkeys aren't entirely free; this unique zoo is more of a cage within a cage, where the humans stroll along enclosed walkways through a large outdoor pen. The monkeys can go wherever they like, which is usually to the top of the walkways where they can drop small feed buckets down to the humans. You're encouraged to purchase monkey chow at the ticket booth.

Monkey Jungle was founded in 1933 by Joseph and Grace DuMond. In the early days, its monkeys and apes performed in goofy costumes for adoring fans, but over the years the general public became less and less comfortable with the shows. The primates were slowly given more freedom, while the humans were put on a tighter leash.

Anyone who has seen *Planet of the Apes* knows this is a recipe for disaster.

14805 SW 216th St., Miami, FL 33170

(305) 235-1611

Hours: Daily 9:30 A.M.–5 P.M.

Cost: Adults $15.95, Kids (3–9) $9.95

www.monkeyjungle.com

Directions: On the northwest corner of 216th St. and Naranja Rd. (147th Ave.).

MONKEYS ON THE LOOSE!

Over 2,000 primates escaped from the Mannheimer Primatological Foundation when their cages near the Everglades were blown apart during Hurricane Andrew. Five hundred baboons at the nearby University of Miami's Perrine Primate Center got loose as well. Not all were recaptured.

Strange Times at Miami International

Who says airline travel isn't entertaining? Hang out at Miami International and you're bound to see something weird. Watch your fellow passengers' trousers. . . .

- Amelia Earhart's final halfway-around-the-world journey originated from Miami Municipal Airport on June 1, 1937. She had stopped in Miami to visit her stepson before heading on to Puerto Rico. You can find her memorial plaque near the airport's E Concourse metal detectors.
- Paranormal investigators claim that decades ago a National Airlines commercial jet disappeared from the radar screens for 10 minutes while on approach to MIA. All the passengers' watches were later found to be 10 minutes slow!
- A Northwest Orient flight crashed north of Miami on February 12, 1963, killing 43 passengers and crew.
- Six flights were hijacked in one week, coming from or heading to Miami, in August 1980. All ended up in Cuba.
- After a shootout near the airport in late 1988, police officers dressed as drug dealers arrested several drug dealers dressed as police officers.
- In the 1990s, 17 flight attendants were caught smuggling heroin and cocaine in their underwear from Colombia to MIA.
- Several years ago, Guillermo Rosales hitched a ride from Bogotá, Columbia, to Miami in the wheel well of a DC-8. When the 13-year-old tumbled out of the undercarriage, a witness claimed he "look(ed) like a ball of snow." He was not repatriated.
- On May 11, 1996, ValuJet Flight 592 crashed into the Everglades after taking off from MIA, killing all 110 aboard. The crash was caused by improperly stored oxygen generators that began burning in the cargo hold of the DC-9.
- In 1997, MIA purchased 625 automatic toilet seat covers for $8,219 . . . each.
- Rodney Carrington, from Barbados, was detained in 2000 with 55 red-footed tortoises in his pants, each one about four inches long.
- A Cuban tourist was stopped by U.S. customs officials in 2001 with 44 songbirds crammed in his trousers.

- Dionne Warwick was busted with 11 joints in her carry-on lipstick holder on May 12, 2002. The charges were dropped when the singer agreed to make an antidrug public service announcement.
- A Canadian cargo plane flew between 60 and 100 feet off Biscayne Boulevard through downtown Miami on July 24, 1997, just missing the Hard Rock Cafe sign (401 Biscayne Boulevard). The Boeing 707 also flew between the towers of the six-story Royal Caribbean International building. Trouble with the yaw damper was corrected in flight, and the plane continued on to New York.

Miami International Airport, PO Box 59205, Miami, FL 33159

(305) 876-7000

Hours: Always visible

Cost: Free

www.miami-airport.com/html/home.htm

Directions: The airport is bounded by Rtes. 953, 836, 948, and 969.

The Voodoo Squad

Santaria, a Caribbean blend of Catholicism and African animism that is popular in Cuba, has a strong toehold in South Florida. Is it any wonder that it shows up in Miami's halls of justice? Hardly. In fact, a group of janitors at Dade County's criminal justice building has been dubbed the Voodoo Squad. Every morning they remove Santaria offerings left by victims, defendants, and families of both. Most are left on the western side of the building at a spot dubbed the Chicken Corner, where unlucky cluckers are often sacrificed.

For those untrained in voodoo, what works best? An offering of corn is said to speed up a trial, while eggs cause a case to collapse. Black pepper will keep a defendant in jail, while a cake will sweeten a judge's disposition. A lizard with its mouth tied shut will silence a witness.

And a horse's head in your bed? That's not Santarian, that's Sicilian.

Miami-Dade Metro Justice Building, 73 W. Flagler St., Miami, FL 33130

(305) 275-1155

Hours: Early morning, before 8 A.M.

Cost: Free

www.co.miami-dade.fl.us/clerk/Criminal.htm

Directions: On the western side of the building, at 1st Ave.

Miami Beach
Al Capone's Home and Death Site

Even gangsters need a vacation. Al Capone wasn't the Club Med type, so he bought this home, Casa Contenta, on an island off Miami Beach in 1928. He was reportedly here at the time of the St. Valentine's Day Massacre in Chicago, providing Scarface with a convenient alibi. Casa Contenta was also where he spent his final days.

In late 1939, Capone was released from prison and retired here. He was suffering from the advanced stages of syphilis, and authorities didn't believe he posed much of a threat. The disease had already done a number on his brain, and his body was not far behind. His speech was slurred and rambling, and he had become increasingly paranoid. Most days he would be propped up on the dock with a fishing pole, in his pajamas, to fish. He finally suffered a brain hemorrhage and died a week later, on January 25, 1947. He was only 48 years old.

Capone's wife Mae sold the estate in 1952.

Palm Island, 93 Palm Ave., Miami Beach, FL 33139

No phone

Hours: Always visible

Cost: Free

Directions: Take General MacArthur Causeway (Rte. 41/A1A) toward Miami; Palm Island is on the right, accessed via Fountain St.

MIAMI BEACH

Eric Clapton recorded "Layla" and "I Shot the Sheriff" at Miami Beach's Criteria Studios (461 Ocean Boulevard).

The Beatles' second *Ed Sullivan Show* performance, aired on February 16, 1964, was broadcast from the Napoleon Room at the Deauville Hotel (6701 N. Collins Avenue) in Miami Beach.

Sam Moore, the emcee at Miami's King of Hearts, met Dave Prater, a short-order cook, on stage at amateur night in the 1960s. They went on to form the two-man group **Sam and Dave**.

Cunanarama

He was America's favorite spree killer of 1997, and left a trail of death across the nation that ended in Miami Beach. You could claim that you aren't the least bit intrigued by the events that unfolded, but you'll probably read on. . . .

The beginning of the end came when Andrew Cunanan arrived in Miami Beach, having left two dead bodies in Minnesota, one in Chicago, and another in New Jersey. He checked into Miami Beach's Normandy Plaza Hotel (6979 Collins Avenue) on May 10, 1997, registering under the name Andrew DeSilva. He paid in cash, and stayed in Room 116 for the first week, Room 201 for the next, and finally Room 322, paying a month's rent in advance.

During the evenings he hit the nightclub circuit, including Twist, Liquid, and the KGB Club. During the day he tried to raise a little cash. On July 7, 1997, Cunanan pawned a gold coin he had stolen from Chicago victim Lee Miglin for $190 at the Cash on the Beach pawnshop (243 71st Street), just up the street from the Normandy Plaza. Remarkably, he gave his *real* name, *real* address, and *real* thumbprint on the pawn document. As required by law, the pawnshop forwarded the information to the Miami Beach police department. Nobody there got around to looking at the document until after Cunanan had murdered Gianni Versace.

A few days before the Versace murder, the police missed another opportunity. A Miami Subs cashier named G. Kenneth Benjamin spotted Cunanan at his store (7140 Collins Avenue), having recognized him from a segment on *America's Most Wanted*. Benjamin called 911 while Cunanan bought a junior tuna combo to go and paid with three silver dollars. The killer departed a minute before the squad car arrived.

Gianni Versace began the morning of July 15, 1997, with his usual routine: he walked four blocks from his mansion to the News Café (800 Ocean Drive) and bought a cup of coffee and five magazines, then headed home. Little did he know that Andrew Cunanan had been casing his mansion for some time, often from the 11th Street Diner (1065 Washington Avenue). Exactly what motivated Cunanan is still open for debate, but he approached the designer and the two spoke briefly outside the gate. Cunanan then pulled a gun from his coat and shot Versace in the head. After Versace fell to the steps, Cunanan shot the designer again.

Casa Casuarina, 1116 Ocean Dr., Miami Beach, FL 33139
Private phone
Hours: Always visible
Cost: Free
Directions: At the corner of 11th St. and Ocean Dr.

The end of the line.

Cunanan was chased briefly by Versace's longtime partner, Antonio
D'Amico, but Cunanan scared him off by threatening to shoot him too.
Versace was taken to Jackson Memorial Hospital's Ryder Trauma Center,
where he was declared DOA. Cunanan fled to the Thirteenth Street
Municipal Garage (Collins Avenue and 13th Street, Level 3B) three
blocks north of the murder scene. He changed his clothes inside the red
truck he'd taken from his New Jersey victim, Bill Reese. Police later
found Lee Miglin's wallet in the truck's glove compartment. Also,
Cunanan had written his own name in the truck using his own blood.

A crowd quickly gathered at the murder site. Ghouls dipped Versace
magazine ads in the pool of blood for creepy souvenirs. Amazingly,

Cunanan returned to the scene three hours later to gawk along with the rest of the crowd. Miami Beach was a-twitter as to who would be next. Rumors circulated that Cunanan wanted to kill Madonna, Julio Iglesias, and Sylvester Stallone.

Yeah, yeah, join the club.

But Versace turned out to be Cunanan's final victim. The killer gained entry to an unoccupied houseboat docked on Indian Creek. Caretaker Fernando Carreira stumbled upon Cunanan on July 23 and called the police. Before they arrived, Cunanan ran upstairs and shot himself through the roof of his mouth. After a long standoff against a dead perpetrator, SWAT teams shot in tear gas and rushed the houseboat, only to find Cunanan's lifeless body.

Police tried to deny Carreira the $45,000 reward since he had not actually identified the man he spotted as Cunanan, just as an intruder. Public pressure eventually forced the department to release the funds, and Carreira was a little richer. A good thing, too, since he soon didn't have a houseboat left to take care of; it sank at its moorings and was later scrapped.

Cunanan Death Site, 5250 Collins Ave., Miami Beach, FL 33140

No phone

Hours: No boat; it sank

Cost: Free

Directions: Opposite Beach View Park on Rte. A1A (Collins Ave.), where the concrete fountain stands on the west side of the street.

MIAMI BEACH

Actor **Sidney Poitier** was born in Miami on February 20, 1924.

Men may not, by law, wear strapless gowns in Miami.

"Miami Beach is where neon goes to die." —Lenny Bruce

North Miami Beach
The Oldest Building in the United States

Strange as it sounds, this Roman Catholic monastery was built 351 years *before* Columbus arrived in the Western Hemisphere. How could that be? It was originally constructed in Seville, Spain, in 1141 by King Alfonzo VII, and remained there for almost eight centuries until William Randolph Hearst bought it for $500,000 to add to his private collection of . . . well . . . everything under the sun.

Hearst also purchased a Spanish forest for use in building crates to ship the monastery, block by block, to San Simeon. When the crates reached New York in 1920, customs officials feared the packing straw might be infected with hoof and mouth disease, and demanded that it be destroyed. The boneheads at the docks emptied all 10,751 crates, burned the straw, then tossed the pieces back into whichever boxes were closest. The boxes had been meticulously labeled as to which piece went where, and now these instructions were all hopelessly mixed up.

All 38,000 pieces were moved to a New York warehouse and abandoned until Hearst died in 1951. The next year, two enterprising men bought what was being called the World's Largest Jigsaw Puzzle through Gimbel's Department Store, brought it to Florida, and spent almost two years reconstructing it. The $1.5 million project drove them into bankruptcy, and they sold it to the Episcopal Church. It has been renamed the Cloisters of the Monastery of St. Bernard de Clairvaux, though it is neither a monastery nor affiliated with the Catholic Church. Today, it is used mostly for weddings.

Cloisters of the Monastery of St. Bernard de Clairvaux, 16711 N. Dixie Hwy., North Miami Beach, FL 33160

(305) 945-1461

Hours: Daily 10 A.M.–4 P.M.

Cost: Adults $4.50, Seniors $2.50, Kids $1

www.spanishmonastery.com

Directions: Four blocks north of Miami Beach Blvd. (163rd St.) on Rte. 1 (Dixie Hwy.).

MIAMI LAKES
Rapper **Vanilla Ice** was born in Miami Lakes on Halloween in 1967. His real name? Robert Matthew Van Winkle.

Miami's Marrakesh.

Opa-Locka
Opa-Locka City Hall

Opa-Locka City Hall looks more like it belongs in Saudi Arabia than it does southern Florida, and there's a reason: it's because the whole town was designed to glamorize the world described in *The Thousand and One Nights*. Incorporated in 1925 by aircraft pioneer Glenn Curtiss, Opa-Locka is short for Opatishawockalocka, the Moorish town from the fairy tales. Curtiss hired architect Bernard Muller to design buildings that fit his image of a Baghdad of Dade County. They were to be laid out on streets with such evocative names as Ali Baba Avenue, Cairo Lane, Harem Avenue, and Sesame Street (but no Bert or Ernie here!).

The crown jewel of this now run-down planned community is Opa-Locka City Hall. Topped by six onion domes and minarets, it will make you think twice about fighting city hall, lest you lose your hands.

777 Shaharazad Blvd., Opa-Locka, FL 33054

No phone

Hours: Always visible

Cost: Free

Directions: At 135th St. and 27th Ave. NW.

Sunny Aisles
Haulover Beach

Have you ever longed to run naked and free, as you did when you were a child (and during a few college parties)? Have you tried, only to find yourself soon sitting in the backseat of a police cruiser heading downtown for a very embarrassing mug shot? Then come to Haulover Beach in Sunny Aisles, just north of Miami Beach, where it's very in to let it all hang out.

Haulover Beach is one of the nation's few public clothing-optional beaches, and one of the only ones with easy access to a major metropolitan area. About 300 yards of beachfront between two storm fences has been reserved for nude sunbathing, with signs clearly posted to warn joggers that nekkid people are ahead. The nude section is hidden from Route A1A rubberneckers by a high dune covered in scrub brush.

The atmosphere at Haulover Beach is remarkably laid back, and about the only way you'll feel awkward is if you don't remove society's Victorian shackles—better known as your clothes. C'mon, it's a fantastic, liberating feeling! But before you toss those trunks aside, make sure you've spread out your towel in the designated area—not all of Haulover Beach is clothing-optional. And neither is the parking lot.

15000 Collins Ave., Sunny Aisles, FL 33160

(305) 947-3525

Hours: Daylight hours

Cost: Parking $3

Directions: Rte. A1A (Collins Ave.) at about 150th St.; park in the northernmost lot.

J-J-J-Jive Talkin'

Songwriters never quite know where their next idea will come from—a bad breakup, a chance encounter, or a drive to the studio. That's what happened one night when the Bee Gees were headed to a recording session. Barry Gibb's wife Linda began crooning along to the sound of the limo tires hitting the gaps on the Sunny Isles Bridge. Ba-dump, ba-dump, ba-dump . . . that's right . . . ba-dump, ba-dump, ba-dump . . . she was . . . ba-dump, ba-dump, ba-dump . . . dr-dr-dr-drive talkin'!

Nope, that sounded kind of stupid. What was she doing, then? Oh, oh, oh—she was j-j-j-jive talkin'! And so it was that one of the group's biggest hits was born. You can get some sense of that inspirational rhythm as you whisk across the causeway today, but frequent traffic jams can funk up your groove.

Sunny Isles Bridge, Rte. 826, Sunny Aisles, FL 33160

No phone

Hours: Always visible

Cost: Free

Directions: The bridge links North Miami Beach to Sunny Aisles at 163rd St.

9

THE KEYS

 here's no denying that the Florida Keys* are a world apart from the rest of the state. Something happens when you hit the first stretch of the 115-mile Overseas Highway; life slows down, and so does the traffic. Nowhere are you more than a few miles from the ocean, and the desire to drop out of the worka-day world sweeps over you like a storm surge from a Force 5 hurricane.

Nowhere will you feel this more than in Key West, the end of the line. In fact, the residents here even tried to secede from the Union . . . in April 1982. The federal government had set up roadblocks on Route 1 with the goal of snaring drug runners. Instead, the operation trapped thousands of tourists in Key West, and prevented others from going there. Frustrated, a band of tequila-soaked citizens formed the Conch Republic and drew up articles of secession. (Check out www.conchrepublic.com.)

The conch shell had long been the de facto symbol for the laid-back island life, but following the blockade it landed at the cen-ter of the new republic's flag. And what better symbol for a Key West–based government? While you might think the shell comes from an industrious creature, like a spunky hermit crab, it is in fact the home of a slowwwww-moving species of marine snail.

So welcome to the Keys—now slow your ass down!

*The sites discussed in this chapter have been arranged in the order you will encounter them while driving from Miami to Key West.

The Upper Keys
Key Largo
Jules' Undersea Lodge

Getting a little tired of humans? Maybe it's time for a break from your terrestrial friends; maybe it's time to *go under the sea*. That's right, 30 feet beneath the surface of Emerald Lagoon in Key Largo Undersea Park is a one-of-a-kind hotel: the Jules' Undersea Lodge (JUL). It began its life as La Chalupa Marine Research Center off the shores of Puerto Rico, but the 50-by-20-foot facility has been converted to sleeping quarters for up to six diver guests.

And what a getaway! It has two private bedrooms, private, that is, if you overlook the schools of fish peering in at you through the 42-inch bubble windows. The lodge has placed a fake wreck—a wrecklica?—of the sunken Spanish galleon *San Pedro* on a nearby coral reef, which you can explore using the lodge's 100-foot hookah lines. No heavy scuba gear required! When you're hungry, you can make your own meals from the well-stocked fridge or, for an additional fee, a Mer-chef will dive down and prepare a gourmet dinner. The JUL will even deliver pizza from a Key Largo pizzeria, but don't gripe if the crust is a little soggy.

For all you Jacques Cousteau wannabes who haven't yet learned to dive, but still want to stay at the JUL, you can take a three-hour class before descending with an instructor as your guide. The lodge has hosted such dignitaries as former Canadian Prime Minister Pierre Trudeau, Aerosmith frontman Steven Tyler, and Jon Fishman of Phish, but not all at the same time. Wouldn't *that* have been a wild party?

51 Shoreland Dr., MM 103.2 Oceanside, PO Box 3330, Key Largo, FL 33037

(305) 451-2353

E-mail: info@jul.com

Hours: By appointment only; Office hours, daily 9 A.M.–3 P.M.

Cost: $250–$350/night (Diving instruction $75)

www.jul.com

Directions: Turn east on Transylvania Ave. from the Overseas Hwy. (Rte. 1), and drive three blocks to the lagoon.

Christ of the Deep

Hey, isn't this guy supposed to walk *on top of* the water? Well, there's no miracle behind Key Largo's *Christ of the Deep*, a nine-foot-tall Jesus statue placed 20 feet below the ocean's surface at John Pennekamp Coral Reef State Park. The two-ton artwork is a replica of *Christ of the Abyss* by Guido Galletti, which is similarly sunk in the Mediterranean. To see the piece you have to take a glass-bottom boat tour, or dive to it with scuba gear. With his arms up, the figure looks disturbingly like somebody who double-crossed the Mob, his feet in cement, reaching out with a final plea for air from the briny depths.

Some have complained that having a religious statue in a state park, underwater or not, is a violation of the separation of church and state. To date, none of the lawsuits to remove it have been successful. Christ may have risen from the dead, but he's not rising from the Atlantic any time soon.

John Pennekamp Coral Reef State Park, MM 102.5 Oceanside, PO Box 1560, Key Largo, FL 33037

(305) 451-1621

E-mail: jpcrsp@terranova.net

Hours: 8 A.M.–Sunset; Glass-bottom boat tours 9 A.M., Noon, 3 P.M.

Cost: Boat tours, Adults $20, Kids (12 and under) $12; Snorkel tours, Adults $26.95, Kids (18 and under) $21.95; sailing, boating, and scuba diving packages also available

www.pennekamppark.com

Directions: Turn east off the Overseas Hwy. (Rte. 1) at Mile Marker 102.5.

SLEEPING WITH THE FISHES?

Christ might not be the only famous figure off the keys. CBS News paid $10,000 to a Mafia informant to learn about **Jimmy Hoffa**'s whereabouts. They ended up looking for a concrete slab off Key West, but the Teamsters president was never found. Neither was the informant . . . after his check cleared.

KEY LARGO

The town of Key Largo was named Rock Harbor until the movie *Key Largo* was released. Residents voted to change the name in 1952 to attract tourists.

A delightful dinky dinghy.

The African Queen

Bogart and Bacall fans won't find much from *Key Largo* that looks familiar here—the movie was shot almost entirely in California—but they will find something from another famous Bogart film: *The African Queen.* Contrary to what you saw in the movie, the 30-foot boat was not destroyed for the 1951 film. That was only a scale model. The craft, whose real name is the *SL Livingston,* was built in 1912 in Lytham, England, and spent most of its life ferrying passengers across Lake Albert between Uganda and the Belgian Congo.

James Hendricks, the owner of the local Holiday Inn, purchased the craft and brought it here a few years ago. For the most part, it rests on a boat lift above a canal beside the resort. Though technically not up to code—who is at age 90?—it has been issued a special permit to carry passengers on short excursions. You must make advance reservations to take a cruise on it. Otherwise, you'll only be able to see it in dry dock.

Holiday Inn Sunspree Resort & Marina, 99701 Overseas Hwy., MM 100 Oceanside, Key Largo, FL 33037

(305) 451-4655

Hours: Always visible; excursions by special request

Cost: Free; excursions extra

www.holidayinnkeylargo.com or www.africanqueen.net

Directions: On the east side of Rte. 1 (Overseas Hwy.).

King Kong crustacean.

Plantation Key

World's Largest Lobster

Don't worry, the 30-foot lobster guarding the Treasure Harbor Trading Company is not a mutant from the cooling ponds at the local nuclear power plant. It's a fiberglass creation intended to lure tourists into the store's tacky—not that there's anything wrong with that!—gift shop. And it works.

As far as gigantic roadside animals go, it's about as realistic a creature as you're likely to find, painstakingly sculpted and painted. The effect is a little creepy; you can almost imagine it coming to life and attacking someone with a bib, tiny fork, and cruet of melted butter.

Treasure Harbor Trading Co., 86701 Overseas Hwy., MM 86.7 Oceanside, Plantation Key, FL 33311

(305) 852-0511

Hours: Always visible

Cost: Free

Directions: On the southeast side of Rte. 1 (Overseas Hwy.), opposite Gimpy Gulch Dr.

You'll be blown away.

Islamorada (Upper Matecumbe Key)
Hurricane Memorial

Measured against other Florida hurricanes, the Labor Day Hurricane of 1935 was one of the worst. A crew of World War I veterans, who had been working on Henry Flagler's overseas railroad, loaded onto a northbound train on September 2, not knowing they were too late to outrun the storm. As it reached Islamorada, the train was struck by an 18-foot-high storm surge that pushed it off the tracks. Officially, 423 were killed, but there were likely more victims who were never found. All that was left on Upper Matecumbe Key was a single tombstone from an old cemetery. That marker is now in the possession of the Cheeca Lodge & Spa.

Three hundred of the unidentified victims were cremated and placed in a tomb in Islamorada beneath a tall marker made of keystone. Its official name is the Florida Keys Memorial, and it depicts several coconut palms bent over in the gale force winds. Some have pointed out that the trees seem to be angling *toward* the storm instead of away from it, but what's with all the nit-picking?

Florida Keys Memorial, 82000 Overseas Hwy., MM 82, Islamorada, FL 33036

No phone

Hours: Always visible

Cost: Free

Directions: Just west of the Cheeca Lodge & Spa on Rte. 1 (Overseas Hwy.).

UPPER AND LOWER MATECUMBE KEYS

The name *Matecumbe* is a variation of the Spanish term *matar hombre*, translated from the Keys' original name of *cuchiyaga*, a Native American word meaning "kill man."

LIGNUMVITAE KEY

Accessible only by boat, Lignumvitae Key has the highest land point in the Keys, at 16 feet.

FIESTA KEY

Fiesta Key was once owned by the Greyhound Bus Company.

MORE FUN WITH HURRICANES

Southern Florida and the Keys have a "significant hurricane event" on average every seven years, so if you're not lucky enough to experience a tropical storm firsthand, here are a few facts and destinations to whet your appetite:

★ A Spanish settlement established in Pensacola in 1559 was wiped out by a hurricane two years later. Nobody made a second attempt to colonize here until 1696.

★ The barometer dropped so low during Miami's September 18, 1926, hurricane that some people fainted from lack of oxygen. The storm killed 400.

★ A spooky sculpture of a family fleeing the September 16, 1928, hurricane stands outside the **Belle Glade Library** (530 S. Main Street). Gale force winds caused the massive Lake Okeechobee to slosh over the communities on its shores, killing almost 2,000 inhabitants. The disaster was central to **Zora Neale Hurston**'s novel *Their Eyes Were Watching God*.

★ Feel the power of hurricane-force winds at the **Gulf Coast Hurricane Exhibit** in Tampa's Museum of Science and Industry (4801 E. Fowler Avenue, (800) 995-6674, www.mosi.org). Visitors are required to strap on a pair of safety goggles before they fire up the blowers to re-create 74 MPH winds.

★ At 5:30 A.M. on August 24, 1992, **Hurricane Andrew** roared through Homestead with 140 MPH winds, with gusts as high as 200. The storm cut a 20-mile-wide path of destruction, wiping out 28,000 homes and leaving a quarter million people homeless in South Florida. Thirty-nine Floridians were killed, as were four people in the Caribbean and nine in Louisiana where the storm leveled its final blow two days later. During the cleanup, beer sales in South Florida went up 50 percent, to say nothing of the hangovers, damage was estimated in the neighborhood of $20 billion.

★ During the off-season, December to May, you can visit the **National Hurricane Center** in Coral Gables (11691 17th Street SW, (305) 229-4470, www.nhc.noaa.gov) to see how the big storms are identified, measured, and tracked. The facility is open for tours on Tuesday and Thursday, but call ahead for a reservation.

High class on the high seas.
Courtesy NautiLimo

NautiLimo

If you've ever fantasized about being a head-banging rock star, trashing hotel rooms and driving limousines into the pool, NautiLimo can help you achieve at least half of your dream, and at a fraction of the expense. You see, the NautiLimo was *designed* to be driven into the water—it's a seaworthy boat! But here's the best part: from the shore, it still looks like a white stretch limo.

Putting around in the Shell Key Channel on the surface of the waves, you'll look like a modern-day Jesus on his way to a very classy revival. Dress appropriately. NautiLimo has a sunroof to allow you a better view of the Keys' famous sunsets, or wave to awestruck tourists on chartered fishing boats.

La Siesta Marina, 80500 Overseas Hwy., MM 80.5 Gulfside, Islamorada, FL 33060

(305) 942-3793

Hours: Reservations required

Cost: $75–$135 depending on time of cruise and number of passengers

www.nautilimo.com

Directions: Ask when you make your reservations.

The mighty Mitzi.

The Middle Keys
Grassy Key
Dead Flipper

Sorry, kids, but the world's most famous dolphin is dead. Flipper's real name was Mitzi. She was one of five dolphins used during the run of the series. Mitzi was used for all the close-ups, while others, like Mr. Gipper, did the tail-walking and flipping stunts. Mitzi was trained at Santini's Porpoise School, the forerunner of today's Dolphin Research Center (DRC).

Most of the television show was filmed in the lagoon at the Miami Seaquarium (4400 Rickenbacker Causeway, (305) 361-5705, www.miamiseaquarium.com), which has since renamed its dolphin arena the Flipper Lagoon. For two years Flipper—the Mr. Gipper Flipper— also performed stunts in a tank in the Orange Bowl's endzone during games. He liked to leap into the air following a home-team touchdown and retrieve any footballs kicked into his tank during extra points and field goals.

Mitzi died of a heart attack in 1972 and was buried beneath a statue on the grounds of the DRC. (Does anyone else wonder why wasn't she buried at sea?) You can't lay a flower on her grave unless you visit the facility, but the DRC is worth the entrance fee. Your DRC admission gets you into all the shows and educational programs. The center also offers interactive programs such as Meet the Dolphin ($15), Dolphin Splash ($75), and Dolphin Encounter ($155), where you can wade or swim with Mitzi's descendants.

Dolphin Research Center, 58901 Overseas Hwy., MM 59 Gulfside, Grassy Key, FL 33050
(305) 289-1121
E-mail: DRC@dolphins.org
Hours: Daily 9 A.M.–4 P.M.
Cost: Adults $17.50, Seniors (55+) $14.50, Kids (4–12) $11.50
www.dolphins.org
Directions: On Rte. 1 (Overseas Hwy.) northeast of Guava Ave.

Marathon (Vaca Key)
Hidden Harbor Turtle Hospital

How often can you say that your night in a motel benefited a worthy cause? At the Hidden Harbor Motel in Marathon, the profit from your room fee goes to finance the work of the adjacent Hidden Harbor Marine Environmental Project, Inc., better know as the Turtle Hospital. The hospital was opened in 1986, housed in a former strip club called Fanny's. Its primary goal was to nurse injured sea turtles and return them to the wild, as well as educate the public and lobby for a better environment.

As a guest at the motel, you're given access to the hospital's facilities to observe the day-to-day work of founders Richie Moretti and Tina

Brown. The greatest threat to sea turtles today is a tumor-causing viral disease called fibropapilloma, and it ain't pretty. There are dozens of very large photos of tumor-covered turtles in the motel office, illustrating the problem that affects more than 50 percent of sea turtles worldwide. It's more than enough to guilt you into booking a room.

2396 Overseas Hwy., MM 48.5, Marathon, FL 33050

(800) 362-3495 or (305) 743-5376

Hours: Call for reservations

Cost: $75/night and up

www.turtlehospital.org and www.hiddenharbormotel.com

Directions: On the north side of Rte. 1 (Overseas Hwy.) opposite 24th St.

6.79 Mile Bridge

You'd think that constructing the world's longest segmented bridge would be honor enough, but noooooooo, the folks who built this structure in 1982 had to *exaggerate* their accomplishment by 1,109 feet. The misnamed Seven Mile Bridge runs parallel to the old bridge of the same name that was constructed back in 1935. That road was built after the deadly Labor Day Hurricane (see page 224) wiped out Henry Flagler's key-to-key railroad, and sat atop the 546 concrete piers installed for that earlier project. The old rails were ripped up and used for a guardrail.

The new 6.79 Mile Bridge sits on only 288 piers and rises 65 feet in the center allowing ships to pass beneath it. The bridge is one of 43 that connect the keys along the 115-mile Overseas Highway, and yeah, it's the longest. But it isn't seven miles, that's for damn sure!

Rte. 1, Marathon, FL 33050

No phone

Hours: Always visible

Cost: Free

Directions: Rte. 1 (Overseas Hwy.) connecting Marathon to Little Duck Key.

THE TORCH KEYS

Little, Middle, and Big Torch Keys are named for the torchwood tree that, when burned, produces hallucinations in those who breathe the smoke.

Who're you calling Shrimpy?

The Lower Keys
Big Pine Key
Shrimpmobile

Big Pine's Bait Shack has some mighty healthy bait for sale, but none as plump as Shrimpy, a 12-foot pink shrimp mounted atop a station wagon that's usually parked in the lot. The Shrimpmobile is a real eye-catcher, and pulls in more than a few tourists from the adjoining highway to take a photo. But here's a question: Can a shrimp as long as two grown men are tall still be called a *shrimp*?

Bait Shack, MM 30.2 Oceanside, Big Pine Key, FL 33043

(305) 872-0650

Hours: Always visible

Cost: Free

Directions: On the south side of Rte. 1 (Overseas Hwy.) at Mile Marker 30.2.

Summerland and Cudjoe Keys
Playboy Bunnies

Imagine a tropical paradise where Playboy bunnies run carefree and nude, protected as an endangered species—could such a place really exist?

Well, it *does*, smack dab in the middle of the Lower Keys! However, these Playboy bunnies are a little . . . you know . . . *hairier* than you might expect. In fact, they're completely covered in fluffy fur. That's right, Summerland and Cudjoe Keys are home to a species of rabbit named *Palustris hefneri*, named in honor of *Playboy* founder Hugh Hefner. The magazine has long contributed to environmental causes, so when a new rabbit species was discovered, scientists felt it was only appropriate to make them Playboy bunnies.

24000 Overseas Hwy., MM 24, Cudjoe Key, 33042

No phone

Hours: Always visible

Cost: Free

Directions: All over the islands.

CUDJOE KEY

Fat Albert, a weather balloon permanently moored to Cudjoe Key, is said to be used by the federal government to monitor drug trafficking.

KEY LOIS

Key Lois, near Cudjoe Key, is the exclusive home to a colony of Rhesus monkeys bred for use in medical testing.

Full of crap.

Sugarloaf Key
Perky Bat Tower

Back in the 1920s, Richter Clyde Perky learned an interesting fact about bats: a single bat consumes about 3,000 mosquitoes *every night*. So, he thought, what better way to solve the mosquito problem on Sugarloaf

Key than to start a colony of bats to gobble the bloodsuckers up? (Perky owned 25,000 acres of the key by 1929, and was hoping to attract investors as well as the flying mammals.)

Sure, they laughed at Columbus, too.

Perky constructed a 35-foot-tall wooden structure capable of holding 100,000 bats. To attract them to their new home, he filled it with bat guano mixed with the ground-up sex organs of other bats. But the bats never came. Who knows, maybe they live in crap-filled caves not because they like the smell, but because they have no choice. So why would they fly all the way to the middle of the Gulf of Mexico for the privilege?

The Perky Bat Tower still stands, batless, a monument to one man's unique but misguided vision. The structure has been listed on the National Register of Historic Places, so Perky's been somewhat vindicated.

Sugarloaf Lodge, 17075 Overseas Hwy., MM 17 Gulfside, Sugarloaf Key, FL 33042 (305) 745-3211

Hours: Always visible

Cost: Free

Directions: Turn north off Rte. 1 onto the dirt road just past the airplane sign, head north, keeping to the right until you reach the tower.

STOCK ISLAND

Key West residents refer to the mound on Stock Island (MM 5) as Mount Trashmore, for it is here that the city's dump is located.

KEY WEST

The World's Largest Key Lime Pie was baked at Key West's Historic Memorial Sculpture Garden (Mallory Square between Whitehead and Wall Streets) in 1997. It was seven feet in diameter and took 1,152 limes.

Key West is the only town in the continental United States that has never experienced a frost.

Key West
Count von Creep-me-out

You want *weird*? How about this? In 1931, a week before Halloween, a beautiful but unfortunate woman named Elena Milagro Hoyos Mesa died of tuberculosis in Key West. She was only 22. Elena was mourned by her family, but even more so by a local X-ray technician named Carl von Cosel, or Count Carl Tänzler von Cosel as he crowned himself.

This eccentric German immigrant had become infatuated with Elena after meeting her at Key West's Marine Hospital (in Truman Annex) where he worked. The count was secretly convinced that she was his reincarnated soulmate, Ayesha. During Elena's final months, von Cosel showered her with gifts and, eventually, a marriage proposal. After she died, he offered to put Elena's body to rest in a mausoleum he'd constructed at the city cemetery, and her poor family accepted. Though they didn't think much about it at the time, von Cosel kept the crypt's only key.

Two years after her death, von Cosel removed Elena's rotting body and took it to a room in a wingless airplane he'd constructed on the beach behind the hospital. Over the next several years he rebuilt a body around the rotting flesh and bones using beeswax, piano wire, plaster of paris, papier-mâché, and a pair of glass eyes. When the base commander died, his replacement asked von Cosel to take his airplane elsewhere, and he moved the plane and Elena to Rest Beach.

The years von Cosel spent with his wife at Rest Beach were his happiest, but they didn't last forever. The count started arousing suspicion around Key West because he kept buying kimonos, and they weren't his size. Eventually he moved Elena to a shack on Flagler Street. It was here, seven years after Elena's death, a paperboy spotted von Cosel dancing with a life-sized "doll" and tipped off Elena's family. A sister went to the shack to confront von Cosel, and when she entered its back room, she came face-to-artificial-face with her long-dead sister . . . who was wearing a wedding dress!

Von Cosel was taken into custody and charged with abusing a corpse, but authorities didn't know the half of it. An autopsy on Elena revealed the count had rebuilt her body in such a way that he could consummate their disturbing union. But the charges were dropped because the statute of limitations on the original grave robbery had expired. The judge refused the count's request to have Elena returned to his custody. She was given instead to the Mesa family, but not before she was put on public display at a local funeral parlor. The Mesas then had Elena broken into pieces and reburied in a secret location. Von Cosel gave 25¢ tours of his airplane "laboratory" to local ghouls and hopeless romantics who found his necrophilia strangely charming. (Emphasis on *strangely*.) When the tourists stopped coming, von Cosel skipped town, but not before dynamiting his beloved Elena's empty tomb. Eleven years later he died in Zephyrhillis, on Florida's Gulf Coast. A new Elena doll was found by his side, and was buried with him.

Rest Beach, Atlantic Blvd. & White St., Key West, FL 33040
No phone
Hours: Gone; nothing visible
Cost: Free
Directions: At the southern end of White St.

AND IF YOU LIKED THAT . . .
Due to the fact that there isn't a whole lot left to see of Elena or the count, you're probably going to have to summon up their dead spirits in another way. Luckily, Key West has a few options. Every evening two **Ghosts & Legends of Key West** tours depart from the corner of Caroline and Duval Streets (www.keywestghosts.com, (866) 622-GHOST, Adults $15, Kids $8) at 7 and 9 p.m. For an even eerier experience, take a seat at an old-fashioned **Séance** (429 Caroline Street, (305) 292-2040, $30). The opportunity to talk to the dead scared even Ozzy Osborne, the reigning Prince of Darkness. Call ahead; seating around the candlelit table is limited.

KEY WEST
Key West is a derivation of *cayo hueso*, Spanish for "isle of bones."

Actor **Stepin Fetchit** was born in Key West on May 3, 1902.

Gimme seven.

Hemingway Home and Museum

Jimmy Buffett aside, nobody is more closely associated with Key West than Ernest Hemingway. The hard-drinking author first visited Key West in 1928, then returned in 1931 when his second wife Pauline's family bought the newlyweds a house on Whitehead Street. Considering that Pauline's kin ponied up the dough for this place, it seems almost obnoxious that Hemingway threw a fit when she had a swimming pool installed (the first in Key West) for $20 Gs. Near the end of the project, Papa tossed a single penny into the wet cement on the patio and screamed, "Here! Take the last penny I've got!" The penny is still there.

Hemingway spent his Key West days writing; he penned *A Farewell to Arms*, *For Whom the Bell Tolls*, "The Snows of Kilimanjaro," *Death in the Afternoon*, and *To Have and Have Not* here. At night, he and his Key West Mob were the terror of Old Town. Papa's favorite watering hole was Sloppy Joe's, named for its owner Joe Russell. One evening, in a typical display of drunken hyper-masculinity, Hemingway ripped out the bar's urinal and brought it back to his house. He wanted to use it as a planter. (Again, you'll see this on the house tour.) Sloppy Joe's was located in the old city morgue, where Captain Tony's stands today (428 Greene Street, (305) 294-1838); Sloppy Joe moved his operation to the bar's current digs (201 Duval Street, (305) 294-5717) when, in 1937, his landlord raised the weekly rent from $3 to $4.

When he wasn't drinking or writing, Hemingway was going to boxing matches or cock fights or getting into scraps of his own. During one Key West party he learned that his sister had been talking to poet Wallace Stevens, a man who unwisely admitted to not liking her brother's work a whole lot. Papa called him outside where he broke Stevens's jaw with a single punch. Both men later received Pulitzer Prizes, but not for brawling.

Following Ernest's and Pauline's divorce in 1939, Hemingway dumped a load of old papers and a few unfinished works in a back room at Sloppy Joe's and moved to Cuba. The room was never opened because everybody thought he'd return one day. He still owned his home on Whitehead when he committed suicide in Idaho in 1961. Eventually, the papers were turned over to the local library. They contained, among other gems, the manuscript for *A Movable Feast* about Hemingway's Paris years.

Today the Hemingway Home seems pretty quiet, comparatively speaking. Though many tourists come to the home to soak up the aura of a great American writer, others are mostly interested in the 50-odd polydactyl cats running free on the grounds. This inbred kitty community produces cats with more toes on each paw than is usual.

Each July Key West hosts a Hemingway Days Festival (www.hemingwaydays.com) where the most popular event is a look-alike contest. Still, you don't have to visit during the event—it seems like every other fat, middle-age bastard you come across in Key West looks like Papa. It's *always* been that way; Hemingway sometimes hired a guy who looked like him to hang out in front of the house to distract the tourists while he wrote.

907 Whitehead St., Key West, FL 33040

(305) 294-1136

E-mail: hemingway@bellsouth.net

Hours: Daily 9 A.M.–5 P.M.

Cost: Adults $10, Kids (6–12) $6

www.hemingwayhome.com

Directions: At the corner of Whitehead and Olivia Sts.

Key West City Cemetery

A cemetery might not sound like the best place to be cracking jokes, but don't tell that to the dead of Key West. They're having their last laughs. Take the tombstone of Bertha Roberts; this vindicated hypochondriac chides her living relatives, "I Told You I Was Sick." Other headstones read "Call Me for Dinner" and "The Buck Stops Here." The widow of a philandering S.O.B. penned her husband's epitaph: "At Least I Know Where He's Sleeping Tonight." And even in death, one resident proclaims herself "A Devoted Fan of Singer Julio Igelsias." That's no laughing matter . . .

OK, maybe it is.

The Key West City Cemetery is also the final resting place for 24 victims, 17 of them unknown, of the USS *Maine* explosion. Remember the *Maine*? When this U.S. ship exploded and sank in Havana Harbor on February 15, 1898, claiming 266 lives, newspaper mogul William Randolph Hearst used the event to drum up support for what became the Spanish–American War. (He was said to have told artist Frederic Remington, who was in Cuba on assignment, "You furnish the pictures, I'll furnish the war.") Recent analysis point to a massive structural failure within the ship itself, not foul play, caused the disaster. Sure, a lot of people ended up dead in the war, but Hearst sold a lot of papers!

Margaret & Angela Sts., Key West, FL 33040

(800) 352-5397 or (305) 296-3913

Hours: Daylight hours

Cost: Free

Directions: The cemetery entrance is on Margaret St.; cemetery bordered by Francis St., Angela St., Margaret St., Passover Ln., and Olivia St.

KEY WEST

Key West was Florida's largest city in the late 1800s. It was also America's richest city, per capita, in 1890.

James Bond parachuted into a wedding at the St. Mary Star of the Sea Church (1010 Windsor Lane) during the opening sequence of *License to Kill*.

All innuendo has been provided.

Rooster Graveyard

Poor Big Dick. He lived hard, he fought hard, and he died hard. At least that's what his tombstone says . . .

Big Dick was a cock, a fighting cock, who battled with other roosters in the side yard of what is now the Blue Heaven restaurant in Key West's Bahama Village neighborhood. Back when Hemingway lived a couple blocks away, the building was a whorehouse—excuse me, *bordello*—and speakeasy that put on boxing matches and cock fights every Friday night.

Papa refereed (and participated in) more than a few matches in what is now the *al fresco* dining area. Just imagine the Nobel prize–winner punching out some sailor's lights as you enjoy your blackened mahi-mahi.

Big Dick isn't the only rooster buried in the restaurant's small cemetery. Many of the other birds' tombstones have similarly suggestive epitaphs.

Blue Heaven, 729 Thomas St., Key West, FL 33040

(305) 296-8666

Hours: Monday–Saturday 8 A.M.–3 P.M., 6–10:30 P.M.; Sunday 8 A.M.–2 P.M., 6–10:30 P.M.

Cost: Free; Meals $5–$36

blueheavenkw.homestead.com/Blue_Heaven_Key_West.html

Directions: At the corner of Thomas and Petronia Sts.

Southernmost Point in the Continental United States, Almost

The red-and-yellow buoy at the foot of Whitehead Street proclaims this plot of land to be the southernmost point in the continental United States, but don't you believe it. In actuality, it's the southernmost point on which *you* are allowed to set foot and pose for photos. There's another point on the island that is farther south, but it's on the navy base and off limits to you, civilian.

And why doesn't the military trust you, a taxpayer, to enjoy its unique bit of geography? Your track record, that's why. The sign that stood where the buoy does today was stolen on a regular basis. Not until it was replaced by this enormous marker in 1983 did people leave it alone. Do you think the navy wants a bunch of hooligans on its base?

Whitehead & South Sts., Key West, FL 33040

No phone

Hours: Always visible

Cost: Free

Directions: At the south end of Whitehead St.

KEY WEST

Key West's Smathers Beach has been named Blood Beach because cattle used to be slaughtered there.

Good-time grandma.

Sunset Celebration

Though very few Key West residents go anywhere near Mallory Square to watch the sun go down, there is a faithful bunch of mimes, jugglers, psychics, escape artists, and house cats who do—just to keep the tourists entertained.

Oh sure, some dismiss it as a overrated, staged event ("It used to be about the sunset, man!"), but those wet blankets should order themselves another margarita, or two, or three. Where else can you go to see such fabulous acts as Dominique LeFort and his Flying House Cats? If you think kitties cannot be trained the same as dogs, check out www.catmankeywest.com or the nightly performance in front of the Key West Hilton. And what about Parrot Bill's Bird Show (www.e-isle.com/parrot/)? Or Will Soto, tightrope walker? Or Joseph, the Silver Statue? Or Rick and his Tricky Dogs, Chico, Comet, and Twinky (www.trickydogs.com)? Or the Great Rondini? Don't let anyone talk you out of attending this one-of-a-kind event.

Mallory Square, Duval & Front Sts., Key West, FL 33040

No phone

Hours: Two hours before sunset to sunset

Cost: Free

www.sunsetcelebration.org

Directions: At the north end of Duval St., between Front & Greene Sts.

Tennessee Williams at Sunset

Ernest Hemingway was only one in a long list of authors who have called Key West home. The sea air, mellow lifestyle, and free-flowing booze inspired more than a few writers, including Tennessee Williams.

The playwright first arrived in Key West in 1941, staying for several years in the converted slave quarters of the Tradewinds guesthouse (Caroline and Duval Streets), a building that burned down in 1966. He returned in 1947, checking into a sixth-floor suite at the Hotel La Concha (430 Duval Street). Williams had come back to Key West to work on the final draft of a play called *The Poker Night,* but by the time it hit the Broadway stage it had been renamed *A Streetcar Named Desire.* The island life must have helped his creative juices; he didn't check out of La Concha until 1949.

But Williams didn't move far. He bought a place on Duncan Street in 1950. He had a writing studio built out back, a room he called the Mad House, that had no outer doorknob and only one key, which he alone kept. It was here that he wrote *The Night of the Iguana* in 1959. Some credit Williams with ushering in the gay-friendly nature of this town, but not everyone was tolerant; he was a victim of a gay bashing on Duval Street in 1979. Williams's home was sold following his death in 1983 with the stipulation that it never be made into a museum or other tourist trap. It remains in private hands.

Williams's most enduring Key West legacy is the Sunset Celebration. The story goes that this nightly tradition started when Williams, gin and tonic in hand, would applaud the setting sun from one of his many favorite bars.

1431 Duncan St., Key West, FL 33040

Private phone

Hours: Always visible; view from street

Cost: Free

Directions: Four blocks south of Truman St., just west of Leon St.

Truman's Little White House

Every U.S. president has had a vacation home away from the White House, and for Harry Truman, that place was in Key West. Rather than accept offers from well-to-do supporters, which he thought unseemly, he chose the little-used commandant's house, Quarters A and B, on the island's naval base.

Why Key West? Truman's daughter Margaret had a theory: her mother Bess rarely wanted to accompany Harry to the island, so it gave him a chance to relax away from a woman he half-affectionately called "the Boss."

During the 175 days Truman spent in Key West during his presidency, he acted more like a Shriner at a convention than a commander-in-chief. Sporting his Key West uniform—a loud Hawaiian shirt—Harry would start the day with a glass of bourbon and an orange juice chaser. Off he would go around the navy base where he would harass the enlisted men, waking up the sailors before reveille, lining up with them in the mess hall, or making them snap to attention in the showers. When he learned that the navy had a two-person Japanese submarine captured in Pearl Harbor, he demanded a ride in the small craft. He got one on November 21, 1946. (You can see the sub today at the Lighthouse Museum, 938 Whitehead Street, (305) 294-0012.) Most of Truman's evenings revolved around a poker game he hosted in his quarters.

Years after Truman left office, the building was pressed into service as the command post for the failed Bay of Pigs invasion of April 17, 1961. Later it was abandoned, and during the 1980s was said to be used as a crack house. In 1991, it was restored to its late-1940s appearance and many Truman-era artifacts were brought back, including his custom-built poker table, designed to be hidden under a false top whenever Bess dropped by to conduct an inspection. Framed on the wall is a copy of the infamous "Dewey Defeats Truman" cover of the *Chicago Tribune*.

111 Front St. (Truman Annex), Key West, FL 33040

(305) 294-9911

Hours: Daily 9 A.M.–5 P.M.

Cost: Adults $8, Kids (4–12) $4

Directions: Enter the Truman Annex at Eaton St. and Whitehead St., head west one
   block to Front St.

Garden Key
Your Name Is Mudd

Dr. Samuel Mudd thought he was doing the right thing by setting the broken leg of John Wilkes Booth in 1865, but he couldn't have been further
from the truth. Booth had broken his leg while jumping from the presidential box at Ford's Theatre after shooting Abraham Lincoln, but Mudd
said he didn't know that at the time. No matter—Mudd was sentenced to
life imprisonment at hard labor at the most remote federal prison imagi-
nable: Fort Jefferson on Garden Key in the Dry Tortugas, 68 miles west of
Key West. He went there along with three conspirators to the assassination; most of the other inmates were Union deserters from the Civil War.

Though the prison sat on a 10-acre rock in the middle of *nowhere*, it
was still susceptible to tropical diseases. From August to November 1867,
a yellow fever epidemic swept the prison, infecting 270 of the 300 inmates
and guards. Before it was over, 38 had died, including the island's garrison
surgeon. Mudd, being a doctor, was pressed into service assisting the ill.

His efforts to save lives bought him a few brownie points with
Andrew Johnson, the man who succeeded Lincoln as president. On
Johnson's final day in office, he pardoned the doctor. Mudd was released
from Fort Jefferson on March 11, 1869, and returned to Maryland.

Contact: Dry Tortugas National Park, PO Box 6208, Key West, FL 33041

(305) 242-7700

Sunny Days Ferry: (800) 236-7937, www.drytortugas.com

Yankee Fleet Ferry: (800) 634-0939, www.yankeefleet.com

Hours: Daily 8 A.M.–7 P.M.

Cost: Free (if you can get there)

www.nps.gov/drto

Directions: Sixty-eight miles west of Key West.

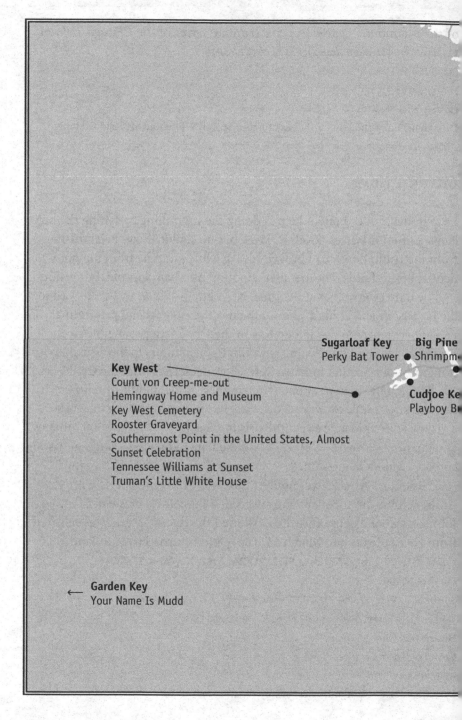

Sugarloaf Key
Perky Bat Tower ●

Big Pine
Shrimpm●

Key West
Count von Creep-me-out
Hemingway Home and Museum
Key West Cemetery
Rooster Graveyard
Southernmost Point in the United States, Almost
Sunset Celebration
Tennessee Williams at Sunset
Truman's Little White House

Cudjoe Ke
Playboy B●

← **Garden Key**
Your Name Is Mudd

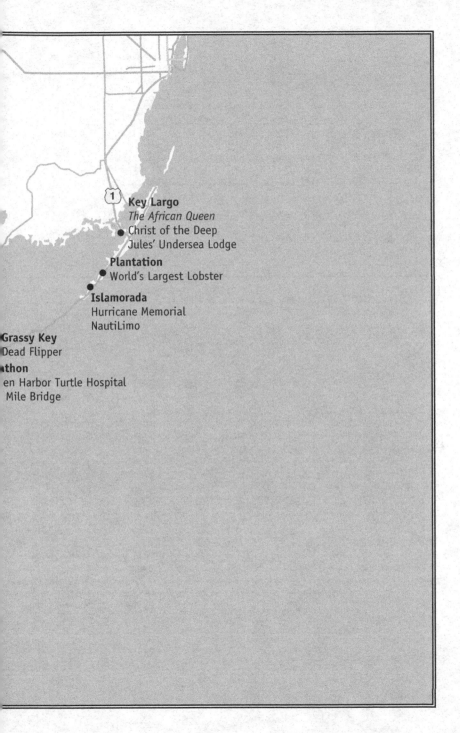

Key Largo
The African Queen
Christ of the Deep
Jules' Undersea Lodge

Plantation
World's Largest Lobster

Islamorada
Hurricane Memorial
NautiLimo

Grassy Key
Dead Flipper

athon
en Harbor Turtle Hospital
Mile Bridge

10

BUSTED TOUR

Celebrities and politicians beware! You might think that
when you're in Florida you're far enough from Hollywood or
Washington, D.C., that nobody will care how you behave. Not
so. Just ask Jim Morrison. Or Jim Bakker. Or Paul "Pee-wee
Herman" Rubens. Or Carmen Electra and Dennis Rodman.

Or Richard Nixon or Marla Maples or Gary Hart. Or Miss Cleo or
O. J. Simpson or Andy Dick. Or Manuel Noriega and his wife
Felicidad. Or Miami Mayor Joe Carrollo, or 2 Live Crew. Or the
Bush family. Or the Kennedys, all of them.

You get the picture? If you want to trash your hotel room,
subvert the Constitution, cheat on your wife, take a dump on
the beach, snort cocaine, whack a loved one with a tea canister,
expose yourself to a crowd of onlookers, forge prescriptions,
shoplift buttons, pick up hookers, run stop signs, or any
combination of the above, do it somewhere else. If you don't,
the Florida authorities are gonna bust you, and it'll be all over
the papers. And I can promise you the story will end up in the
second edition of this book.

Until then, here's a themed tour of the Sunshine State's most
embarrassing celebrity moments, arranged in chronological
order—tales of those who loved a little too much, partied a little too hearty, and dropped their drawers when they should have
kept them up.

Miami
Jim Morrison, Unplugged

Fans of Jim Morrison had come to expect a certain level of obnoxiousness from the usually drunk performer, but the concert at Miami's Dinner Key Auditorium on March 1, 1969, was a new low, even by Morrison's minimal standards.

The trouble actually began before the concert started. Morrison's flight to Miami had been delayed, and he had spent his afternoon in an airport lounge. By the time he arrived at the auditorium he was tanked to the gills, and he argued with police backstage. (In retrospect, not a smart move.)

Morrison started the concert by saying, "You're all a bunch of slaves. What you gonna do about it?" and went downhill from there. At some point a lamb was placed onstage, which he cuddled, then observed, "You know, if it wasn't so young, I'd f--- it." Later, for a grand finale, he announced, "You didn't come here for the music, you came for something else, something greater than you've ever seen." At this point he removed his shirt, held it over his crotch, and simulated masturbation. The concert continued, but four days later he was charged with a list of naughty violations. Morrison turned himself over to the FBI in Los Angeles to avoid additional charges of flight to avoid prosecution.

Before Morrison ever went before a jury he was tried, convicted, and sentenced in the court of public opinion. At least 30,000 Miami-area residents attended a Rally for Decency at the Orange Bowl (1501 NW 3rd Street). Jackie Gleason, no stranger to vices, and Anita Bryant, no stranger to finger-wagging, were headliners.

A jury in 1970 acquitted Morrison of lewd and lascivious behavior, but he was convicted of indecent exposure. Strangely, no witness even testified that Morrison had exposed himself. Morrison was sentenced to six months of hard labor and given a $500 fine. His case was on appeal when Morrison died in a Paris bathtub two years later.

Coconut Grove Exhibition Center (former Dinner Key Auditorium), 2700 S. Bayshore Dr., Miami, FL 33133

(305) 579-3310

Hours: Always visible

Cost: Free

www.doors.com/miami/

Directions: Now part of the Coconut Grove Exhibition Center at 27th St. S, at the water.

Key Biscayne
Nixon's Florida White House

Though Richard Nixon was a California native, it wasn't until he started hanging out with the wrong crowd—the *Florida* crowd—that he started getting into big trouble. The president's Florida White House in Key Biscayne was actually more of a compound. It included five homes surrounded by one very high security wall. Inside, Nixon used two of the structures for living quarters and leased another pair to the federal government. The fifth home was owned by his good (and possibly only) friend Bebe Rebozo.

After closing on the property in 1968, Nixon began $1.1 million worth of improvements. Because he lumped the entire project "security upgrades," the American taxpayers foot the bill . . . for a while. When it was later learned that the government had paid for such assassin-stopping items as an ice maker, clubhouse chairs, a swimming pool heater, a sofa, and decorative pillows, Nixon refiled his 1973 income taxes to the tune of an additional $432,787.13. Ouch! (But don't feel too sorry for the fella. Though he paid $79,000 in taxes in 1969, his first year in office, he paid only $702 in 1970, and $878 in 1971.)

Nixon drew heavily on his south Florida connections to launch the criminal activity that eventually cost him the presidency. In March 1972, during a meeting held in a Key Biscayne hotel, the Committee to Re-elect the President (CRP, better known as CREEP) first entertained G. Gordon Liddy's plan to bug Democratic Party leaders. Attorney General John Mitchell, head of CREEP, approved $250,000 to bug the Watergate complex.

Four of the five "plumbers" Liddy hired for the break-in were from Miami, and all had worked for the CIA. When they were busted in the offices of the Democratic National Committee on June 17, 1972, burglar Bernard Barker had $5,000 in sequential $100 bills on him. Investigators learned the bills came from the Federal Reserve branch in Miami and had been issued to a Republic Bank office on LeJeune Road. Paperwork led back to a Boca Raton account under the name Kenneth Dahlberg who, it turned out, had recently deposited a check for $25,000 from—you guessed it—CREEP. Deep Throat was right: follow the money.

Bebe Rebozo tried to provide an alibi for Nixon during the Watergate break-in. He claimed that Tricky Dick was bobbing around in his Key Biscayne pool when he heard about the burglary. "What in God's name were they doing there?" he was said to have bellowed. Of course, he already knew.

500–516 Bay Lane, Key Biscayne, FL 33149

Private phone

Hours: Always visible

Cost: Free

Directions: Follow the Rickenbacker Causeway to Key Biscayne, turn right on Harbor Dr., and follow the road for about 8 blocks until Bay Lane veers off to the right.

Lake Buena Vista
"I'm Not a Crook"

If Richard Nixon is remembered for saying one thing, it was a less-than-accurate proclamation in front of a group of 400 Associated Press managing editors on November 17, 1973. Nixon had traveled to Orlando to give a speech at the University of Central Florida, but he stopped off at Disney World to give an unconvincing, often contradictory press conference. He must have known the hounds were closing in when Air Force One took off from Key Biscayne that morning; the White House had passed on sending its routine back-up plane, and Nixon observed, "If this one goes down, they don't have to impeach." No such luck.

The hour-long Q&A focused primarily on the unfolding Watergate investigation, but it was a response to a question about his refiled income taxes on the Florida White House that elicited the now-famous remark: "(I)n all my years of public life I have never obstructed justice. People have got to know whether or not their president is a crook. Well, I'm not a crook."

Okey-dokey . . .

Disney World, Lake Buena Vista, FL 32830

(407) W-DISNEY

Hours: Times vary; check Web site

Cost: Prices vary

disneyworld.disney.go.com/waltdisneyworld/index

Directions: West of I-4 on Rte. 192 (Irlo Bronson Hwy.), then north on World Dr.

Clearwater
Jim and Jessica

"Jessica, by helping the shepherd, you're helping the sheep."

Wow, you don't hear a pickup line like *that* every day! But that's the smooooooth line Jim Bakker ultimately used to convince church secretary Jessica Hahn to meet with him at a Clearwater hotel suite on December 6, 1980. And he wasn't talking about typing and filing.

The shepherd was pleased, for a while, until he started to worry the sheep would bleat. Fearing that news would destroy his PTL ministry, Bakker paid Hahn $265,000 in hush money out of church coffers. Hahn stayed hushed until Jimmy Swaggert found out and blabbed it to the whole darn world.

Sheraton Sand Key Hotel, Room 538, 1160 Gulf Blvd., Clearwater, FL 33767

(727) 595-1611

Hours: Always visible

Cost: Free

www.beachsand.com

Directions: Take Rte. 60 west, over the Memorial Causeway, to Clearwater Beach, left at
 Gulf Blvd., heading south; Sheraton is on the right, just over the bridge.

Orlando
Jim and Tammy Faye at the Mall

In the short period between Jim and Tammy Faye Bakker's fall from grace and Jim's indictment on fraud charges, the pair ran a radio ministry out of an Orlando strip mall. At the time, Shopper's World was barely hanging on with only one tenant: a bar. But when the Bakkers showed up, so did business.

The couple christened their ministry the New Covenant Church. A local preacher, unhappy the pair was in town, tried to intimidate them by dumping a casket in the parking lot with a sign on it reading "Bury Jim and Tammy!" Even worse, a local DJ brought Jessica Hahn to Orlando for a live show from the mall bar. A near-naked Hahn lounged on a waterbed and invited Bakker to pay her another visit. He passed.

Shortly after Bakker made it known that he was going to try and wrestle Heritage USA back from Jerry Falwell, like Moses coming down from Mount Orlando, the feds indicted him. Now Tammy Faye had bigger issues to cry about.

6303 Grand National Dr., Orlando, FL 32819

No phone

Hours: No longer there

Cost: Free

Directions: One block southwest of the intersection of International Dr. and W. Oak Ridge Rd.

THE END WAS NEAR

Tammy Faye filed for divorce from **Jim Bakker** in a Tallahassee courtroom on March 13, 1992, ending their 31-year marriage. Jim was in a federal prison at the time.

Eglin Air Force Base
Watergate to PTL-gate

Celebrities who get busted rarely go to the clink, but the criminal element that assists them often does. Richard Nixon was pardoned for any role he played in the Watergate break-in and cover-up, but four of the plumbers, Bernard Barker, Virgilio Gonzalez, Eugenio Martinez, and Frank Sturgis, did their minimal time in a minimum-security prison near Fort Walton Beach. They didn't get the same red-carpet treatment that Nixon's top aides got—the golf course at Eglin is strictly for military personnel—but this place isn't exactly Alcatraz, either.

Years later, PTL vice-president/vice-conspirator Richard Dortch did his time here, writing his memoirs, and finding God . . . *again*!

Eglin Air Force Base Prison, Eglin AFB, FL 32542
Private phone
Hours: Always visible
Cost: Free
Directions: Between the airport and Ft. Walton Beach on Rte. 85, inside the main gate.

Miami
Monkey Business

Who can forget that touching photo of Donna Rice on Gary Hart's lap aboard the Bimini-bound yacht *Monkey Business* in 1988? Certainly not Gary Hart! More than anything else, it was that image that torpedoed his quest for the 1988 Democratic presidential nomination. That and being caught by a *Miami Herald* reporter leaving his Georgetown townhouse with Rice early one morning. And it didn't help that he shared the pad with notorious womanizer Warren Beatty.

Some time earlier Hart had thrown down the gauntlet to reporters questioning rumors about infidelity. "Go ahead. Put a tail on me. You're not going to find anything," he suggested. They did, and they did. The *Monkey Business* photo came out after the reports of Hart's early-morning exit in Washington, and only served to put a grinning, guilty face on the affair. The *Monkey Business* had been chartered from a Miami yacht club.

Turnberry Yacht Club, 19735 Turnberry Way, Miami, FL 33180
Private phone
Hours: Always visible
Cost: Free
Directions: North of the William Lehman Causeway (192nd St.), three blocks west of Rte. A1A.

DANNY BONADUCE GETS BUSTED
The ugliest member of the Partridge Family, **Danny Bonaduce**, was arrested in March 1990 at a Daytona Beach housing project while buying $20 of crack.

Hollywood
2 Live Crew Gets Busted
As it is often said, no publicity is bad publicity. It's true—ask 2 Live Crew. Few who did not listen to rap knew of the band, but when Governor Bob Martinez asked prosecutors to charge anyone selling their album, *Nasty as They Wanna Be*, with obscenity, *everyone* suddenly knew about them.

Fort Lauderdale record storeowner Charles Freeman challenged the ruling, and was dragged into court. Following a trial, a judge ruled on June 6, 1990, that the album could not be sold, nor could the group perform its works in concert. Many were concerned about the First Amendment implications, but busybody prudes such as Tipper Gore were thrilled.

Four days later, on June 10, police busted 2 Live Crew at the adults-only Club Futura in Hollywood. Band members were charged with violating local obscenity laws. They were eventually found not guilty by a jury.

Club Futura, Dixie Hwy. & Hollywood Blvd., Hollywood, FL 33020

No phone

Hours: No longer there

Cost: Free

Directions: Rte. 820 (Hollywood Blvd.) at N. 2nd Ave. (Dixie Highway), three blocks west of Young Circle Park, along the railroad tracks.

Palm Beach
The Kennedys' Party Central
While most folks limit their Florida party days to a few spring breaks during college, the Kennedy family had the money and stamina to make it a full-time operation for nearly 60 years. Joseph Kennedy purchased La Guerida, better known as the Kennedy Compound, in 1933. Joe had a soft spot for Palm Beach, for it was there in 1928 at the Royal Poinciana Hotel that he first romanced (or as she described it, hopped on) Gloria Swanson. Joe broke it off with the actress about a year later, but he returned to Palm Beach often, and eventually bought the oceanfront property for $100,000, a bargain even during the Depression.

Joe Kennedy loved to lounge nude beside the pool at La Guerida, conducting business while the underpaid servants (who nicknamed the mansion the House of the Minimum Wage) waited on him hand and foot. Women other than his wife were constantly coming and going, but Rose seemed resigned to her husband's womanizing.

It was a pattern his children and grandchildren would continue. John F. Kennedy also liked to hang around the pool naked, usually with a woman in a similar state of giddy undress. JFK had a room on the first floor with a private exit, which he used often. Drunken brother Ted, six months before Chappaquiddick, crashed his car on Ocean Boulevard near the country club, then got the family's chauffeur to hush it up.

A third-generation Kennedy, Robert's son David, was too out-of-control for even their party-hearty family. In and out of drug treatment programs, he was not allowed to stay overnight at La Guerida. David came to Palm Beach for the family's Easter get-together in 1984, but stayed at the nearby Brazilian Court Hotel (301 Australian Avenue). On April 26 he overdosed in room 107 from a mixture of cocaine, Mellaril, and Demerol he'd stolen a few days earlier from Grandma Rose. Caroline and John Jr. had to identify his body.

La Guerida was also the scene of the notorious William Kennedy Smith/Patricia Bowman incident. On March 29, 1991, Smith and Bowman met at Palm Beach's Au Bar (366 Royal Poinciana Way), then returned to the compound before heading to the beach. When Smith went skinny-dipping, Bowmen headed inside. Before she got to the house, however, he had gotten out of the water and caught up with her. Bowman claimed Smith raped her on the lawn; Smith claimed their intercourse was consensual. A Palm Beach jury agreed with Smith.

The Kennedy Compound was sold in 1993 for $7 million, so there's less chance of running into one of the clan here these days. Kennedyphiles might want to check out St. Edwards Church (144 N. County Road, (561) 832-0400) where they can sit in the "Kennedy Pew." It's amazing that nobody seems as interested in the "Kennedy Confessional." If those walls could talk . . .

La Guerida, 1095 N. Ocean Blvd., Palm Beach, FL 33480

Private phone

Hours: Always visible; view from street or water

Cost: Free

Directions: Ten blocks north of the Palm Beach Country Club on the ocean side of the southern peninsula.

Sarasota
Pee-wee's Porn House

On July 26, 1991, a Sarasota police dragnet nabbed one of the 1990s' most diabolical celebrity criminals. No, not O. J. Simpson—Paul Reubens, better known as Pee-wee Herman. The crime? Exposing himself in an X-rated theater. Sometime during a screening of *Nancy Nurse*, the comedian reportedly took out his . . . well, you know . . . and . . . well, *you know*. . . .

Who would have thought that polishing your bayonet in a porno theater was against the law? Apparently it was an "affront to community standards"—not the X-rated movie–going community, but the greater Sarasota community. Perhaps the locals thought guys were going to see *Nancy Nurse* for a checkup.

With all the problems the police have to keep them busy, wouldn't you think that sending four officers to an adult theater looking for lonely guys would be a pretty low priority? Apparently not in Sarasota. Reubens pleaded no contest to the charges. He was fined and ordered to make an anti-drug PSA. It's about all they could have done—they caught him red-handed.

Manhattan Bar & Grill (former site of South Trail Adult Theater), 6727 S. Tamiami Tr., Sarasota, FL 34231

No phone

Hours: Torn down; restaurant on the site today

Cost: Free

Directions: Just southeast of the Gulf Gate Mall.

LIKE HUSBAND, SORT-OF LIKE WIFE

Panamanian strongman **Manuel Noriega**, captured in 1990 during Operation Just Cause, has been in federal custody since 1992 at the Federal Metropolitan Correction Center in Miami, serving out a 40-year sentence for drug trafficking and money laundering. Because he is technically a prisoner of war, he is allowed to strut around in his khaki dictator's uniform. Guards report that other prisoners, on seeing the outfit, have taken to calling him "sissy." (You can write to him at Prisoner #38699-079, 15801 SW 137th Avenue, Miami, FL 33177.)

Meanwhile, his wife **Felicidad** was busted in 1992 for cutting off and shoplifting 27 buttons from designer clothing at a Burdines in the Dadeland Mall (7303 N. Kendall Drive). She pleaded guilty and paid $1,340 in damages.

Coral Gables
Jennifer Capriati Gets Busted

Jennifer Capriati was tennis's Girl Wonder in the 1980s, but she became a Girl-Wonder-Gone-Astray in the 1990s. It started innocently enough in 1993 when she was caught shoplifting a cheap ring at a Tampa mall. Kids will be kids, the lawyers said, and the judge gave her a slap on the wrist.

But, as often happens to kids with plenty of money, Capriati had no problems finding friends and new ways of getting in trouble. The particular friends she ended up with were the type that always needed money for drugs. One of her pals turned police informant, and when cops raided a hotel party in Coral Gables on May 16, 1994, Jennifer was arrested and charged with possession of marijuana. It could have been worse; one guy who was there was busted with crack and a crack pipe, and a teenage runaway had heroin on her. Capriati was eventually sentenced to 23 days in rehab.

Gables Inn, Room 208, 730 S. Dixie Highway, Coral Gables, FL 33146

(305) 661-7999

Hours: Always visible

Cost: Free

Directions: Three blocks north of Granada Blvd. on Rte. 1 (Dixie Hwy.).

OOPS, OUR MISTAKE!

Playwright **Edward Albee** was arrested for indecent exposure on a Key Biscayne beach in 1992. The cops conveniently overlooked the fact that he was on a private nude beach at the time. No charges were filed.

Ocean Ridge
A Trump Dump

If you're under the delusion that the rich and powerful don't eat and sleep and poop like the rest of us, you're right. They're *worse*.

Take the case of Marla Maples Trump, the post-Ivana mate of comb-over king Donald Trump. In late 1996 the oh-so-glamorous Ms. Maples couldn't wait to get back to Mar-A-Lago, Trump's sprawling Palm Beach estate, so she asked her bodyguard Spencer Wagner to pull over at Ocean

Ridge Beach so that she could use the facilities. And by "facilities" she meant the beach. While Trump was off doing her doody, a police officer came upon Wagner and asked what he was up to at 4 A.M. The bodyguard was making a lame excuse when Marla stumbled out of the dunes, much relieved.

Was she busted? Heck no—she was Palm Beach royalty! But The Donald did sue Wagner after the latter spilled the beans to *The Globe*.

Ocean Ridge Beach, Rte. A1A, Ocean Ridge, FL 33435

No phone

Hours: Always visible

Cost: Free

Directions: Along Rte. A1A.

GOD WORKS IN *VERY* MYSTERIOUS WAYS . . .

Football star **Eugene "The Prophet" Robinson** of the Atlanta Falcons was busted for offering an undercover policewoman $40 for oral sex on January 30, 1999, the day before he was to play in the Superbowl. While being arrested at the corner of Biscayne Boulevard and 22nd Street, the devoutly religious player stated, "I have accepted the Lord as my savior. . . . I have disappointed my team, my coach, and my God." (Earlier that morning he had been given an award for his high moral character.)

Miami Beach
Carmen Electra vs. Dennis Rodman

It was a fight between two West Coast celebrities . . . and the hotel lost.

Police were called to a disturbance at the Bentley Hotel on November 5, 1999. In room 302 they found Tara Patrick, better known as Carmen Electra, and her ex-husband (and soon-to-be-ex-ex-boyfriend) Dennis Rodman. Their accounts varied, but it seemed that Rodman had flown off the handle while watching MTV after another of Electra's former boyfriends, Fred Durst of Limp Bizkit, appeared on the screen. Items were tossed. Clothing was ripped. Furniture was overturned. Jewelry once gifted in love was hastily returned.

Both stars were arrested at the scene. A local judge ordered them to stay away from each other—good advice!—and both were charged with misdemeanor battery.

Bentley Hotel, 510 Ocean Dr., Room 302, Miami Beach, FL 33139

(305) 538-1700

Hours: Always visible

Cost: Free; Rooms $150–$1,500

Directions: At 5th St. and Collins Ave., at the beach.

THIS GUY COULD GET AWAY WITH MURDER . . . *TWICE*

On December 4, 2000, motorist Jeffrey Pattinson got into a traffic altercation with the wrong guy. According to police reports, Pattinson was approaching the intersection of SW 106th Street and 92nd Avenue when a Lincoln Navigator, driven by **O. J. Simpson**, blew the stop sign at 92nd. Pattinson slammed on his brakes and honked at the ex-football player, who then followed him to a spot farther down 92nd Street. Simpson reportedly blocked in Pattinson's vehicle, got out, and confronted him. "So I blew the stop sign! What are you going to do, kill me and my kids?" He then reached into the driver's window and ripped the sunglasses off Pattinson's face.

Simpson denied it all, but he was arrested and later released on $9,000 bond. Pleading not guilty, he was later acquitted in a trial on October 24, 2001.

Miami, Tallahassee
Bushes Gone Wild!

Type the Bush family name into a search engine of police reports like The Smoking Gun (www.thesmokinggun.com) and it shows up like a rash. It seems that most Bush family members lead a pretty active social life—drinking, carousing, getting into trouble—until, sometime in their late 30s or early 40s, an older family member sits them down, tells them it's time to grow up, and installs them in positions of political or economic authority far above their competence, kind of like the Kennedys. Florida Governor Jeb Bush's young 'uns were no exception. In fact, their rap sheets could be made into a cable-access video: *Bushes Gone Wild!*

Jeb's oldest, George P. Bush, couldn't take no for an answer, even though it had been proffered 18 months earlier. On December 31, 1994, the Rice University student tried to break through the bedroom window of a former girlfriend at 4 A.M. This woman happened to live with her parents, and her father confronted the no-doubt future president while he was half-in and half-out of his home. Bush fled, but returned a short time later in his Ford Explorer to perform a "lawn job" on the family's yard and the one adjoining (10025 SW 130th Terrace).

Bush was charged with burglary and criminal mischief, but the victims in this case decided not to press charges. Does anyone wonder why?

10005 SW 130th Ter., Miami, FL 33176

Private phone

Hours: Private property, view from street

Cost: Free

Directions: One block east of 102nd Ave., five blocks north of 135th St.

Scene of the non-crime.

George Bush III's high jinks were mild in comparison to his sister Noelle's troubles, though at least she can blame her rap sheet on a medical addiction. At 1:15 A.M. on January 29, 2002, Noelle Bush pulled her white VW bug up to the Walgreens prescription window to pick up a phoned-in prescription for the depressant Xanax. The pharmacist suspected something was awry— in part because the doctor on his answering machine had identified herself as Noelle *Scidmore*, and sounded a whole lot like his customer Noelle Bush—so he called the cops. An officer placed the 24-year-old Bush under arrest at the scene. Bush was eventually convicted of prescription fraud, and made to spend two weeks in a drug rehabilitation facility.

It didn't take. While Bush was staying at the court-ordered facility in July, a worker found her in possession of another prescription that wasn't hers. The judge tossed her in jail for a couple days on contempt-of-court charges. After she was released, she was packed off to the Center for Drug Free Living in Orlando. Bush must have thought it was the Center for Free Drug Living, because on September 9, counselors (tipped off by other residents) found Bush with a 0.2-gram rock of crack cocaine in her shoe. Police summoned to the center reported that while they were talking to the staff who had called them in, their supervisor appeared and told the pair to stop talking, then grabbed their half-written statements and tossed them in the garbage. The police retrieved the papers from the trash and entered them into evidence anyway.

For this third strike, did the First Niece receive the same punishment as, say, an inner city black youth might? Puh-lease. She was sentenced to a whopping 10 days in jail on October 17, 2002.

Walgreens Pharmacy, 2349 N. Monroe St., Tallahassee, FL 32303

(850) 385-7141

Hours: Always visible

Cost: Free

Directions: One block southeast of the Tallahassee Mall On Rte. 27 (Monroe St.).

Brother John Bush, better known as Jebby, ran into his own trouble in the parking lot of a Tallahassee mall on October 7, 2000. Security guards noticed the windows of a Jeep Cherokee were excessively fogged in the north parking lot, outside Parisian's. When they investigated they found the 16-year-old Bush and a female companion inside. Neither was wearing anything from the waist down, though Jebby still had his socks on, and they were engaged in sexual intercourse. Jebby was on the bottom.

Whether you think it was a case of the kids being half-naked or half-clothed depends on whom you asked. The security guards went for half-naked. But they soon realized who they'd just turned over to police, noting "political ties" in their complaint report. Too late to change it to half-clothed. . . . The minors were turned over to their parents, and the charges were eventually dropped because, as the original report stated, the windows were fogged and there was no danger of anyone witnessing the act.

Parisian's, Tallahassee Mall, 2415 N. Monroe St., Tallahassee, FL 32303

No phone

Hours: Always visible

Cost: Free

Directions: At the corner of Monticello Dr. and Rte. 27 (Monroe St.).

JOE GOES NUTS!
Miami Mayor Joe Carollo spent the night of February 7–8, 2001, in jail for hitting his wife in the head with a cardboard tea canister.

HEY, IT'S YOUR DIME . . .
When actress **Natasha Lyonne** was pulled over for drunk driving in Miami Beach on August 28, 2001, she asked the police, "I'm a movie star—can I call my entertainment lawyer?" She pled guilty, paid an $887 fine, and lost her license for six months.

SHOULDN'T SHE HAVE SEEN THIS COMING?
Television psychic **Miss Cleo** was let go from the Fort Lauderdale–based Psychic Reader's Network after federal authorities levied a $5 million fine against the company for deceptive advertising. The company was also ordered to pay back $500 million in customer fees.

Only a small part of the problem.

West Palm Beach, Miami, Sarasota
The 2000 Election Fiasco

There's little point in trying to convince anyone who followed the 36-day, postelection fiasco in Florida whether George Bush or Al Gore rightfully won the right to assume the nation's highest office. Instead, for the purposes of a weirdo travel guide, there are three indelible images worth recalling: the West Palm Beach recount; the Button-Down Riot; and the grinning, clownlike face of Katherine Harris.

Most of the attention during the recount (or attempted recount) focused on returns from Palm Beach County. There, a Democratic election official had created a poorly designed butterfly ballot—an illegal ballot, actually—that was approved by the Florida Secretary of State's office, the governmental body charged with conducting a fair election. The ballot resulted in a weird spike of support for third-party candidate Pat Buchanan in a district that was both liberal and Jewish. Neither of these demographic groups were known to support the right-wing Buchanan for *anything*, much less the presidency.

As provided under Florida law in the case of a close election, candidates can request a recount. Vice President Al Gore stupidly asked for recounts in a few select counties, opening him to legitimate complaints that he was selectively fishing for missed votes. The Bush camp, on the other hand, tried to act as though nobody had the right to challenge the results via a recount, which was clearly not the case under both state and federal law.

The nation watched as election officials and uptight observers from both parties pored over the punchcard ballots. Dimpled chads . . . pregnant chads . . . court injunctions . . . it was a *mess*, and all the while protesters for both sides stood outside the Palm Beach Government Center Complex screaming at one another.

Those who should have been shouting were those inside, the admirable citizens who volunteered their time to be election judges and poll-watchers in the first place. *Where were all you lazy, Wednesday-morning loudmouths when you were asked to do your civic duty to monitor an honest, fair election? Too busy to sit at a card table for one damn day every two damn years? Screw you!* Instead, these folks did their best to rectify the situation while cable-TV commentators belched hourly that they were all incompetent.

No good deed goes unpunished.

Palm Beach Government Center Complex, 301 N. Olive St., West Palm Beach, FL 33401
(561) 355-2040
Hours: Always visible
Cost: Free
Directions: Four blocks south of the Flagler Memorial Bridge and one block east of the Dixie Hwy.

On November 22, the Miami-Dade Canvassing Board was preparing to start its own recount at the Stephen P. Clark Governmental Center in downtown Miami. Again, protesters were outside the meeting room screaming, even though both sides had monitors *inside* watching the board's every move. When the three-member board and the official observers tried to move to a 19th-floor office for a little quiet, a small band of Bush supporters ran through the halls, kicking and shoving state employees while the TV cameras rolled. The dozen or so "Button-Down Rioters" pounded on the doors outside the canvassing board chanting "Stop the count! Stop the count!"

And the canvassing board did. It was probably the battle that turned the tide against the recount statewide. Conservative pundits tried to pass off the rioters as a band of local citizens exercising their constitutional right to free speech.

But then somebody hit the replay button. *Who were those rabble-rousers with male-pattern baldness? They looked too chubby and untanned to be Floridians....*

As it turns out, none of them were Florida residents at all, but were in fact GOP Capitol Hill staffers who had traveled to the state on the tax-payers' dime. Suddenly the riot looked a bit more ... what's the word? ... *criminal.* Federal employees crossing state lines to intimidate local election officials—partisan politics paid for by the American public—it was beyond the pale.

Their punishment was swift and brutal. On Thanksgiving Day, the rioters found themselves trapped in a ballroom at the Fort Lauderdale Hyatt on Pier 66 (2301 SE 17th Street) where they were serenaded by a thankful Wayne Newton, crooning "Danke Schoen." Certainly this crossed the constitutional protection against cruel and unusual punishment. And for those who actually *enjoyed* the show? Clearly they were not responsible for their actions, for they obviously didn't know the difference between what is right and what is very, very, very wrong.

Stephen P. Clark Governmental Center, 111 NW 1st St., Miami, FL 33128

(305) 375-2500

Hours: Always visible

Cost: Free

Directions: Two blocks east of I-95, two blocks north of Flagler St.

It would be easy to blame Katherine Harris for much of Florida's 2000 election debacle. It would also be *correct* to blame her. After all, as secretary of state, she was the person responsible for making sure that the election was run properly, and regardless of which side of the political fence you fall on, it's hard to make a case that the 2000 election was properly managed.

Now to be fair, everyone makes mistakes—just look at your hairstyle from, say, 1984. And I'm sure there are a few folks in West Palm Beach who wish they'd looked at their ballots a little more carefully. But what seems a little odd—no, *suspicious*—is that every time Katherine Harris made a boo-boo—and she made a lot of boo-boos—it ended up favoring Republican candidates. The $4.3 million she used to "scrub" the state's voter rolls of ineligible voters disenfranchised an estimated 8,000 legal voters, a majority of whom were from predominantly Democratic districts, something the contractor described as "a minor glitch." *Ooops! Mistakes happen.* . . . Shortly after Norman Schwarzkopf endorsed George W. Bush for president, Harris approved $30,000 in taxpayer funds to make a "nonpartisan" get-out-and-vote PSA featuring the general. *The man is a national hero!* Ten laptop computers used to check voter eligibility were sent to Tampa by the secretary of state, but none of them were given to predominantly African American precincts where the disproportionately large number of voters had been improperly disenfranchised by her "scrubbing" efforts. *Must have been an oversight.* When Jeb Bush used the governor's office to encourage GOP voters to exercise their absentee ballot option, even if they weren't going to be absent, Harris was mum, even though filing for an absentee ballot without cause was illegal. *Really? News to me!* And when an estimated 10,000 mangled absentee ballots arrived in the mail, 26 counties had workers "re-create" the ballots by hand on Election Day. *Wasn't that helpful?* As overseas ballots trickled in during the tension-filled days following November 7, questionable ballots were rejected 80 percent of the time in Gore-leaning counties, but only 40 percent of the time in Bush-leaning counties. *Hmmmmm, now how could that be?* And when 700 overseas military ballots arrived a week later without postmarks, the secretary of state, a self-described "stickler for the rule of law," accepted them anyway. *Just being patriotic.*

In the end, Harris certified a 537-vote "win" for George W. Bush, and boy was she thrilled. After all, she was co-chairperson of the Bush for President campaign in Florida, and she had made it widely known that she wanted to be an ambassador. Someplace fun. In Latin America. Harris came right out and said so.

Can you say "conflict of interest"?

Harris was a hero to the GOP, but she was also a political hot potato. In the end, George W. Bush (the ingrate!) never offered her an ambassadorship. And because the office of the secretary of state was to be abolished in 2002 due to government restructuring, she decided to run for the U.S. Congress. Though she qualified to run in mid-July 2002, she did not resign her state job until August 1, thereby violating Florida's resign-to-run law, a statute her office was responsible for enforcing. Again, ooops.

It was the kind of attention to detail the voters had come to expect from Harris, and they didn't hold it against her. In November she was elected to Congress, beating out a field of candidates that included a spirited write-in challenge from Percy the Border Collie.

Harris's District Office, 1991 Main St., Suite 181, Sarasota, FL 34236

(800) 453-4184

Hours: Call for an appointment

Cost: Free

Directions: One block south of Fruitville Rd. (Rte. 780) on Rte. 301 (Main St.).

Harris's Congressional Office, 116 Cannon House Office Building, Washington, DC 20515

(202) 225-5015

Hours: Call ahead for an appointment

Cost: Free

www.house.gov/harris or katherineharrissucks.com

Directions: It's that big white building to the southeast of the Capitol Building, at Independence Ave. and 1st St. SE.

EPILOGUE

When I first started traveling to Florida, there was a fantastic museum on the north side of St. Augustine called the Tragedy in U.S. History Museum. Its owner and curator, Buddy Hough, had the foresight to make a beeline to Dallas just after the Kennedy assassination. Once there, he snagged up artifacts from that tragic event: Lee Harvey Oswald's pocket comb and boarding-house furniture, the car that Oswald's coworker used to drive him to the Texas School Book Depository on the morning of the shootings, and the ambulance and gurney that carried Oswald's body away from the Dallas police station after Jack Ruby gunned him down. To broaden his museum's scope, Hough purchased other bizarre items for his collection: Jayne Mansfield's deathmobile, a 1966 Buick Electra 225 with its top sheared off; *Bonnie and Clyde*'s death car (from the movie), a 1934 Ford riddled with 137 bullets; a smashed engineer's watch and whistle from the "Wreck of Old '97"; and an old Egyptian mummy. He then added a picnic area in his backyard, next to Mansfield's unintended convertible, just in case visitors wanted to make a day of it.

City leaders in St. Augustine were not impressed with Hough's efforts to bring a little historic tragedy into their cultural landscape, and tried to shut him down by strictly interpreting the local zoning laws. Hough's private museum was located on the first floor of his residence, which was not supposed to be used as a place of business. When courts sided with Hough, the city acted as if his creepy collection just didn't exist, and refused to mention the museum in any of its tourist brochures. When Hough died in 1996, his wife, Debra, tried to keep the museum going on her own. But in 1998, she gave up and the collection was scattered in a ghoulish auction.

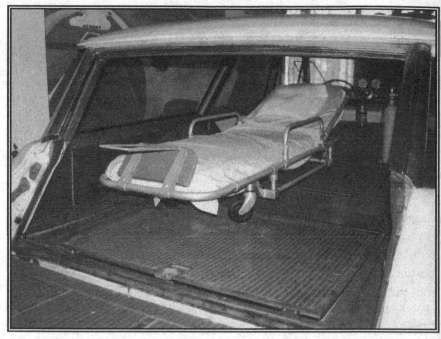

A real tragedy.

The story of the Tragedy in U.S. History Museum has been repeated over and over in the Sunshine State. After Dave Shealy of Ochopee was denied a $44,000 tourist tax–funded grant to keep his World Headquarters for Skunk Ape Research solvent ($20,000 was to be spent on two tracking expeditions through the swamps to gather evidence on this Florida Big-foot, and the remaining cash was earmarked for a toll-free Skunk Ape Tourist Hotline), he sold off his family's campground in Ochopee and moved away from the Everglades forever.

The Orlando area, as you can imagine, has fared worst of all. The last decade has seen the closing of the World of Orchids; the record-breaking Guinness World Record Experience museum; Terror on Church Street, a year-round, walk-through spook house; the Stars Hall of Fame Wax Museum; the Gold Box, a two-story jewelry mall shaped like a treasure chest; and, saddest of all, the Tupperware Museum.

Gone, too, are Jungle Larry's African Park and Caribbean Gardens in Naples, a nude car wash in Sarasota, the Tiki Gardens restaurant and gift shop at Indian Rocks Beach, the two-story Sisson's Coffee Pot percolator in Port Malabar, and the Museum of Torture and Execution in Key West. And what happened to the Burt Reynolds Dinner Theater in Jupiter? Ask Loni Anderson.

The message should be clear. If it's not, let me be more direct: Go. Now! Florida's theme park cancer is spreading and you haven't got much time. When the She-inal or Xanadu or the Jackson 5 station wagon are gone, you'll never get a chance to see them ever again. Can you live with yourself after that?

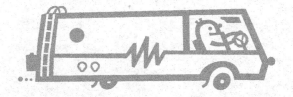

ACKNOWLEDGMENTS

This book would not have been possible without the assistance, patience, and good humor of many individuals. My thanks go out to the following people for allowing me to interview them about their roadside attractions: Adrian (Sarasota Classic Car Museum), Lowell Bassett (T. T. Wentworth, Jr., Museum), Carol Beck (Key West Sunset Celebration), Pia Dahlquist (Mai-Kai), Lisa Diaz (*Titanic: The Exhibition*), Pam Dunmire (Shell Factory), Elaine Faser (Oldest Wooden Schoolhouse), Joe Fox (NautiLimo), Don Garlits (Don Garlits Museum of Drag Racing), George (SkyVenture), Alan Haines (South Florida Museum), Jerome Holton (Bonita Rib Room & Club Royale), Cobi Kagin (Jungle Adventures), Gordon Lovestrand (Florida Cactus, Inc.), Carole Lowe (Water Ski Hall of Fame and Museum), Alice Moss (Ripley's Odditorium), Dean Murphy (Solomon's Castle), Mary Anna Murphy (Florida International Museum), Robbie Musgrove (National Museum of Naval Aviation), John Nathanison (Weeki Wachee Springs), John Robinson (Koreshan State Park), Lisa St. John (Water Ski Hall of Fame and Museum), Donald Schaafsma (Liberty Bell Memorial Museum), Sherry (Possum Monument/Wasau), Howard Solomon (Solomon's Castle), Jerry Theriault (Memphis Gold), Buddy Wilkes (Miracle Strip Amusement Park), and Jan Zweiffel (Presidents' Hall of Fame).

For research assistance, I am indebted to the librarians in the Florida communities of Apalachicola, Fort Lauderdale, Fort Pierce, Key West, Kissimmee, Leesburg, Mandarin, New Smyrna Beach, Panama City, Perry, Port Orange, St. Augustine, St. Petersburg, Sarasota, Wauchula, West Palm Beach, and Winter Park. Thanks also to the visitors bureaus and/or chambers of commerce in Bartow, Bradenton, Clearwater, Daytona Beach, Destin, Fort Lauderdale, Fort Myers, Homestead, Jacksonville, Key Largo, Key West, Kissimmee, Lake Wales, Melbourne, Miami, Miami Beach, Orlando, Panama City Beach, Pensacola, Polk City, Pompano Beach, St. Augustine, St. Cloud, St. Petersburg, Seaside, Tallahassee, Tampa, Tarpon Springs, Titusville, Vero Beach, and the Space Coast.

Thank you, Carol Beck, for enthusiastically posing for a sunset shot. To Jeffrey Glover who, with a little Photoshop, transformed a tame turn on the Tea Cups into a death-defying Disney "disaster," my thanks. And to Harry Sperl, champion of all things hamburgery, and his photographer/agent Harrod Blank (the living patron saint of art cars), thank you for your contribution. The world needs more wackos like you.

To my godparents, Uncle Jerry and Aunt Ethel, Floridians for some time now, I hope you enjoy the book—I promise I'll get to Destin some day when you're not on the road. To my Florida friends Sandi Simpson; Chuck Shepherd; Theresa Volpe; Tom and Isabel Shea; and Tess, John, and Jack Shea, I hope I did your state proud. Failing that, I hope you at least get a kick out of it.

Many thanks (as always) to everyone at Chicago Review Press for supporting the Oddball travel series, particularly its champion from the get-go, Cynthia Sherry, and this book's editor, Lisa Rosenthal. To everyone at WBEZ, Chicago Public Radio, thanks for the continued support of *Cool Spots*.

And finally, to Jim Frost, for inviting me along to all those Southern Florida Growers conventions, and letting me drag you through the swamps afterward, you certainly got the ball rolling on this one—so thank you.

RECOMMENDED SOURCES

If you'd like to learn more about the places and individuals in this book, the following are excellent sources. The best sources are listed first within each section.

General Florida Guides

An Uncommon Guide to Florida by Nina McGuire (Lake Buena Vista, FL: Tailored Tour Publications, 1997)

Florida Off the Beaten Path, Sixth Edition by Diana and Bill Gleasner (Guilford, CT: Globe Pequot Press, 2001)

Irresistible Overnights by Bob Rafferty and Loys Reynolds (Nashville, TN: Rutledge Hill Press, 2000)

Quick Escapes, Florida, Second Edition by W. Lynn Seldon, Jr. (Guilford, CT: Globe Pequot Press, 2000)

Backroads of Florida by Ann Ruff (Houston, TX: Gulf Publishing Company, 1992)

Up for Grabs by John Rothchild (Gainesville, FL: University Press of Florida, 2000)

Unique Florida by Sarah Lovett (Santa Fe, NM: John Muir Publications, 1993)

One Tank Trips by Bill Murphy (St. Petersburg, FL: Seaside Publishing, 1999)

More One Tank Trips by Bill Murphy (St. Petersburg, FL: Seaside Publishing, 2001)

Florida (History)

200 Quick Looks at Florida History by James C. Clark (Sarasota, FL: Pineapple Press, 2000)

Historical Traveler's Guide to Florida by Eliot Kleinberg (Sarasota, FL: Pineapple Press, 1997)

A Treasury of Florida Tales by Webb Garrison (Nashville, TN: Rutledge Hill Press, 1989)

Dreamers, Schemers, and Scalawags by Stuart McIver (Sarasota, FL: Pineapple Press, 1994)

Murder in the Tropics by Stuart McIver (Sarasota, FL: Pineapple Press, 1995)

Touched by the Sun by Stuart McIver (Sarasota, FL: Pineapple Press, 2001)

Florida Ramble by Alex Shoumatoff (New York: Vintage Books, 1974)

Florida (Weirdness)

Awesome Almanac Florida by Cima Star and Jean F. Blashfield (Walworth, WI: B&B Publishing, Inc., 1994)

Weird Florida by Eliot Kleinberg (Atlanta, GA: Longstreet, 1998)

Pop Culture Florida by James P. Goss. (Sarasota, FL: Pineapple Press, 2000)

Florida Curiosities by David Grimes and Tom Becnel (Guilford, CT: Globe Pequot Press, 2003)

More Great Southern Mysteries by E. Randall Floyd (Little Rock, AK: August House, 1990)

Haunt Hunter's Guide to Florida by Joyce Elson Moore (Sarasota, FL: Pineapple Press, 1998)

Florida (Trivia)

Florida Trivia by Ernie and Jill Couch (Nashville, TN: Rutledge Hill Press, 1994)

Florida Fun Facts by Eliot Kleinberg (Sarasota, FL: Pineapple Press, 1995)

Fabulous Florida by B. J. Bergman-Angstadt (Nashville, TN: Premium Press America, 1999)

Florida Firsts by Beverly Bryant Huttinger (Philadelphia, PA: Camino Books, Inc., 2002)

You Got Me! Florida by Rob Lloyd (Sarasota, FL: Pineapple Press, 1999)

Florida Almanac, 2002–2003 by Del Martin and Martha J. Marth (Gretna, LA: Pelican Publishing, 2002)

Florida Place Names by Joan Perry Morris (Sarasota, FL: Pineapple Press, 1995)

1. The Panhandle

The Gulf Breeze Sightings

The Gulf Breeze Sightings by Ed and Frances Walters (New York: Avon Books, 1990)

UFO Abductions in Gulf Breeze by Ed and Frances Walters (New York: Avon Books, 1994)

Gideon's Trumpet

Gideon's Trumpet by Anthony Lewis (New York: Vintage Books, 1964)

Wakulla Springs

Watery Eden: A History of Wakulla Springs by Tracey J. Revels (Wakulla Springs, FL: Wakulla Springs, 2003)

2. The North

Lynyrd Skynyrd

Lynyrd Skynyrd: Remembering the Free Birds of Southern Rock by Gene Odom and Frank Dorman (New York: Broadway Books, 2002)

Freebirds: The Lynyrd Skynyrd Story by Marley Brant (New York: Billboard Books, 2002)

The Germans Have Landed

Shadow Enemies: Hitler's Secret Terrorist Plot Against the United States by Alex Abella and Scott Gordon (New York: Lyons, 2003)

War in Paradise by Eliot Kleinberg (Melbourne, FL: Florida Historical Society Press, 1999)

Potter's Wax Museum

Potter's Wax Museum, Collectors Edition Guidebook by Peter Carsillo (St. Augustine, FL: White & White, Ltd., 2000)

Old Sparky

The Electric Chair: An Unnatural American History by Craig Brandon (New York: McFarland & Company, 1999)

Blood and Volts by Th. Metzger (New York: Autonomedia, 1996)

3. The Gulf Coast

Cyrus Teed and Koreshanity

The Cellular Cosmogony by Cyrus Teed (Philadelphia, PA: Porcupine Press, 1975)

Kooks by Donna Kossy (Portland, OR: Feral House, 1994)

Edison and Ford

Uncommon Friends by James Newton (San Diego, CA: Harcourt Brace Jovanovich, 1987)

Don Garlits

Top Secrets on How to Build Record Breaking Chryslers by Don Garlits (Ocala, FL: Self-published, 1960)

Ma Barker

Mean Men: The Sons of Ma Barker by Robert Winter (Danbury, CT: Rutledge Books, 2000)

Sanibel Shells

A Gift from the Sea by Anne Morrow Lindbergh (New York: Pantheon Books, 1955)

4. Tampa/St. Petersburg Area

The Murder of Lobster Boy

Lobster Boy by Fred Rosen (New York: Pinnacle Books, 1995)

The Cinder Lady

Ablaze! by Larry E. Arnold (New York: M. Evans and Company, 1995)

The Cuban Missile Crisis

Thirteen Days by Robert Kennedy and Arthur Schlesinger, Jr. (New York: W. W. Norton & Co, 1968)

Jack Kerouac

Kerouac: A Biography by Ann Charters (New York: St. Martin's Press, 1973)

5. Orlando Area

Orlando (General)

Exploring Central Florida by Benjamin D. Brotemarkle (Gainesville, FL: University Press of Florida, 1999)

Orlando's Other Theme Parks by Kelly Monaghan (New York: The Intrepid Traveler, 1997)

Celebration

The Celebration Chronicles by Andrew Ross (New York: Ballantine Books, 1999)

Celebration, U.S.A. by Douglas Frantz and Catherine Collins (New York: Henry Holt, 2000)

Walt Disney World

Team Rodent by Carl Hiaasen (New York: Library of Contemporary Thought, 1998)

Inside the Mouse by the Project on Disney (Durham, NC: Duke University Press, 1996)

Disney: The Mouse Betrayed by Peter and Rochelle Schweizer (Washington, DC: Regnery Publishing, 1998)

Mouse Tales by David Koenig (Irvine, CA: Bonaventure Press, 1995)

Married to the Mouse by Richard E. Foglesong (New Haven, CT: Yale University Press, 2001)

6. The Atlantic Coast

Kennedy Space Center

Kennedy Space Center Official Tourbook by the Kennedy Space Center (Cape Canaveral, FL: Kennedy Space Center, 2002)

How Do You Go to the Bathroom in Space? by William R. Pogue (New York: Tom
   Doherty Associates, 1999)

Cassadaga Spiritualist Camp
Cassadaga by John J. Guthrie, Jr., Phillip Charles Lucas, and Gary Monroe
   (Gainesville, FL: University Press of Florida, 1997)
Cassadaga Spiritualist Camp 2002/2003 Annual Program by the Cassadaga Spiri-
   tualist Camp (Cassadaga, FL: 2002)
Cassadaga, Florida: Then and Now, Fourth Edition by Elizabeth Owens (Cas-
   sadaga, FL: Pisces Publishing, 2001)

Daytona 500
Daytona 500: An Official History by Bob Zeller (David Bull Publishing, 2002)

7. The South

The Ghost of Flight 401
The Ghost of Flight 401 by John G. Fuller (New York: Berkley Medallion, 1976)

The Bermuda Triangle
The Bermuda Triangle by Charles Berlitz (New York: Doubleday, 1974)
The Bermuda Triangle—Solved! by Lawrence Kusche (New York: Harper & Row,
   1975)
On Atlantis by Edgar Cayce (New York: Warner Books, 1968)

The Coral Castle
Coral Castle by the Coral Castle (Homestead, FL: Self-published)
Mr. Can't Is Dead by Orval M. Irwin (Self-Published, 1996)
How to Read His Writings by Edward J. Marlinski (Lansdale, PA: Passels Information
   Network, 2000)

Henry Flagler
Henry Flagler: Visionary of the Gilded Age by Sidney Walter Martin (Tailored
   Tours Publications, 1998)

8. Miami Area

Elian Gonzalez
Betrayal of Elian Gonzalez by Michael John (Miami, FL: Self-published)

FDR Near Assassination
The Five Weeks of Giuseppe Zangara by Blaise Picchi (Chicago: Academy Chicago
   Publishers, 1998)

Al Capone
Al Capone by Rick Hornung (New York: Park Lane Press, 1998)
Mr. Capone by Robert J. Schoenberg (New York: Quill, 1992)

Andrew Cunanan
Vulgar Favors by Maureen Orth (New York: Delacorte Press, 1999)
Death at Every Stop by Wensley Clarkson (New York: St. Martin's Paperbacks, 1997)
Andrew Cunanan: An American Tragedy by the Cunanan Family (Minneapolis, MN: Piper Publishing, 1998)
Three Month Fever by Gary Indiana (New York: Cliff Street Books, 1999)

9. The Keys
The African Queen
The Making of The African Queen, *or How I Went to Africa with Bogart, Bacall, and Huston and Almost Lost My Mind* by Katharine Hepburn (New York: Knopf, 1987)

Florida Hurricanes
Florida Hurricanes and Tropical Storms by John M. Williams and Iver W. Duedall (Gainesville, FL: University Press of Florida, 1997)
In the Eye of Hurricane Andrew by Eugene F. Provenzo, Jr., and Asterie Baker Provenzo (Gainesville, FL: University Press of Florida, 2002)

Count von Creep-me-out
Undying Love by Ben Harrison (New York: St. Martin's, 1997)
Ghosts of Key West by David L. Sloan (Key West, FL: Mirror Lake Press, 1998)

Hemingway in Key West
Papa: Hemingway in Key West by James McLendon (Key West, FL: Langley Press, 1990)

Tennessee Williams in Key West
Literary Sands of Key West by Patricia Altobello and Deirdre Pierce (Washington, DC: Starrhill Press, 1996)

Harry Truman in Key West
Harry Truman and the Little White House in Key West by Arva Moore Parks (New York: Centennial Press, 1994)

Dr. Samuel Mudd

The Escape and Capture of John Wilkes Booth by Edward Steers, Jr. (Gettysburg, PA: Thomas Publications, 1992)

10. Busted Tour

Scandals (General)

The Smoking Gun Web site, www.thesmokinggun.com

The Smoking Gun by William Bastone, Daniel Green, and Barbara Glauber (Boston: Little, Brown & Company 2001)

Sex, Sin, and Mayhem: Notorious Trials of the 1990s by Edward Knappman (Detroit, MI: Visible Ink Press, 1995)

Jim Morrison

Break on Through: The Life and Death of Jim Morrison by James Riordan and Jerry Prochnicky (New York: Quill, 1992)

Watergate

All the President's Men by Carl Bernstein and Bob Woodward (New York: Warner Books, 1974)

Jim Bakker and the PTL Scandal

Tammy: Telling It My Way by Tammy Faye Messner (New York: Villard, 1996)

Integrity: How I Lost It, and My Journey Back by Richard Dortch (Green Forest, AR: New Leaf Press, 1991)

Anatomy of a Fraud by Gary Tidwell (New York: Wiley, 1993)

2 Live Crew

They Fought the Law by Stan Soocher (New York: Schirmer Books, 1999)

The Kennedys in Palm Beach

Palm Beach Babylon by Murray Weiss and Bill Hoffmann (New York: Birch Lane Press, 1992)

The 2000 Presidential Election

Jews for Buchanan by John Nichols (New York: The New Press, 2001)

36 Days by Correspondents of the *New York Times* (New York: *Times* Books, 2001)

Down & Dirty: The Plot to Steal the Presidency by Jake Tapper (Boston: Little, Brown & Company, 2001)

The Betrayal of America by Vincent Bugliosi (New York: Thunder's Mouth Press, 2001)

INDEX BY CITY NAME

INDEX BY SITE NAME

Jerome Pohlen is the author of *Oddball Minnesota, Oddball Colorado, Oddball Indiana, Oddball Illinois,* and *Oddball Wisconsin.* He is an award-winning commentator on the *848* show on WBEZ, the Chicago affiliate of National Public Radio. He lives in Chicago.